THE
SOCIAL SKILLS
GUIDEBOOK

MANAGE SHYNESS,
IMPROVE YOUR CONVERSATIONS,
AND MAKE FRIENDS,
WITHOUT GIVING UP
WHO YOU ARE

CHRIS MACLEOD, MSW

ISBN: 978-0-99498-070-0

Editor: Vicki Adang
Cover and interior design: Victoria Valentine/Page and Cover Design

TABLE OF CONTENTS

INTRODUCTION

THIS BOOK IS FOR ANYONE who feels they need to brush up on their social skills. Maybe you feel shy, anxious, and insecure around people. You struggle to make conversation and leave a good impression on others. You're lonely and isolated and don't go out nearly as often as you'd like, or you only have a few casual acquaintances and want some closer relationships. Maybe all of the above. Maybe you feel like you somehow missed out on learning the unwritten social rules that everyone else seemed to have gotten the hang of by the time they were thirteen.

If you have these social difficulties, you're not alone. You may feel like a uniquely broken outcast, but they're all common issues. Millions of people feel the same way you do.

The good news is that these social problems can be fixed. The concept of a "late bloomer" exists for a reason. Lots of people were shy or lonely for a period in their lives before they developed their interpersonal skills and put the shyness or loneliness behind them. You can increase your self-confidence. You can learn to manage shyness and anxiety and the counterproductive thinking and behaviors that feed them. You can practice and hone your conversation skills. You can learn a reliable process to meet friends and build a social life. Even if aspects of socializing don't come that naturally to you and you'll have to work a little harder at it than most, nothing about your situation makes you a lost cause.

You don't need to completely change who you are to become more socially successful either; you can leave your interests, values, and personality traits intact. You just need to fill in the skills or confidence gaps that are currently holding you back. Then you'll be a more socially polished version of yourself. The goal of this book is to give you the tools you need to become socially happy in whatever way works for you, whether that involves partying all the time with a dozen casual acquaintances or mostly keeping to yourself except to occasionally meet with a few really close friends. It doesn't want to turn you into someone who acts fake so they can appeal to as many people as possible.

This book is a comprehensive guide to catching up socially. There are titles that cover shyness or conversation skills separately, but this one tells you everything you need to know in one place. The author struggled with all of these issues himself when he was younger and wrote this as the guide he wished he'd had at the time.

This book teaches the fundamentals you somehow missed learning as you were growing up. It addresses barriers that only come up for people who have been struggling socially for most of their lives.

If social skills could be rated on a ten-point scale, it's about helping you get from an unhappy 3 to a content, functional 7 (or higher). It's not a collection of little-known tricks that will let you move from average to advanced. It won't reveal five secret tricks that CEOs use to make their handshakes extra memorable and influential. That said, charismatic people are that way not because they have access to a bunch of techniques most of us don't, but because they execute many of their social fundamentals a little better than normal. In that sense, this book may help you someday have lots of charisma by making you aware of the core skills you could develop beyond a typical level.

This title focuses on day-to-day socializing. It doesn't cover workplace-specific issues like how to manage difficult colleagues, influence your boss, or nail that product demonstration. It also doesn't go into dating and flirting. However, if you're struggling socially, most of the topics covered here should help your career or love life. You can hardly woo someone or get along with your coworkers if you have trouble with conversation or can't manage your anxiety around people.

What's ahead

After a few opening chapters about the process of working on social issues, the book covers three core areas of social skills:
1. Dealing with shyness, anxiety, and insecurities, and feeling more comfortable and confident with yourself and others
2. Making conversation and interacting with people
3. Meeting people and making friends

The sections build on each other—you're going to struggle to make conversation if you're anxious and insecure, and you're going to have a hard time making friends if you can't keep an interaction going—but you don't have to read them in order. If you feel your confidence and conversation skills are already okay, then using the suggestions in the "Forming and Growing Friendships" section may have the biggest and quickest impact on your social life.

1

THE OVERALL PROCESS
OF IMPROVING
YOUR SOCIAL SKILLS

As you work to improve your social skills, you must approach the process in the right way. Many people struggle to improve their social skills not because they're up against impossible challenges, but because they approach the task from the wrong angle and get unnecessarily discouraged. With the right mind-set, expectations, and approach to improving, you'll make more progress. This chapter covers some things you should know before working on your issues. Chapter 2 troubleshoots some common questions and concerns people have about improving their social skills.

FIGURING OUT WHICH SKILLS AND TRAITS TO WORK ON AND WHICH TO LEAVE ALONE

As the Introduction said, you don't need to change everything about yourself to do better socially. Of course, you'll want to address clear-cut problems that most people would be happy to be rid of—shyness and anxiety, low self-confidence, unpolished conversation skills, and lack of knowledge about how to make friends.

The traits listed below can also cause social problems. They're all perfectly valid variations from the norm that you shouldn't have to change. However, they can lead to practical social inconveniences when either people misunderstand and look down on the traits, or the traits cause you to have competing needs.

Acceptable, though sometimes impractical, social differences

- Having an introverted personality
- Liking to spend a lot of time alone
- Not needing or wanting a ton of friends
- Being selective when choosing who you want to be friends with
- Preferring to socialize for shorter periods of time, and then head home to relax and recharge your batteries; having a tendency to get drained by socializing
- Being into low-key types of socializing and choosing to avoid rowdy parties or getting drunk
- Preferring to hang back and listen more in conversations, rather than talking a lot and trying to hold the spotlight
- Not having a bubbly, expressive, excitable personality
- Being able to take or leave aspects of socializing, like making chitchat with strangers waiting in a line with you
- Preferring your conversations to have lots of substance
- Being into "uncool," non-mainstream hobbies
- Not caring about seemingly popular interests like team sports or reality TV
- Living an alternative lifestyle or being part of a non-mainstream scene or subculture
- Having beliefs and values that differ from the mainstream
- Having a more quirky personality

As examples, having non-mainstream hobbies may hinder you if they cause your peers to stereotype you and write you off without giving you a chance. Liking to spend time alone may cause a conflict in your social goals. Part of you may want to go out more to make new friends, but your urge to hang out by yourself may get in the way.

You'll have to decide for yourself how to approach your acceptable differences in light of your social goals. Wherever possible, you should be true to yourself and try to find your niche, which includes looking for friends who get you and like you for who you are.

No one is socially perfect. As long as they bring enough positives to the table, they can still get by. If you read a piece of advice in this book you aren't crazy about following, ask yourself, "Would it make me happier on the whole to skip this suggestion? Could I handle the consequences of not following it?" For example, maybe you're at peace with having a blunter communication style and can live with the fact that it will occasionally put some people off. Maybe you'll even decide you're okay with aspects of your being mildly shy, even if it is technically a "problem." Be your own judge of what works for you.

At times you may weigh the pros and cons of a situation and find it suits you to go along with certain social conventions. For example, in your perfect world you'd never devote a second of thought to fashion, but you realize other people value it and so learn to dress a little better. Or you like spending a lot of time alone, but you push yourself to be around people slightly more than you'd prefer so you have enough time to practice your social skills and be with your friends.

You'll have to decide for yourself where you are and aren't willing to compromise. Changing isn't an option if something violates your deepest values or you outright dislike it. The pragmatic approach can work if you feel indifferent toward something and it doesn't take that much effort to go along with it. However, there are always going to be parts of the social world, where even if you realize intellectually it would be practical to go along with them, you're just not going to be able to play along. Most people aren't going to give up their religious or political views to fit in. As a lighter example, some men don't care about sports, but know they'd have an easier time relating to other guys if they were into them. Some never come to love sports, but can make themselves follow just enough news about game results and trades to grease their conversations. Others can't bring themselves to do even that, and they're fine living with the minor hassles that causes.

Keep an open mind

Although you don't need to completely change or sell yourself out to do better socially, you should try to keep an open mind. Be open to new experiences and the possibility that one day you may develop traits or come to appreciate things you never thought you'd enjoy. People change throughout their lives. It's important to be true to yourself, but not to the point where you become locked in place and dismiss anything new with "No, that's not who I am." Say a friend invites you to an introductory salsa class, and you've never done much dancing. Even if you sense it's not something you'd get a lot out of, it's too rigid to blindly say, "No, that's not me! I don't like dancing and never will!" You don't have to mindlessly try everything everyone suggests, but you never know—you may actually love partner dancing and just not realize it yet.

REALIZING YOUR INTERPERSONAL SKILLS DON'T HAVE TO BE FLAWLESS TO HAVE A SATISFYING SOCIAL LIFE

Countless people in the world have fun social lives even though they're a bit shy and insecure, or they sometimes stumble in their conversations, or they don't have a ton of fascinating hobbies, or they have a few irksome personality quirks. Even charismatic people make bad jokes or have their invites turned down. You don't need to perfectly execute every skill in this book 100 percent of the time, and you don't have to get every last person on the planet to like you. You just need to be good enough to get by and have friends who accept you for who you are. You don't need all of your interactions to go flawlessly. You just need enough of them to go well that you can meet your social goals (if you invite ten people to hang out and only three accept, but they go on to become your good friends, that's a win).

PRACTICING YOUR SOCIAL SKILLS
TO IMPROVE THEM

Social skills are skills like any other. Reading advice can give you an idea of what you need to work on and help the learning process go more smoothly, but in the end you have to practice to really get things down. You've probably socialized for fewer overall hours than many of your peers, and you have to put in the time to catch up.

That seems obvious, but when it comes to interpersonal skills, some people think they can be gained all at once through the right trick, insight, psychology "hack," or confidence booster. They likely think that because social skills are non-physical and mundane. People instinctively understand it takes time to learn complex physical abilities like skiing or drawing. However, when it comes to socializing, their thought process is, "It's just talking. I already know how to do that. So just give me some secret super-effective conversation formulas, and I'll be off to the races."

Additionally, most people have found that navigating a social situation was easier when they were temporarily more confident than usual. So they figure there must be a way to be extra-confident all the time. However, although you can fleetingly become unusually self-assured, there's no way to call that feeling up on command or lock it in place for life. There really are no shortcuts. If there were, they'd be common knowledge, and this book wouldn't be needed.

Knowing what are you working on when
you practice your social skills

As you practice socializing, you'll develop the following overall abilities. In some interactions, you'll draw on only a few of them, while other interactions will require you to juggle many at a time.

1) Your ability to think on your feet. When it's your turn to say something, you can't take forever to come up with your response. Also, aside from the relatively predictable first minute or two, interactions can quickly go in countless directions. It's unfeasible to try to plan out everything you're going to say ahead of time or map out how to handle every scenario in advance. The best you can do is learn some general guidelines and then sharpen your ability to improvise.

2) Your ability to multitask. When you're interacting with someone, you have to continually attend to several things at once. The other person is constantly sending signals through their words, actions, and nonverbal communication; you have to take it in, evaluate it, and decide on the fly how to act on your conclusions ("They just said they're not familiar with cycling. I'll have to adjust how I tell my anecdote."). At the same time, you have to manage the signals you're sending ("I'm curious about what time it is, but I won't check my watch now because it may make me look like I'm not interested in their story."). As you get better at socializing, taking in all of that information and deciding what to do with it starts to feel less overwhelming.

3) Your proficiency in a variety of concrete subskills like listening, asserting yourself, or phrasing an invitation. Like with any skill, at first you'll be clumsy and exaggerated when you listen actively, assert yourself, or extend an invitation, but in time you'll develop a defter touch and be able to calibrate your behavior to the situation at hand. For example, when you're first getting the hang of listening skills, you may sometimes come across as an over-the-top therapist. With more practice, you'll be able to show you care and that you're paying attention in a more subtle way.

4) Your comfort level with various subskills, like making eye contact or starting conversations. Some subskills, like making eye contact or initiating a conversation, will make you feel nervous or unnatural at first, but the more you do them, the more normal they'll feel.

5) Your general knowledge of people, what makes them tick, and how they tend to react to various things. Every person is different, but with enough social experience, you'll start to notice broad patterns you can act on. For example, you may notice that people who are into a certain hobby also tend to share the same political beliefs and conversation style, and you can adjust accordingly.

6) Your knowledge of various social situations and how to navigate them. You can learn this through firsthand experience or by observing other people who are more socially experienced than you. It's possible to find advice on common scenarios, like how to approach people at a party or turn down an unreasonable request, but in your day-to-day life, you'll come across other scenarios that are too rare and esoteric to end up in any book. When you come across these novel situations, you may not always handle them perfectly, but with time you can build up an overall sense about how to approach them.

7) **Your knowledge of the unwritten social guidelines of your particular culture, subculture, or group of friends, and how to adjust the general communication-skills rules to fit them.** This is another reason it's impossible to explain how to deal with every situation ahead of time. What may be considered an appealing conversation style in one country or among one circle of friends may be seen as obnoxious elsewhere. The only way to learn the rules for your social context is to be in it and observe them for yourself.

8) **Constructive mind-sets toward socializing.** A well-intentioned, but unhelpful, variety of social advice is to suggest you adopt useful, but easier-said-than-done, mind-sets like, "Don't care too much about people's opinions of you" or "Just go out to have fun and don't fret about how well you socialize." It's great if you can think like this, but you don't instantly acquire those worldviews just by reading they're good to have. Instead, as you socialize more and more, you'll have many small experiences and successes that show firsthand these are good ways to think, and you'll gradually add them into your worldview.

9) **Your personal social style.** There are some general guidelines for what makes for a better or worse interaction, but there isn't a single right way to socialize. Everyone has his or her own personality and strengths and weaknesses. There are usually multiple ways to handle any situation. What works well for another person may not fit you at all. Your friend may be good at cheering people up by being a good listener. You may be better at being funny and helping them take their mind off their worries.

Ways to practice socializing

You can practice your social skills in three ways. First, if you feel you're socially inexperienced all around, you can simply find ways to spend more time socializing. This method is unstructured, but you'll still learn new things from all the extra hours you'll rack up, and hone a variety of skills. You can

- socialize more with the people you already know (existing friends, coworkers, classmates, roommates, family members);
- get a job that involves lots of interaction with people (for example, retail, restaurant server, bartender, call center, sales);
- sign up for a volunteer position that involves socializing (for example, fundraising, talking to seniors, helping out at a festival);
- join a club, team, or organization;
- attend online-organized meet-ups (for example, from a forum you use, through sites like Meetup.com);
- take advantage of natural opportunities to have brief, friendly interactions with people who are generally expected to be pleasant and chat with you, such as store clerks and restaurant servers;
- go to a venue where people can show up alone and be social with the other patrons (for example, a board game café, a pub or pool hall);
- interact with people online (for example, chatting with people while playing a multiplayer game). Of course, this can't be a complete substitute for face-to-face practice, but it shouldn't be dismissed entirely either; or
- if it's a realistic option, travel and stay in busy, social hostels.

A second method is to practice in a deliberate, structured way, especially if you want to work on specific skills. For example, if you have trouble starting conversations, you could attend one online-organized meet-up a week and talk to at least five new people each time. If you have trouble with a specific type of interaction, like inviting someone out or turning down an unreasonable request, you could practice by role-playing the scenario with a friend or family member. Some organizations and counseling agencies run social skills training groups that provide opportunities to practice in a safe, supportive environment.

A third way to practice socially is to take a class to learn a performance-oriented interpersonal skill like public speaking, acting, or improv or stand-up comedy. These more specialized skills don't fully carry over into day-to-day situations. A rehearsed, memorized speech isn't the same as a spontaneous, casual conversation. However, they still provide a lot of benefits. For example, speech classes may teach you how to project your voice and use confident body language. Performing in a play may help you deal with your nerves and fear of being on the spot. Improv teaches you to be more loose, playful, and spontaneous in your conversations. Many people also find they get a small confidence boost in their daily interactions from knowing they're getting the hang of a more intimidating skill like speaking in public.

You don't have to spend a lot of time talking to strangers in public to practice your social skills. Some people think they have to chat with a bunch of randoms at the mall or grocery store. If you're specifically trying to get used to starting and carrying on conversations with people you don't know, that's one thing. If you generally want to rack up some social experience, talking to strangers is usually too stressful and inefficient. It's better to practice with people whom you know and are already somewhat comfortable with, or strangers you meet in more structured situations like an art class.

INDIRECTLY IMPROVING YOUR SOCIAL SUCCESS

Although directly addressing the less-practiced aspects of your social skills is essential, you can also indirectly help your cause by becoming a more well-rounded, knowledgeable, interesting person. This works in a "wax on, wax off" kind of way. Imagine you did nothing to directly practice your social skills for three months, but spent that time traveling, discovering new music, and learning to mountain bike. At the end of those three months, many social situations would likely go more smoothly for you. You'd have more to talk about and relate to people over, and you'd really notice a difference if you ended up in a conversation with a traveler, cyclist, or music fan. The struggles of traveling and learning to mountain bike would have increased your overall confidence or maybe made you more fun and adventurous. The experiences you had on vacation may have some cachet and make people want to chat more with you so they could learn more about them.

That's not to say that if you pick up a bunch of new hobbies, you'll be able to duck out of the direct practice requirement. Also, some people hear this advice and they try to learn about and do everything, hoping to get the maximum social benefit. Of course that's not feasible.

KNOWING HOW LONG IT WILL TAKE TO CATCH UP IN YOUR SOCIAL SKILLS

Of course, it's hard to estimate how much time you'll need to polish your social skills because everyone starts from a different place. One to three years is a reasonable amount of time to expect if you're behind all around, as opposed to needing help with a smaller area or two. It generally takes a few years to get half-decent at many skills.

Reading that may leave you feeling discouraged: "It may take me three years? Are you kidding me?!" That estimate isn't meant to bring you down, but to be straightforward and realistic about the process. In the long run, knowing what to expect prevents more discouragement than it creates. Hearing the news doesn't feel good up front, but when you're six months in and have a bad day, you can put it in perspective and not see it as a sign that you're hopeless. If this book falsely led you to believe social skills are quick and easy to obtain, you'd feel worse— and maybe even give up entirely—if everything didn't fall into place after a few weeks.

One to three years may seem long, but the process of improving won't be a grind the entire time. As with learning anything, it will be roughest at the beginning and then get more enjoyable and comfortable once you've developed a basic foundation. It's like learning to play the guitar: In the first month it hurts your fingers to hold down the strings, and it's an accomplishment to play a chord properly, let alone to switch between several of them quickly and smoothly. At the six-month mark, the situation is far different. You're still a clueless beginner in the grand scheme of things, but you know enough that practicing isn't a complete struggle, and is often fun when you get the hang of a new song. It's the same with socializing. At first it may be nerve-racking to make polite chitchat with someone for a few minutes. A year in you may confidently head to a party with a bunch of friends and know you'll get in some mingling practice while you have a good time with everyone.

Not all progress comes slowly either. Some areas are easier to make improvements in than others. For example, there are some simple, common mistakes people commit when trying to make friends, and after they know how to avoid them, their social lives often improve quickly.

You have more time than it seems. Late bloomers often worry that their best years have passed them by and they've missed the window for having a fulfilling social life. That's not true at all. Social skills can be learned at any time in your life. After you're caught up, you're caught up. Learning social skills isn't like learning languages, where our brains are wired in such a way that it's harder to learn new ones after childhood. There's no door that closes when you reach 20, 25, 30, or any other arbitrary age. You will have opportunities to enjoy yourself and socialize throughout your life. If you're in your early twenties or younger, you may believe that after college all the fun dries up and everyone becomes boring and bogged down by responsibilities. Not true. People never stop socializing and having fun together.

It can be frustrating to hear you have to wait before you can get what you want, but try not to succumb to impatience. If you're impatient, you may give up on helpful suggestions because they're not working instantly. You also might chase one supposed quick fix after another, instead of sticking with proven approaches that are slower and less glamorous. When you do get discouraged or impatient, remind yourself that social skills take time to develop; it's not realistic to expect to become an expert overnight. Also, look at where you are now compared to where you began. You'll be more likely to keep going when you can show yourself you're making improvements.

EXPECTING YOUR EMOTIONS TO SWING UP AND DOWN

You can broadly divide the process of putting your social problems behind you into an initial, more frustrating phase, and a later one where the sailing is smoother. As you improve your social skills, practicing them becomes easier and more encouraging, and you have a sense the worst is behind you—success is just a matter of time if you stay the course.

Your moods can be rocky during that first phase. Whatever happens, you'll tend to read too much into what it means for the future. If you have a good day, you'll be overly excited and feel like you've finally turned a corner and everything will be okay. When you inevitably have an off day, you'll conclude you're hopeless and you'll never have better social skills.

With more practice and a few more tastes of success, you'll calm down. You'll also realize that even if you have a few shaky interactions, your progress is still steadily ticking upward; if you keep at it, you'll get there eventually. One way to maintain perspective is to keep a record of your progress. That way you have an objective reminder that you're making positive changes ("I feel like I'm still as shy as I've always been, but it says this month I started more conversations than I ever have, and I've hung out with three new people.")

REALIZING IT'S OKAY TO SEEK PROFESSIONAL SUPPORT

This is a self-help book, but when it's appropriate, it will point out situations where it may be helpful to get some extra assistance from a counselor or support group. Sometimes you'll face challenges that are too difficult to deal with on your own. Seeing a professional isn't a shameful last resort for "weak," "broken," "crazy" people. It's just a way to get some knowledgeable experts on your side. If you're in college, your school may offer free counseling services. Many communities also have affordable mental health agencies.

2

ADDRESSING SOME COMMON CHALLENGES AND CONCERNS ABOUT WORKING ON YOUR SOCIAL SKILLS

THIS CHAPTER FIRST COVERS common practical challenges to improving your interpersonal skills; then it goes over some concerns people have about the process.

PRACTICAL CHALLENGES

Even when you want to make changes in your social skills, the following challenges can make it hard to start, and continue, working on them. These barriers are all surmountable.

"I want to practice my social skills, but I get drained quickly in certain situations."

It's not uncommon for people to quickly become mentally drained when they're socializing. They can handle a dinner party conversation for an hour or two, but after that they feel depleted, like they want to leave. After a few hours, they're too tired to properly listen to everyone and craft their responses. Afterward they usually need some downtime to recover from their interactions.

Getting drained easily can interfere with your ability to practice, or just stay out with friends as long as you'd like. From an "acceptable, but inconvenient, differences" perspective, you may also be annoyed when people don't understand you're wired this way; some less-sensitive people may give you a hard time when you want to take off from an event early, or they may take it personally when you look tired around them.

Short-term ways to feel less drained once the feeling has started to set in

- **Have some caffeine to give yourself a quick burst of energy.** This suggestion especially helps if you're out late and you're feeling sleepy on top of being depleted from socializing.
- **Have a snack or full meal if you haven't had any food in a while.** Your energy levels can subtly slip if you've gone hours without eating. However, don't eat so much that you go into a food coma.
- **Wait until you get a second wind.** Tiredness tends to come in waves, and your energy will usually rebound if you can gut out the grogginess for twenty minutes or so.
- **Take mini-breaks to recover some of your energy.** Bathrooms are a classic hideout. At a bigger function, moving from the hectic indoors to a more low-key conversation outside may be enough to give you a breather.
- **Consciously throw yourself into another gear and try to re-engage with everyone.** After you've started feeling drained, it's easy to give in to those feelings and sit back, zone out, and wait until you can go home. Hanging back and doing nothing is dull and usually makes you even more tired and checked out. Instead, try to find a fun interaction to join, which may perk you up and make you feel more enthusiastic.
- **If you know about a draining event ahead of time, take a strategic nap beforehand so you'll have more energy.**

Becoming less susceptible to feeling drained over the long term

Even taking the above suggestions into account, you can only do so much to hold back the drained feeling after it's already started. Here are some things you can do to reduce your tendency to get socially drained over a long haul:

- **Get more proficient at socializing in the situations that tire you.** Anything is more mentally taxing if you're unpracticed at it. Also, you'll start to feel drained and disengaged more quickly if you're bored and not having a good time. As you get more skilled at handling a situation, it will easier to have fun in it.
- **Get more comfortable in the situations that tire you.** Anxiety is very physically and mentally draining. When you're more relaxed in a situation you won't waste your energy feeling tense and worried.
- **Over time push yourself to stay in social situations longer and longer.** You can "exercise" to build up your social endurance. When you're out with friends and want to take off, tell yourself you'll stick around for another half hour, and then later, an hour or more. After you've decided to stay, actively socialize rather than retreating to wait out the clock.
- **Hang around people who are more your style.** You'll be more prone to feel drained if you're with people who you don't have much in common with and are either too dull or too go-go-go for you.
- **Be around people more often.** Everyone has a baseline level of social contact they prefer, but it has some wiggle room. If you spend a lot of time alone, then when you do socialize, it's more of a shock to your system, and it won't be long before you want to be on your own again. If your life circumstances constantly put you around classmates, coworkers, family, and roommates, you get used to being around people constantly. Your need to escape and recharge doesn't totally go away, but your tolerance for having company is higher.

"I want to work on my social skills, but I just can't motivate myself to get started or stick with practicing for very long."

To improve your social life you need to be motivated to work on it, and push through the difficult patches. That motivation is sometimes hard to find even if you feel you logically *should* have it. There are a few reasons this can happen:

- **Your anxiety is holding you back.** It's only natural you'd want to avoid the kind of social practice that makes you nervous. At times you're well aware that you'd like to make changes but are too scared of getting rejected, embarrassing yourself, or having to dwell on your failures. At other times your anxiety will provide you with an excuse to procrastinate, like "I'll try to make more friends in the summer, when I'm not so busy with school."
- **If you have a personality where you have a lower need to socialize and are happy to be alone, you can get caught in a stagnant middle ground**. You wish your social life was better, but having to spend a lot of time on your own doesn't bother you *that* much, so you never feel enough of the pain or loneliness that lights a fire under you and compels you to make big changes.
- **Your goals aren't your own.** You may truly not care about improving aspects of your social skills at the moment, but have absorbed messages from society that you should want to address them. If you're younger, your family may be pressuring you to change before you feel ready.
- **You're not sure how to begin tackling your problems and are overwhelmed.**

If you struggle with motivation, here are some things you can do:
- **Learn to handle your anxiety**. The book's next section goes into detail on this topic.
- **Accept that you may not be fully ready to change yet.** Regardless of how you think you *should* feel, your heart may not fully be in it at the moment. If you don't have an inner drive to tackle your issues, no rah-rah speech or quote is going to fix that. At best that'll make you

feel psyched up for a day or two before you go back to the status quo. There's nothing wrong with deciding to wait until a greater sense of urgency sets in.

- **Set aside some time to figure out what you really want.** Are you telling yourself you should try to become an outgoing party animal because that's what society says is important, when deep down it doesn't interest you? Would you feel more enthusiastic about trying to develop a more low-key social life?

- **Realize the hardest part is often getting started.** After you're over that initial hump it will feel rewarding to make progress.

- **Break your goals down into manageable chunks.** Rather than having a vague objective of "I'm so lonely" or "I'm so bad with people. I don't want to be like that anymore," try to define exactly what you'd like to change. Would you like to make three friends you see regularly? Would you like to be able to chat to your coworkers without feeling tongue-tied and self-conscious?

- **Focus on the next immediate step.** It's important to keep your long-term goals in mind so little hiccups don't discourage you. However, when it comes to motivation, your overall objective may feel impossible and overwhelming. You may not know where to start with "Have a full and rich social life," but it's easy enough to tackle "Step 1: Research some places in town where I may be able to meet people."

- **Don't try to work on every social skill or goal at once.** Figure out the few core things you'll need to get half-decent at to feel better about your social situation. Save all the smaller tweaks for later. For example, if you're shy and lonely, but okay at making conversation after you're past your initial nerves, focus on meeting new people and being able to feel comfortable enough to chat to them. Don't spread yourself thin by also trying to perfect your posture and use of humor.

- **Do what you can to practice socializing in ways that are fun and convenient.** There's no way to avoid feeling uncomfortable at all times, but as much as possible try to get your practice through types of interactions you'd enjoy anyway.

- **Alter your environment so it nudges you toward getting out and being social.** You could decide not to watch TV or play video games on the weekend, so you'll feel bored and look for something else to do. If you have a specific social task you're putting off, tell yourself you can't do certain fun things until you've completed it (for example, "I can't go on the Internet until I text Karen and ask her if she wants to hang out this weekend.").

"I'm too busy to work on my people skills."

Everyone gets really busy from time to time, and if you have more important priorities, there's nothing wrong with putting your social skills development on the back burner for a while. However, try to be honest with yourself about whether you're really too busy or if you're using that as an excuse. Don't hide behind a job or graduate program that has a culture that glorifies having no life. If you want to try to work around your hectic schedule, here are some ideas:

- **Make socializing a priority.** Don't see it as something you'll get to if your schedule happens to work out.
- **Boost your energy level.** If being too tired to go out is the problem, a nap after work or class or a strategic dose of caffeine may be all you need to get your energy and motivation back.
- **Manage your time better.** Figure out ways to use your time more efficiently and free up some hours in the day, for example, by improving your study or assignment-writing skills.
- **Streamline your social life.** Tweak your social life so it's less time-consuming and fits into your schedule. For example, make plans to see your friends after work, when you're already downtown.
- **Spend quality time with people instead of hanging out aimlessly for hours on end.** For example, have a shorter conversation-filled dinner instead of spending an evening watching TV and barely talking.
- **Organize group activities.** If you don't mind that kind of thing, try to hang out with lots of people at once instead of catching up with every person individually.

"I don't think I can get past my social problems without an exhaustive structured roadmap with hands-on exercises for each subskill."

Some people like to have every step of a process spelled out before they feel ready to start. This book offers lots of details that you can apply to your life as you see fit, but the content still may not be as fine-grained as you'd like. Every author has to decide what to leave out so the book can stay at a reasonable length. If you want in-depth clarification on a specific topic, you can look for it elsewhere, perhaps from a book in the Further Reading section.

Another possibility is you're not giving yourself enough credit to figure out how to improve on your own. To learn any complex skill, you need to know how to direct your own development at times. Everyone is different, and your needs aren't always going to fit a template. You need to know how to decide what to focus on and how to come up with your own practice exercises if none are available. As a side effect of being less socially successful, some people develop a sense of helplessness and passivity around the issue. They think, "I'm clueless at socializing. I could never figure out how to get better by myself. The only way I'll have a chance is if someone holds my hand every step of the way." Not so. Figuring out how to improve is something you have the ability to do.

This is not to pooh-pooh the idea of having a detailed, personalized plan entirely. Just don't default to thinking you can't do anything without one. If you think having a personalized plan would benefit you, a counselor can help with that.

"I feel like I'm a lost cause. I'm an especially bad case. I have too many factors stacked against me to ever get past my issues."

It's not uncommon to feel discouraged in this way. However, very few people are hopeless cases when it comes to their social skills. The ones who have limits on their potential have real impediments, like congenital intellectual deficits, lower-functioning autism, or significant mental health issues like severe schizophrenia. Even then, they can still make some improvements. If you're more typically functioning, you're more than capable of developing good social skills, even if it takes a while.

When people see themselves as a hopeless case, the biggest barrier that prevents them from getting over their problems is, ironically, their belief that they're a lost cause. If you actively, consistently work on your issues, it may be tough at times, but you'll overcome them eventually. However, if you give up and don't do anything to address your problems, they are guaranteed to stay with you. Chapter 5 goes into more detail about how you can identify and dispute some of the beliefs that may be feeding this sense of being beyond help.

"I have Asperger's syndrome/mild autism, which makes it harder for me to improve my social skills."

Asperger's syndrome is an inborn condition on the mild, higher-functioning end of the autism spectrum. Those who have it find socializing more difficult in a variety of ways. However, Asperger's is relatively rare, and most people who struggle socially don't have it. Appendix A goes into detail about the challenges Asperger's can cause and provides some approaches for working on your social skills if you have the condition.

CONCERNS ABOUT THE IDEA OF WORKING ON YOUR PEOPLE SKILLS

A fear of having to change too much and sell out to do better socially is a common concern. This book has already touched on some of these worries, and here are some more:

"I'm not sure if I want to work on my people skills. I don't lead a very social life, and I'm happy with it."

Odds are you're reading this book because you're motivated to change your social situation. However, maybe you're feeling more ambivalent. Maybe someone bought this book for you, and you're noncommittally flipping through it.

If you're content with your current social situation, this book isn't going to try to persuade you to change. However, it's important to make that decision with full self-awareness and honesty. Issues like anxiety, discouragement, and past resentments over being picked on or over-looked can cloud your motivations. You can trick yourself into believing you don't want what you think you can't have.

If you want to spend all of your time at home and not have many friends, and you've arrived at that choice with a clear head, that's fine. If you think you want to live a mostly solitary life because a) your anxiety has gotten out of hand, b) you're convinced no one would like you if you did try to make friends, and/or c) you're bitter about the idea of being social because you got picked on for being "weird" in high school, that's a different story. It's okay if you're not operating at 100 percent self-awareness at all times; no one is. Just check in on yourself occasionally and adjust course if needed.

"I'm on the fence about working on my social skills. I just don't enjoy socializing and don't see how I'd get any personal benefit from improving at it."

If you truly don't get much out of socializing, then you should live your life in a way that reflects your personality. However, many people who express this view are younger. They think they don't like socializing because they haven't experienced how rewarding it can be. Simply put, they don't know what they're missing. They associate "conversation" with all the awkward or insulting interactions they've had, instead of associating it with interest-ing, affirming exchanges with good friends who get them.

If your social skills are less developed, you have a lower ability to "unlock" the fun in many situations. For example, attending a party is going to feel like a chore if you don't know how to mingle and partic-ipate in engaging conversations, and are uncomfortable with letting loose or dancing. Of course, if you don't get a lot out of parties even after you know how to navigate them, that's okay too. It's also okay if you're not that keen on getting good at socializing at parties to begin with. Not everyone has to like all the same activities or be a social but-terfly. However, when you're inexperienced or gun-shy, it can cloud your sense of how appealing certain types of socializing can be. Once your interpersonal skills and confidence are higher you may find you enjoy some activities more than you used to.

**"It's not socializing itself that I dislike. It's that
I generally think other people suck."**

Sometimes when a person says they "don't like people," it's just their semi-facetious way of stating, "I'm not super social by nature. I don't need a ton of friends. I'm selective about who I hang around. My personality is on the less conventional side, and I've come to realize most people don't have a lot to offer me." That's fine. Not everybody has to be mainstream and love everyone.

At other times "I just don't like people" is said in a much more wounded, hostile manner. As with believing you don't like being social, feeling that you don't like people may be a reasonable conclusion based on your life so far. Who wouldn't dislike people if all they've known is cruel classmates, unsympathetic parents, coworkers they have little in common with, and a difficult, nitpicky boss?

It's also easier to form a negative opinion of people when you're at a distance. If you spend a lot of time alone, and your only social interactions are fleeting and superficial, a lot of the information you receive about humanity is more abstract. You read articles about the latest bar-lowering hit TV show or trashy celebrity. When you look at life from that detached viewpoint, it's easy to be down on everyone else. Improved social skills let you have the positive firsthand experiences that reinforce how great people can be.

**"I'm the way I am now socially because I was picked on in
the past. Why should I have to change? It's society in general
and the type of people who bullied me who should change."**

If you were picked on for perfectly acceptable differences like your interests, then I agree you shouldn't have to change those things. However, if being picked on caused you to develop social problems that are having an undeniable negative effect on your life, you probably do want to change by getting rid of them.

It's unjust that you experienced these adversities, but in the end they're still issues you need to deal with. You're only holding yourself back if you refuse to deal with them out of a sense that it's not fair. It's like if you were walking down the street and a stranger jumped out from behind a corner and shot you in the leg. Is it your fault that this happened? Not at all. Is it unfair? Certainly. Is whoever did it a horrible person? Without a doubt. But at the end of the day, you still have a gunshot wound in your thigh that you need to attend to. You can't get everyone in the world to change; you can only work on yourself.

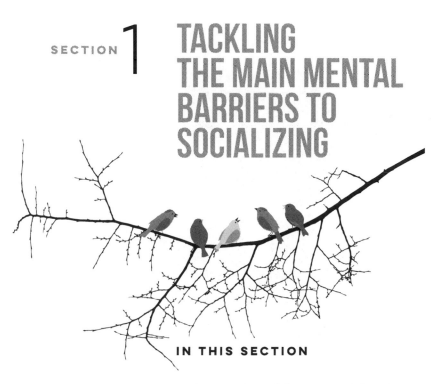

TACKLING THE MAIN MENTAL BARRIERS TO SOCIALIZING

IN THIS SECTION

- An overview of shyness, social anxiety, insecurity, and discouragement
- Important mind-sets for working on these issues
- Four effective approaches for dealing with these issues:
    1. Addressing the counterproductive thinking patterns that sustain them
    2. Knowing some hands-on methods for reducing anxiety
    3. Gradually facing and reducing your fears
    4. Increasing your overall confidence

3

SEEING THE EFFECTS
OF SHYNESS,
SOCIAL ANXIETY, INSECURITY,
AND DISCOURAGEMENT

IF YOU'RE LIKE MANY PEOPLE who want to improve their social situation, the biggest thing holding you back is your own mind. You may be quite socially capable and charming when you feel comfortable with someone, but in many situations, your shyness, anxiety, insecurities, and counterproductive thinking get in the way.

This chapter describes the four main confidence and comfort issues that interfere with people's ability to socialize:

1. Shyness
2. Social anxiety
3. Insecurity
4. Pessimism and discouragement

SHYNESS

Shyness is a multifaceted condition with many variations and nuances, but in short it's when you feel inhibited and uncomfortable in certain social situations because you're worried about how you'll come across to everyone. Just as other social difficulties can range from mild to severe, shyness also comes in degrees. If you're slightly shy, you may seem totally functional and even charming. Even though you may have some inner worries and insecurities, you can socialize in spite of them. Your shyness isn't a huge problem, but even if you're performing well outwardly, it's still draining to be constantly worrying and doubting yourself. If you're moderately shy, you'll be more hesitant and quiet than normal in social situations, but still be able to get by. If you're severely shy, you'll be totally withdrawn, if you get into many interactions at all. Less mild forms of shyness overlap with social anxiety, which will be covered in a second.

The richest aspect of shyness is the thinking patterns and beliefs that fuel it. Shy people think in ways that increase the supposed risks and stakes of socializing. They see other people as mean and judgmental. They see themselves as unappealing and less socially capable. They view interactions as life-or-death tests of their social skills and worthiness as individuals. Chapter 5 goes into more detail about these unhelpful thinking patterns.

People who suffer from shyness often second-guess the meaning behind other people's words. They may be hypersensitive to perceived signs of rejection or hostility ("She only sort of laughed at my joke. She must hate me." "He complimented my hat. He's probably messing with me somehow.") Sometimes they dwell on past social situations, sometimes years after the fact, and beat themselves up over the things they supposedly did wrong.

Overall presentation

Regardless of how shy you are, you're likely to experience some or all of the following effects:
- being hesitant, reserved, and untalkative;
- coming across as meek, soft-spoken, and unsure of what you're saying;
- acting uncomfortable (for example, fidgeting, avoiding eye contact, crossing your arms over your chest);
- having trouble getting your words out or putting sentences together; stuttering;
- coming across as unconfident and self-effacing;
- on occasion, being more outgoing and chatty than normal because

of nerves or because that's how other people expect you to behave;

- on occasion, coming across as cold and aloof because you unintentionally act this way when you're feeling awkward, or because you're purposely trying to manage your discomfort by sending out "don't approach me" vibes;
- reacting physically: blushing; trembling; muscle tension; sweating; clammy hands; dry mouth; tight, quiet voice; increased heart rate; stomach upset; increased need to urinate; feeling amped up and fidgety.

Circumstances that can bring on shyness

You may feel shy in most social situations or only during particular ones. Situations in which people commonly feel shy include

- meeting new people;
- having to work a room and mingle;
- interacting with people you find intimidating and high-status (for example, asking a professor to reconsider a grade she gave you on a paper);
- interacting with people whose opinion you really care about and whom you want to make a good impression on;
- being put on the spot (for example, being handed a microphone out of the blue and asked to record a video message at a wedding);
- being the center of attention or doing something that draws attention to yourself (for example, being called on in class, wearing flashy clothes, calling down a hall to get a friend's attention);
- having to perform (for example, giving a speech or telling a story when everyone at the table is listening intently);
- confronting someone or being assertive (for example, telling a friend you don't like it when they tease you constantly, telling a coworker you don't want to help them move on the weekend);
- during interactions where you may upset the other person (for example, turning down a request, asking someone not to do something annoying, asking a person to go out of their way for you);
- talking on the phone or having to leave a voicemail.

Approaching social situations

Shy people dread many common social settings or interactions because they aren't sure how to act or they aren't sure how they'll be received by others. See if any of these responses for handling social situations sound familiar:

- completely avoiding social situations or interactions that make you feel shy (for example, not going to a party, crossing the street to avoid having to stop and chat with an acquaintance, sending an email when a phone call would be easier, not following up to hang out with someone you met the other day);
- bailing out of social situations early (for example, making an excuse to end a conversation after a few minutes, leaving a pub because you feel so out of your element);
- partially avoiding social situations or interactions (for example, being present in a group conversation but not saying anything);
- being less likely to take social risks (for example, not asking someone to hang out, not approaching a stranger to start a conversation, holding back a mildly controversial opinion).

Overall consequences

Being shy does more than keep you home at night. It also causes these overarching problems:

- The self-doubt and inhibition inherent in shyness prevent you from showing your full personality. When you're in a conversation with people you feel uncomfortable around, you stand there silently, and no one sees what you're capable of. However, if the people were your long-time friends, you'd be making all kinds of hilarious jokes and witty observations.
- It keeps you from going after what you want.
- It simply doesn't feel good to be so hard on yourself or feel so ill-at-ease in certain situations
- Your shy behavior may create a poor impression on other people. It's not that most people think horribly of shyness; it's just that if it comes down to being sure of yourself or being withdrawn, the

former is going to come across better.

- Making friends is difficult. You can still make friends when you're shy, but the process takes longer and you may have less control. You have to hope that you'll spend enough time with the other people for you to feel comfortable around them or that they'll give you a chance and make all the first moves.

Getting a handle on your shyness allows you to reverse the condition. You'll be more willing to show your personality and put yourself out there in social situations. You'll feel better about who you are. You'll feel comfortable instead of being a ball of nerves. On the whole, your interactions will be more effective. Reducing your shyness also frees you up to work on your social skills more effectively. You'll be able to socialize more often, during which time you can take more chances, push yourself harder, and make more mistakes you can learn from.

SOCIAL ANXIETY

Social anxiety is when you feel nervous in social situations. It has a lot in common with shyness; it leads to similar outcomes, like avoidance and impaired social performance, and is often brought on by fears about how you'll come across to people. However, social anxiety and shyness don't always go hand in hand. It's possible to feel shy and inhibited at a party without feeling physically nervous. It's also possible, but less likely, to feel anxious in a social situation without having a ton of worries or insecurities (for example, even though you know everything will turn out fine, you're stressed about meeting your friend's friends just because it's a new situation and you're generally frazzled from problems at work).

With social anxiety, the nervousness can become its own problem. Mild anxiety isn't oodles of fun, but it's relatively easy to tolerate and push through. Physically it doesn't feel that different from excitement. You may feel a little amped up and jittery or have some minor sweating, blushing, or butterflies in the stomach. Moderate anxiety is another story. Besides your fear levels being higher, it can cause unpleasant bodily symptoms like nausea, trembling, dizziness, hot flashes, heart palpitations, and a need to use the bathroom. Severe anxiety—that is, a panic attack—is downright terrifying. You feel incredibly bad physically, you have an intense urge to escape, and you often think you're going to die or go crazy.

Acknowledging social fears

If a social situation made you anxious, a completely understandable reaction would be to become scared of it and want to steer clear of it in the future. Stronger anxiety can also lead you to develop a second-order fear that your anxiety is obvious and noticeable, which in turn can cause you to fear being rejected; you may worry that everyone will be put off by your looking like a shaky wreck, or that you'll do something humiliating, like throw up or freak out in public.

As with shyness, social anxiety can crop up in most social situations or be specific to a particular one. These more specific fears may be the same as the ones a shy person has (for example, meeting new people). Socially anxious people can develop other types of specific fears. First, they may get nervous and self-conscious in day-to-day situations where they feel people are watching or evaluating them, such as eating in front of their friends, writing in view of others, working out at the gym, or, for men, using a urinal with other guys around. Second, they may develop a fear of situations where they're "trapped." In situations where people feel trapped, they worry that if they were to become really anxious, they'd draw attention to themselves and perhaps become a laughing-stock (for example, sitting in the middle seat of a crowded movie theater, getting a haircut, riding the subway).

The problem is that this is all self-reinforcing. You develop a fear of fear. When you're worried about getting anxious, you're almost guaranteed to bring on the very nervousness you want to avoid. It's one more obstacle to improving socially. If you go to a party, you're so preoccupied with managing your nerves that trying to connect with anyone gets pushed to the back burner.

Overcoming avoidance

It's no picnic when your nerves screw up your conversation in the moment, so you may choose to avoid interactions that may be difficult or unpleasant for you. However, over the long run, the avoidance that anxiety encourages is more damaging. Avoiding something that scares you prevents you from feeling bad in the short term, but often runs counter to your long-term interests. Anxiety is manageable if you're afraid of some obscure scenario, but it's another story if you feel nervous about day-to-day social situations that you want to be involved in. A key to handling anxiety is to break the avoidance habit.

Avoiding something you fear plays into a vicious cycle, which strengthens your anxiety. Whenever you avoid a situation, the relief you feel reinforces the behavior and cements the idea that you dodged something truly dangerous. Avoidance can make you miss out on important parts of life when you try to prevent yourself from ever feeling uncomfortable. You can end up rearranging your days into a lonely, sterile rut.

It's one thing to feel blatantly nervous and cancel on a dinner party or decide against trying to start a conversation with a classmate. However, anxiety can be a lot more subtle when it comes to avoiding social situations. People sometimes have a hard time admitting that they're not doing something because it makes them uneasy, and anxiety is great at providing reasonable-sounding excuses and rationalizations. Anxiety can make you think you truly aren't interested in an activity when the situation really just scares you. You can be about to leave for a get-together when you start thinking, "You know what? I really should study tonight instead." Subtle anxiety can also appear as procrastination. You really want to join that running club, but you've been putting it off for the past six months because it's never the perfect time.

Safety behaviors allow you to partially avoid a situation. These behaviors shelter you from the full brunt of an anxiety-provoking situation. For example, if you feel off-balance at parties, you may drink a lot to dull your nerves and have a ready-made excuse for any gaffes you make. Safety behaviors can also be more understated. If you're mildly anxious in social situations, you may be able to have conversations, but only when you stick to neutral topics, keep the focus on the other person, and don't reveal any deeper personal information about yourself. If you have trouble with specific symptoms like blushing or nausea, you may wear your hair in a way that covers more of your face or always carry some stomach-soothing medication around "just in case."

Social Anxiety Disorder

Shyness is a fairly common, if inconvenient trait. Everyone feels socially anxious at times. However, if you experience anxiety in social situations often or intensely enough that it interferes with your life, a professional could decide a diagnosis of Social Anxiety Disorder / Social Phobia is appropriate. Here are the criteria for it from the latest edition of the *Diagnostic and Statistical Manual of Mental Disorders*:

DSM-5 Criteria for Social Anxiety Disorder

A. Marked fear or anxiety about one or more social situations in which the individual is exposed to possible scrutiny by others. Examples include social interactions (for example, having a conversation, meeting unfamiliar people), being observed (for example, eating or drinking), and performing in front of others (for example, giving a speech).
B. The individual fears that he or she will act in a way or show anxiety symptoms that will be negatively evaluated (that is, will be humiliating and embarrassing; will lead to rejection or offend others).
C. The social situations almost always provoke fear or anxiety.
D. The social situations are avoided or endured with intense fear or anxiety.
E. The fear or anxiety is out of proportion to the actual threat posed by the social situation and to the sociocultural context.
F. The fear, anxiety, or avoidance is persistent, typically lasting for 6 months or more.

G. The fear, anxiety, or avoidance causes clinically significant distress or impairment in social, occupational, or other important areas of functioning.

H. The fear, anxiety, or avoidance is not attributable to the physiological effects of a substance (for example, a drug of abuse, a medication) or another medical condition.

I. The fear, anxiety, or avoidance is not better explained by the symptoms of another mental disorder, such as panic disorder, body dysmorphic disorder, or autism spectrum disorder.

If another medical condition (for example, Parkinson's disease, obesity, disfigurement from burns or injury) is present, the fear, anxiety, or avoidance is clearly unrelated or is excessive.

To be diagnosed with Social Anxiety Disorder, your nervousness in social situations has to be at least moderate. There are degrees of severity within the condition. Someone with a mild version of it may feel quite uncomfortable in social situations, but is still able to be functional. In severe cases, people never leave their house, only socialize with family, and panic if they have to speak to anyone else.

If you suspect you have Social Anxiety Disorder, make an appointment to see a professional and get their opinion on what steps to take next.

INSECURITY

Insecurity boils down to having a low opinion of your own value (particularly in social situations), assuming other people won't like you, and believing your flaws will keep you from meeting your goals. Like anxiety, insecurity is often a component of shyness, but it can exist on its own. You could go to a social function and be outgoing and calm, while still having thoughts like, "I'm too lame to be hanging out with this crowd," "Everyone probably thinks I'm annoying," or "He gave me his number and said we should hang out, but if I call, he'll probably think I'm needy."

Insecurity doesn't rear its ugly head only before a social interaction. You may experience some of the following thoughts during a conversation:

- "I'm probably screwing up."
- "They think I'm annoying."
- "They'll only like me if I'm really impressive."
- "They'll only like me if I hide who I really am."
- "He glanced away for a split second after I made that joke. He probably thinks I'm corny and trying too hard."
- "She's talking to me now, but it's probably just out of politeness. She'd never want to hang out later."

When you're facing the opportunity to pursue a friendship, these thoughts may run through your mind, causing you to second-guess whether you should reach out to the other person:

- "They probably don't want to hang out again."
- "If we meet and grab a coffee, they'll realize how awkward I really am. No point in bothering."

Even after you've established relationships, you may feel insecure about your value to the other person:

- "My friends probably don't really like me. They're still hanging out with me only out of inertia or pity."
- "She didn't return my text right away. She hates me."

Signs of insecurity

Sometimes people who are insecure show no signs of it. Some insecure people have it together on the outside, and no one would ever guess that they question their value to themselves and others. But all too often, people who are insecure subtly convey that feeling to those they're talking to. Examples include

- coming across as shy, unconfident, and fearful about saying the wrong thing;
- trying too hard to please people and do whatever it takes to get their approval;

- bragging and trying too hard to impress people; acting overly outgoing and self-assured to compensate for a lack of confidence; putting others down so you'll feel better about yourself in comparison;
- acting needy and clingy with friends (for example, contacting them constantly or always casually mentioning how much they mean to you and how devastated you'd be if they stopped hanging out with you);
- trying too hard to control your friends' behavior and force them to be considerate toward you (for example, "I invited you to my birthday dinner, and you didn't let me know you were coming until a week before it was happening. You should have let me know right away!");
- overreacting to possible signs of rejection, either by giving up entirely, showing needy behavior (sending a bunch of increasingly frantic "u there?" texts if they don't reply to you instantly), or being too quick to stand up for yourself and set them straight over minor issues ("You were half an hour late to my party. You have no respect for me! Don't let it happen again").

DISCOURAGEMENT / PESSIMISM

Feeling discouraged or pessimistic is an issue that is different from the three above, but often goes hand in hand with them. The methods for addressing it are the same as well. A history of poor social outcomes can lead to pessimism and discouragement about meeting your goals to improve your social situation. Feeling discouraged can then cause you to develop a number of counterproductive mind-sets that can hinder you even further. It can also lead to self-sabotaging behavior where you don't try because you "know" you'll fail anyway. Here are some typical discouraging thoughts:

- "I'm too unlikable. There's no point in trying anymore."
- "I could go to that party, but it won't get me anywhere, so I'll take a pass."
- "They'll probably reject me, so I won't bother talking to them."
- "They seem bored by me. I'll bow out of the conversation now to save us both time."
- "He just gave me his number and said we should

grab a beer sometime. It never works out when I
follow up with someone, so I won't bother."
■ "Maybe other awkward people can improve, but
my set of issues is too much to overcome."

The four related problems of shyness, social anxiety, insecurity, and
discouragement need to be tackled directly. You should do some work
on them before working on conversation or social life issues you want
to fix. If you're shy and insecure around people, you can indirectly become more confident by developing your conversation and friend-making skills (assuming they're not already fine and your shyness just blocks
them from coming out). One warning though: If you attempt to practice your social skills but haven't taken steps to address the counterproductive thinking at the core of your shyness and anxiety, you may end
up worse off. You'll put yourself in social situations but still see them as
dangerous and high-stakes; if something goes wrong, you may come to
inaccurate, disheartening conclusions about yourself and your hopes of
improving. You don't have to get your thinking to a flawless place before you start working on your people skills, but your thoughts should
be at a level where they won't completely sabotage you either.

4

SHIFTING YOUR MIND-SET ABOUT YOUR SOCIAL DISCOMFORT

BEFORE YOU CAN START WORKING on any shyness, anxiety, or lack of confidence, you need to develop the right mind-set for dealing with these problems. People often believe two big myths that give their social discomfort too much power and hinder their ability to deal with it:

1. "There must be a way to totally eradicate my shyness, social anxiety, and insecurities (and therefore I'll put improving my social life on hold until I do that)."
2. "I can't show any signs of social discomfort to people. It's shameful and will ruin the interaction."

You'll have to do some work, but you can limit the impact of these counterproductive mind-sets. This chapter presents some useful attitudes to adopt regarding social situations. If you keep these points in mind, you'll be on your way to feeling more comfortable around people and handling any uneasiness that pops up along the way.

KNOW AND ACCEPT THAT YOU'LL NEVER BANISH ALL SOCIAL DISCOMFORT FROM YOUR LIFE

Although the strategies in the following chapters will help you turn down the dial on your social discomfort, you'll never banish those issues completely. Humans just aren't wired to be blissfully happy and self-assured 100 percent of the time. Even if you learn and apply every coping strategy there is, you need to accept that the following things will still happen:

- At times you'll have worried, insecure, or counterproductive thoughts, even if you use every technique you know to try to make them go away.
- Sometimes you'll feel anxious, regardless of how much you try to control it or logically realize there's nothing to fret about.
- Some situations will always make you a little nervous, even if you've successfully gone through them plenty of times (for example, most people never get entirely comfortable with public speaking or trying to start a conversation with someone they're attracted to).
- There will be instances where you'll make a mistake, get rejected, or look bad in a social situation, even if you do everything you can to prevent it.
- You'll feel down on yourself at times, no matter how much you try to psych yourself up or remind yourself of your strengths.
- Even if you seem to have your shyness and insecurities under control, you may go through a stressful period in your life that makes them flare up again.
- You'll never be able to predict the future or have full certainty an upcoming social event will go well.
- You may have been born with a tendency to be more anxious and insecure than average, and it's something you'll have to learn to work around.

Accepting that you may sometimes get uncomfortable in social situations takes away some of the control your shyness and insecurities have over you. For example, if you think awkward silences are terrible, you'll avoid countless conversations in an attempt to only chat to someone under the perfect, safe set of conditions. If you make peace with the fact that lulls happen sometimes, no matter how prepared you are, you'll be willing to talk to more people.

Even when you really don't want a certain outcome, you'll often feel a kind of relief when you know for sure it's going to happen. At least the uncertainty and "what if?" worrying are gone, and you can focus on how you're going to handle it. If you knew with 100 percent certainty you were going to stumble over your words whenever you met someone new, it would be inconvenient, but you could shift your energy toward coming up with strategies to deal with that fact.

AIM TO BECOME SOCIALLY FUNCTIONAL, RATHER THAN 100 PERCENT ASSURED AT ALL TIMES

After you accept that you're still going to encounter some social unease from time to time, your aim should be to become socially *functional*, where even if you're nervous or self-doubting, you can still meet your goals. Don't put your social life on hold until you wipe all shyness from your mind, because that will never happen. A key part of being functional is to realize you can be shy, nervous, or insecure during a social event and still function and ultimately enjoy yourself.

Socializing while experiencing a case of the jitters

When people struggle with social anxiety, they sometimes look at their discomfort in either–or terms when they're deciding whether to attend a get-together. They think if they're not completely confident and relaxed, then they have to skip it. If nerves strike when they're with people, they think the whole outing is ruined.

You can get through most social situations with some self-doubt or jitters. If your nerves or insecurities are mild, they may not interfere with your outward performance at all. Even if they trip you up a little, they won't fully ruin the interaction. Only the most extreme, sustained anxiety will do that. A conversation can easily be a success, even if you trembled or had trouble putting your thoughts together at the beginning of it.

When looking back at an outing, how nervous or unsure you were at the time becomes even less important. If you get nervous in crowds but go to see your favorite band anyway, five years from now you'll be happy you went and cherish the good memories you have; you'll hardly regret the experience because you felt on edge at the start of the show.

Acknowledging that nervousness comes with valued goals

Figure out what is truly important to you in life and commit to going after it, regardless of your fears or insecurities. This will put your discomfort in perspective and help you set your priorities. If you're pursuing something you truly care about, then any nervousness that comes up along the way will be worth it. For example, you might decide it's important to increase your social circle and try new things. If you get an invitation to go rock climbing with some coworkers, but the thought of it makes you anxious, it'll be easier to get yourself to go because you know it aligns with what you want.

Accept that it's okay to show signs of your issues

Shyness and anxiety can have such a powerful hold on you because you're afraid of experiencing their symptoms in front of people. You can take a lot of that influence away if you say to yourself, "You know what? If I look scared in front of people, then so be it. If I turn red while talking to someone, it's not the worst thing ever, if I seem comfortable with myself otherwise." If you can start to care less about the consequences of your self-doubts or anxiety, you'll be less likely to feel insecure or anxious in the first place.

Caring less about your social faux pas is easier said than done. The secret is to make acting against your worries a higher priority than trying to make every interaction go perfectly. You can achieve this by employing two mentalities, either of which may motivate you depending on your personality:

1. Be pleasant and understanding toward your fears and insecurities. You see your anxiety as just trying to help, but it's going too far. If you're nervous about meeting your new friends for drinks, tell yourself, "Anxiety, thanks for your concern, but getting to know new people is a priority for me, so I'm not going to cancel and stay home."

2. Be more angry and defiant. You're tired of letting your shyness and worries push you around, and you won't let them run your life any longer. You may be heading to a meet-up and think, "If I get nervous, I get nervous. At least I showed up and didn't let my anxiety rule my life." On the walk home, you may think, "I was a little inhibited and queasy at the start of the night, but I hung in there. My anxiety wanted me to leave, but I beat it."

Mention when you're shy, nervous, or insecure

Part of accepting your shyness or anxiety can include a willingness to tell people you're feeling shy or anxious at that moment, or have a problem with those issues in general. Being able to talk about your problems takes away the belief that you can't let anyone find out what you're going through. Occasionally someone will respond insensitively, but most people know what it's like to feel nervous and will be understanding. If you tell someone, don't phrase it as a shameful confession or go into the entire backstory of your struggles. Just casually let them know you're a bit nervous and then move on with the conversation. If you set a tone that your nerves aren't that big a deal, everyone else will follow your cues.

Know it's normal to be shy, insecure, or socially anxious at times

It's certainly not fun or helpful to feel shy or nervous, but it's not a sign you're weak or mentally defective. These problems are very common. Just because they may be giving you more trouble than average doesn't change that they're normal human emotions. Go easy on yourself and give yourself permission to feel that way.

KNOWING WHETHER WORKING ON YOUR SOCIAL SKILLS DIRECTLY WILL DECREASE YOUR SHYNESS

Many people who are shy or socially anxious have perfectly good social skills. Their fears and insecurities just get in the way of them using those skills, unless they're around people they're comfortable with. Other people have underdeveloped interpersonal skills in addition to their shyness and anxiety, and the two problems feed into and amplify each other. If your social skills are creaky, you may start to feel more socially confident once you develop them more, or even just learn some strategies on paper and feel more prepared.

The book's other two sections on conversation and making friends have plenty of advice on handling social situations. One warning though: If you attempt to practice your social skills but haven't taken steps to address the counterproductive thinking at the core of your shyness and anxiety, you may end up worse off. You'll put yourself in social situations but still see them as dangerous and high-stakes, and if something goes wrong, you may come to inaccurate, disheartening conclusions about yourself and your hopes of improving. You don't have to get your thinking to a flawless place before you start practicing your people skills, but your thoughts should be at a level where they won't completely sabotage you either.

WHAT IF YOU CAN'T REDUCE YOUR SHYNESS OR ANXIETY BY YOURSELF?

If you have mild to moderate shyness or social anxiety, you should be able to apply the suggestions in the next four chapters using a self-help approach. Sometimes your anxiety will be more severe and too much to handle on your own. If that's the case, consider seeing a therapist or joining an anxiety support group. You'll still go through the same kinds of treatment approaches the following chapters cover, but a professional or others with similar issues can support you through the rough patches and customize everything to your needs. Also, go to a doctor to rule out whether your anxiety has a physical cause, like an issue with your thyroid gland.

Medication may also be an option to look into. Speak to a physician or a psychiatrist about that possibility and to get the most up-to-date information about your options. Medication dampens the physical symptoms of anxiety, but doesn't affect its underlying psychological causes. It needs to be used in conjunction with psychological treatment approaches that address those issues. Medication can reduce your symptoms enough that you can implement a treatment plan you'd otherwise be too nervous to progress through.

Although many people take medication on a short-term basis, a smaller number feel it improves their quality of life enough to justify staying on it long-term. They realize that they were born with an overly high anxiety level, and medication brings it down to a level where they can function better.

Some people are justifiably wary about taking any kind of drug, and it's not a decision to be made lightly. Medication can cause side effects, and it can take people some time and experimentation before they find a drug and dosage that works for them. In more severe cases, it can make the difference though, so at least give it some thought if a professional makes that recommendation.

5

HANDLING COUNTERPRODUCTIVE THINKING ABOUT SOCIALIZING

SHYNESS, SOCIAL ANXIETY, INSECURITIES, AND DISCOURAGEMENT about your chances of improving are all sustained in part by thoughts and beliefs that are counterproductive—that is, thoughts that lead you away from good outcomes. They create unpleasant feelings like nervousness and self-doubt, and cause you to behave in ways that go against your goals, such as avoiding get-togethers or giving up on trying to be friends with people. They can pop up in the present moment or when you're looking back on the past or toward the future. If you can rein in your negative thoughts about socializing, you'll be more content and confident and have an easier time going after what you want.

This chapter explains the two broad ways your thinking can stifle you. Then it covers two approaches for dealing with your counterproductive thoughts. First, it gives you a framework for identifying and disputing these types of thoughts and replacing them with more-balanced alternatives. It then explains an equally effective alternative approach—using mindfulness principles to acknowledge and accept your counterproductive thoughts without getting sucked into them.

COUNTERPRODUCTIVE THINKING PATTERN 1: COGNITIVE DISTORTIONS

When thinking about social interactions, you may have thoughts that psychologists call cognitive distortions. These thought patterns become misleading and irrational in ways that sustain your problems. It's possible to have cognitive distortions about all kinds of things, like your ability to grow tomatoes, but the examples below naturally focus on social situations.

Emotional reasoning

Emotional reasoning is when you think that because your emotions are telling you something is a certain way, it truly *is* that way. For example, thinking that because you feel anxious, something must be happening that is worth feeling anxious about, when in fact maybe you're just on edge because you drank too much coffee. In social situations, it often creates the reasoning of "I'm nervous about doing X, therefore X must be scary, difficult, and complicated."

Jumping to conclusions

When you jump to conclusions, you quickly assume something negative, even though your belief has little or no basis in reality. There are two variations: mind reading and fortune-telling.

- Mind reading is when you believe someone thinks a certain way without any solid evidence to support it (for example, "I just know everyone on my dodgeball team hates me" or "When she said 'hi' she was doing it sarcastically to subtly mock me").
- Fortune-telling is when you assume an event will turn out a certain way (for example, when you "know" you're not going to have fun at the bar later that night because some jerk is going to bother you).

All-or-nothing thinking / Black-and-white thinking

When you see things in simplistic, absolute terms, you're using all-or-nothing or black-and-white thinking. This may involve extreme comparisons like perfect vs. useless or words like "never" or "always." It often comes up when you're thinking about your social goals or evaluating how you're currently doing. For example, "I don't think I'll be able to become incredibly charismatic, so there's no point in trying to work on my social skills at all," or "Not every person in my class loves me, so that means I'm a complete reject."

Overgeneralization

Overgeneralization involves taking a few isolated incidents and making sweeping generalizations about yourself, other people, or your life. For example, "My one coworker didn't invite me out. No one at my job wants to be friends," or "I didn't find those two people that interesting to talk to. I have nothing in common with anybody."

Filtering

You're filtering when you apply a dark-tinted mental lens to your perceptions so you dwell on the bad aspects of something, while ignoring the good. This can involve "seeing what you want to see." Because life offers up a variety of experiences, no matter what conclusion you want to reach, you can usually cherry-pick enough "evidence" to support it. For example, you may be feeling discouraged about getting over your shyness and remember the times you felt self-conscious and inhibited, but "forget" all the instances where you weren't. Or you may believe that other men / women are macho jerks / catty gossips. You overlook all the people who don't fit that stereotype but can't let it go if you spot someone acting like an obnoxious bro / backstabbing Queen Bee.

Magnification and minimization

When you overstate how something really is, once again with iffy evidence to back up your thinking, you magnify the situation; similarly, if you understate a situation with insufficient evidence, you minimize it. For example, you could magnify the supposed importance of the first week of college by believing that if you don't make friends during that time, your social life for the next four years will be ruined. You could minimize the usefulness of a personal talent by telling yourself, "Sure, I'm good at singing, but there's no way that could help me meet people. How much could joining a choir or band really do?"

Catastrophizing

When your mind leaps to the worst possible outcome, you're catastrophizing. It can also mean to see a situation as totally hopeless or unbearable, when it's really just uncomfortable. This cognitive distortion unsurprisingly tends to increase anxiety. Some examples:

- "I have no plans this weekend. I can't take it. I just know I'm going to live a life of complete social isolation."
- "If I seem shy at this lunch, everyone's going to think I'm a weirdo and kick me out of the group."
- "I'm feeling too nervous right now. I can't do this, I can't do this. I need to leave."

"Should" statements

This cognitive distortion involves constraining yourself with unrealistic expectations about how things "should" be (for example, "People should invite their friends to hang out at least once a week, otherwise it's a sign they hate them"; "I should always have brilliant things to say in conversations"; "I should never get anxious in social situations").

Labeling

Labeling occurs when you slap simplistic labels on things in order to explain them, rather than looking at the unique facets of the situation. You'd be labeling if you explained away a strained conversation by saying it was because you're a geek and the other person was a jock, or if you told yourself, "I'm an electrical engineering student. It's a given that I'm awkward around people."

Personalization

Personalization involves thinking you directly caused something to happen, or that something relates to you, when other forces may have been at work. For example, you might think your friends want to leave your place early because you're so boring, when they're really just tired.

Disqualifying the positive

Disqualifying the positive is when you dismiss positive events for no real reason, probably while being all too eager to accept the negative ones (for example, "I had a really nice conversation with Amy at that party, but it doesn't count. She's friendly to everyone. I still suck at talking to people").

Attributional style

Disqualifying the positive ties into a related psychological concept called attributional style, or explanatory style, which is the way people tend to explain events to themselves. People who are socially insecure tend to dismiss positive experiences as being one-off flukes, while seeing negative interactions as being caused by their enduring flaws. If they have a good conversation, they'll write it off as the other person being in a cheerful mood or talking to them out of pity. If they have a stilted exchange, they'll blame it on how boring or awkward they are. Most people are the opposite. They're slightly benignly deluded in a way that helps them function better. If an interaction goes well, they give themselves the credit, but if it doesn't, they look for outside explanations, like that the other person was distracted and in a hurry.

COUNTERPRODUCTIVE THINKING PATTERN 2: UNHELPFUL BELIEFS

A lot of counterproductive beliefs arise from cognitive distortions. Odds are, as you read the preceding section, you recognized a few cognitive distortions you've had yourself. Your thinking can also interfere with your social success when you hold inaccurate beliefs that are related to socializing. A few of these beliefs are straight-up false. Most have a kernel of truth to them, but that element has been blown out of proportion. Unhelpful beliefs can be about several categories. You'll notice some of them contain cognitive distortions like mind reading or fortune-telling as well:

Beliefs about yourself

- "Being shy or socially inexperienced is a very negative trait."
- "I'm flawed and unappealing at my core."
- "People won't like me because I'm too X."

Beliefs about the risks and stakes of socializing

- "My worth as a person depends on how well I perform socially."
- "My social performance has to be 100 percent at all times, or I won't be successful."
- "Every interaction is a test of my social skills and likability."
- "It would be terrible if people thought of me as shy or awkward."
- "Every social mistake I make will have horrible immediate consequences."
- "If I screw up, people will remember it, hold it against me for a long time, and tell everyone they know, and it will ruin my social life."
- "Rejection is terrible and intolerable."

Beliefs that give you responsibility for things you can't control

- "I must make everyone like me."
- "I'm 100 percent responsible for how well an interaction goes."
- "I'm 100 percent responsible for other people's reactions to me."

Beliefs about other people

- "Everyone is really choosy about what they look for in others."
- "Everyone else has their act together socially."
- "Other people are constantly evaluating how I'm coming across socially."
- "This certain type of person is mean and especially likely to reject me."
- "Certain people have the authority to judge my value as a person. If they don't like me, then I'm a loser."
- "People often mock others by pretending to compliment or be friendly to them."

Beliefs about improving your social situation

- "Something about my area makes meeting my social goals too hard." (For example, "The people in my city are too unfriendly" or "There's nowhere good to meet anyone in my town.")
- "Something about me makes it too hard to reach my social goals." (for example, "I'm too old to make friends." or "I have bad skin. No one will want to hang out with me.")
- "It's inappropriate or ineffective to do certain things to try to reach my social goals." (For example, "I can't just start conversations with people I don't know. Who does that? Everyone will think I'm a creep.")

These unhelpful beliefs may only somewhat interfere with your social success. For example, a belief that other people are putting your social skills under a microscope may make you somewhat more nervous around others, but not enough that it prevents you from meeting new friends. Beliefs can limit you when you believe them too strongly and refuse to accept the possibility that you're wrong. For example, you could believe that you'll never make friends in your new city because the locals are too cold and aloof; when anyone tries to say differently, you get angry. These limiting beliefs can be stubborn because the filtering cognitive distortion can kick in and cause you to focus only on things that confirm your existing views.

Now that you have an understanding of how your thinking can get in the way, let's look at the first method for dealing with it.

IDENTIFYING, QUESTIONING, AND REPLACING YOUR COUNTERPRODUCTIVE THINKING

Because counterproductive thoughts are distorted or inaccurate, you can overcome many of them by logically picking them apart and replacing them with a more realistic alternative. Here are the steps to doing this:

STEP 1: IDENTIFY YOUR COUNTERPRODUCTIVE THOUGHTS AND BELIEFS

You can informally do this step and the next one in your head, but they're more effective if you make a proper written exercise out of them. It's an ongoing process. Don't expect to spot and debunk all of your negative thoughts in one twenty-minute brainstorming session.

Areas of counterproductive thinking to delve into

1. Think of what your counterproductive beliefs are. If you're like most shy or less-confident people, you're all too familiar with the messages that scroll through your brain all day and won't have trouble getting a bunch of them down on paper.
2. Follow your negative emotions (for example, anxiety, discouragement, resentment) and see where they lead you. For example, you might start thinking about some acquaintances, feel a bit sad, and then identify some worries about them not wanting to become closer friends with you.
3. Pick a specific social situation you struggle with and then examine your thoughts around it (for example, speaking up in class).

4. Look back on a social interaction you recently had. Say you tried chatting with some coworkers during your lunch break. How do you feel it went? What discouraging or self-critical thoughts are you having about it?

STEP 2: CRITICALLY EXAMINE YOUR COUNTERPRODUCTIVE THOUGHTS AND BELIEFS

Do this step when you have some time to yourself and you're in a fairly neutral, logical mood. It is possible to analyze your thoughts when you're in the middle of a social situation or in the grip of a strong emotion, but it's a lot more difficult to stay objective.

To begin, you want to shift your perspective. When dissecting each thought, imagine it's something a friend told you they were feeling about themselves or a statement your worst enemy made to you. You'll often uncritically accept ideas from your own mind that you would question instantly if they came from an outside source.

You could also try "externalizing" your issues. Instead of seeing your anxiety or insecurity as a core part of you, view it as an outside entity that has taken up residence in your mind and is trying to sabotage it (for example, picture it as a cartoony demon).

Next, ask several questions of each thought and see how well it holds up:

- What is the overall tone of the thought? Sometimes you'll have thoughts that are technically accurate and free of distortions, but you're still being way too harsh and unsympathetic toward yourself.
- Is there a cognitive distortion, self-effacing attribution, or unhelpful belief in the thought?
- Do you have any evidence that the thought is accurate and true? Don't just think about it for a second and come to a knee-jerk conclusion. Write out all the objective arguments for each side, like you were arguing a case in court. Say you believe no one likes you. What real-world encounters are you basing that on? Are you giving too much weight to one negative memory? What about counterexamples of people who enjoy having you around?

- If you feel you do have evidence that the thought is true, is it accurate, or is it the product of counterproductive thinking as well? If you think, "No one likes me," and for evidence you recall that last week one acquaintance didn't respond to your text right away, that's overgeneralizing or jumping to conclusions. If you say, "I just *know* everyone hates me. I just feel it every time I reach out to someone," that's mind reading and emotional reasoning.

- If you have a simplistic black-and-white thought about yourself, like "I'm boring," can you break it down more? You're not either 100 percent dull or 100 percent interesting. What percent interesting would you say you are? What are the individual elements of being interesting? Being funny? Having unique experiences and stories to share? Having insightful opinions? If you made each of those a scale from 0 to 10, where would you come out on them?

What if a belief or observation turns out to be true?

If you're really shy and insecure, you should lean toward assuming your thoughts on socializing are at least somewhat skewed. However, sometimes you'll put a thought or belief through the questioning process, and it will be accurate. For example, you can make a solid argument that two of your acquaintances truly don't want to be closer friends. When that's the case, don't overgeneralize beyond it (two people not wanting to be friends with you doesn't mean you're utterly flawed and hopeless). Even if the conclusion you came to stings, try to get any useful feedback you can from it, such as realizing you were coming on a bit too strong and scared them off.

Finally, ask yourself what the consequences are of holding a particular thought or belief. Even if it's technically true, it may not lead to the best outcomes. For example, you could make a case that humans are inherently selfish; however, socializing under this assumption may lead you to be too guarded, distrusting, and cynical. It's more adaptive to act as if people generally have good intentions.

STEP 3: COME UP WITH MORE REALISTIC, BALANCED ALTERNATIVES FOR YOUR COUNTERPRODUCTIVE THOUGHTS

The key words here are *realistic* and *balanced*. The idea is not to skip around being blindly "positive." An unrealistic counterproductive thought might be, "Everyone at this party will hate me. I'll never make any friends in this city!" An equally unrealistic overly positive thought may be, "I'm an amazing person! Everyone there will love me instantly!" A balanced thought is, "Some people will probably like me, and others won't. The ones who aren't into me probably won't be mean, just kind of indifferent. I can handle that and will concentrate on the ones who seem friendly."

As mentioned, tone is just as important as content. Even if what you're telling yourself is technically balanced and true, you shouldn't need talk to yourself as if you're an incompetent piece of crap. You can work to improve yourself while being compassionate and understanding of your struggles at the same time.

There will be several examples after the final step is explained.

STEP 4: CONTINUALLY QUESTION YOUR COUNTERPRODUCTIVE THOUGHTS

If you have interpersonal issues, you have probably been thinking about yourself and your social skills in a negative light for many years. That's not a pattern you're going to undo in a week. You need to continue discovering and challenging your counterproductive thoughts and beliefs. Written exercises will always be useful, but after you've gotten the hang of analyzing your thoughts, practice noticing and quickly analyzing them as they appear. For example, you may be at a pub and suddenly stop having fun and get the urge to go home early. Why? You may realize you had a thought like, "I don't belong here. My friends don't really want me around. They just invited me because they feel sorry for me." If you can nip that mind-reading thinking in the bud, your night can go on.

You don't necessarily have to sit down for an hour every day to do a full-on written analysis of your thoughts, but you should continually be on the alert for the ways your own mind is trying to hinder you. With time, your thinking really can shift. You'll never completely be free of counterproductive thoughts—no one is—but your outlook can become a lot more self-supportive and optimistic. You'll also become more familiar with the directions your mind tends to go and can learn to cut off many of your counterproductive thoughts before they pick up steam.

COMMON COGNITIVELY DISTORTED THOUGHTS WITH MORE REALISTIC ALTERNATIVES

"I just know everyone at my job hates me." (Mind reading)

Alternative: Unless you have strong, clear-cut evidence, the odds this is the case are really low. You're probably projecting your insecurities onto ambiguous things like one person not giving you a big enough nod when you passed in the hallway. Maybe one or two coworkers aren't fans of yours, but most are probably pretty neutral about you.

"If I go out to the bar with my friends, I know all kinds of annoying things will go wrong with the night." (Fortune-telling)

Alternative: Social events hardly ever turn out exactly as we predict or anticipate, good or bad. The more social experience you get, the more this point will be driven home.

"I can't see myself becoming extremely charismatic so I don't see the point in working on my people skills." (Black-and-white thinking)

Alternative: Even tweaking your social skills a little can make a big difference in the quality of your life. You only need average people skills to enjoy most of what the social world has to offer.

"Not everyone in my class likes me. That means I'm a complete reject." (Black-and-white thinking)

Alternative: Your worth as a person doesn't hinge on having every last person like you. No one is universally liked. You can get by in life by having a smaller group of friends with most other people being indifferent to you.

"My one coworker didn't invite me to his barbeque. No one wants to be friends with me." (Overgeneralization)

Alternative: How one or a few people act doesn't say anything about the rest of the world. There are plenty more chances to make friends.

"The first week of college makes or breaks you socially. If you don't make a ton of friends, your social life for the next four years is ruined." (Magnification)

Alternative: There are lots of chances to make friends at the start of college, but if you don't, you'll have countless other chances to meet people.

"Yeah, I'm a really good singer. But I don't see how that will help me make friends." (Minimization)

Alternative: As with most skills, singing isn't universally useful for meeting people, but it still opens some doors, such as being able to join a band or choir, and those opportunities shouldn't be discounted. All else being equal, singing (and similar skills) is a helpful talent to have in your pocket.

"I have no plans for the weekend. I'm never going to have a social life!" (Catastrophizing)

Alternative: As discouraging or boring as it may be, one slow weekend doesn't mean your social life is doomed for all the decades to follow, especially if you're actively working to make friends.

**"I feel too nervous. I can't take it! I can't take
it! I have to leave!" (Catastrophizing)**

Alternative: Anxiety can be unpleasant, but its worst moments are
short-lived spikes. For the most part, you can handle those episodes,
even if it's not the most comfortable experience.

**"People should invite their friends out at least
once a week." ("Should" statements)**

Alternative: There's no one way people have to act around their friends.
Everyone has his or her own social style. If someone invites you out less
frequently, it doesn't necessarily mean anything bad.

"I should never get anxious." ("Should" statements)

Alternative: This is unrealistic. Anxiety is a core human emotion that
everyone feels from time to time, even the most confident individuals.

**"I'm an electrical engineering student. It's a given
that I'm awkward with people." (Labeling)**

Alternative: Electrical engineering is a field of study. It doesn't automatically doom anyone who's interested in it to have certain social
limitations. Even if you are an engineering student and you feel you're
not good with people, you can work to change that.

**"Everyone left early because I'm so boring
to be around." (Personalization)**

Alternative: They could have needed to leave for any number of reasons that had nothing to do with you; for example, maybe they were
tired or had to be up early the next morning.

**"Sure, I had a good conversation with Amy, but she's nice to
everyone, so it doesn't count." (Disqualifying the positive)**

Alternative: You need to give yourself credit for your successes, even if some of them come more easily than others. There's still a lot you have to do on your end to make good conversation with someone, even if they are nicer than average.

COMMON UNHELPFUL BELIEFS WITH MORE REALISTIC ALTERNATIVES

"Being shy and socially inexperienced is one of the worst things someone can be."

Alternative: Those issues are common. Plenty of people have good friends and satisfying social lives despite not being socially perfect. As far as flaws go, it's hardly comparable to, say, being a con artist who swindles money from unwary pensioners.

"I couldn't withstand rejection, disapproval, or an awkward interaction."

Alternative: Rejection can hurt, but you can bounce back from it, even if it makes you feel bummed out for a few days. No one ever becomes totally immune to it, but it's possible to develop more productive attitudes toward rejection and become more tolerant to it:

- When it happens, rejection often doesn't hurt as much as you expect it to.
- Just because one person rejects you doesn't mean no one else is interested in you.
- Rejection isn't a sign that you're universally flawed; it just means you weren't a good match for that particular person or group.
- Rejection sometimes isn't about you at all. Someone may reject you because they were in a bad mood that day.
- Making new friends is partially a numbers game, and some amount of rejection is inevitable.
- Rejection helps screen out people who are incompatible with you and frees you to put your energy elsewhere.

- Sometimes you'll be rejected for mistakes you make, but at least you'll get feedback on how you can do better next time.
- People often respect someone who has the guts to go for what they want, even if they're rejected.

These mentalities tend to grow as you have more success and build up the real-world experiences that prove that even if some people turn you down, you can go on to have a good social life. Also, when you're purposely trying to get used to rejection, you'll often react to it differently than when you were unconsciously trying to avoid it. You'll tend to treat it as a form of training, like a martial artist trying to toughen his hands, rather than something scary to avoid at all costs.

"I must make everyone like me."

Alternative: It's impossible to make everyone like you. There are too many conflicting types of people in the world for that to happen. You wouldn't want everyone to like you either. If you're progressively minded, would you want to be friends with a bigot? Furthermore, the more alternative your lifestyle and values are, the fewer people who will be receptive to you. Even if you're a pleasant, charming person, some closed-minded types won't give you a chance based on a surface impression. There's more to life than getting approval from the maximum percentage of the population.

"It would be terrible if people thought of me as shy, socially awkward, or nervous."

Alternative: Most people are pretty forgiving of shyness and anxiety in others. They've felt nervous in situations themselves and are understanding. Sometimes shyness or social fumbling is seen as endearing and disarming. A few jerks may give you a hard time for it, but they're relatively rare, especially after high school.

"Every social mistake will have horrible consequences."

Alternative: People make little social errors all the time. Most of them are quickly forgotten and have no lasting effects. Again, aside from the occasional jerk, most people are willing to cut you some slack if you make some gaffes but are otherwise a good person.

"If I do something wrong, people will care about it and think badly of me for a long time."

Alternative: Most people are too busy worrying about themselves to give much thought to whether you said the wrong thing or seemed nervous at the start of the conversation. Even if the odd person does think badly of you, you can handle it.

"Every interaction is a test of my social skills and likability."

Alternative: You're not a failure for all time just because you have one shaky social interaction. Everyone has them. There's no social scoreboard in the sky.

"I'm 100 percent responsible for how well an interaction goes."

Alternative: The other people in an interaction have to pull their weight as well. If a conversation goes badly, it could be just as much a reflection of their social abilities as yours. It's a misconception that if someone's people skills are good enough, they can make every interaction go smoothly.

"I'm 100 percent responsible for other people's reactions."

Alternative: People's reactions are often as much about them as about you. If someone reacts badly to you, it may because they're stressed for any number of possible reasons.

"My social performance has to be at 100 percent at all times."

Alternative: Many people do just fine in social situations even if they're not completely "on." It's possible to socialize effectively if you're feeling a bit distracted, grumpy, or insecure.

"Everyone has super high standards for what they expect in others. I have to come across as really impressive."

Alternative: Some people are choosy, but what most people look for in a friend is someone who they get along with, who they have some things in common with, and who they feel comfortable around. They're not looking for someone who's perfect in every way.

"Everyone else totally has their act together socially."

Alternative: Everyone has weak areas and insecurities. Everyone has nervous moments. Most people are socially average. Only a handful are highly charming and confident, and even they feel unsure of themselves at times.

"He just said he liked my shirt. He's making fun of me."

Alternative: The vast majority of the time, if a person says something positive to you, they mean it at face value. They're not subtly disrespecting you or setting up a trap. The best way to handle a compliment is with a simple, cheerful "Thanks."

"The people in this city have a reputation for being unfriendly to non-locals, and I'm overweight and have a stutter. It's impossible for me to make friends here."

Alternative: All else being equal, it will be harder for you to make friends, but that's not even close to meaning it's impossible. Most people have a few traits or circumstances that get in the way of their social lives, but they manage.

"It's inappropriate to chat with strangers. Who does that? Everyone will think I'm a creep."

Alternative: Although not everyone talks to strangers, it's not unusual to do so, and it often goes well. Sometimes you won't get a warm reaction, even when you approach someone in a polite way, but it doesn't mean the act itself is wrong.

USING MINDFULNESS-BASED TECHNIQUES TO DEAL WITH UNHELPFUL THOUGHTS AND EMOTIONS

The preceding part of the chapter explained how to reframe unhelpful thoughts by logically debunking them. The ideas in this part offer another approach: to deal with unwanted thoughts and emotions by acknowledging their presence, but not getting sucked in by them. The concepts may seem to contradict the suggestions above, but in practice the two approaches are complementary. Some of your unpleasant thoughts and feelings will respond better to a logical reasoning approach, while others are better managed by being mindful, which is covered in the following pages.

Being mindful of unwanted thoughts and feelings

Mindfulness involves focusing your attention on the present moment and experiencing your thoughts, emotions, and bodily sensations without judgment. Rather than seeing anxiety, nervousness, or shyness as horrible things you must fight off at all costs, you can accept that they will sometimes appear, but you don't have to get swallowed up by them. Instead, you can learn to experience them in a more detached way.

Our minds are thought generators. Some of our thoughts are useful and valid, but others are mental noise. The anxious and unconfident parts of the mind in particular tend to send out a steady stream of worried or insecure chatter. These thoughts aren't bad or evil. They're just a by-product of how our brains work. You can learn to simply observe these thoughts and choose not to take them at face value or act on them. You don't need to debate or break them down. That would give them too much credit and power. Instead, you can briefly note them in a distant, nonjudgmental way and then let them pass.

Try this: Think to yourself, "There's a hungry dragon nearby." When you did this, you probably thought, "'There's a hungry dragon nearby'…. Uh… Okay?" You had the thought, but you didn't automatically go, "Oh no! A dragon! I've got to hide!" However, when you have thoughts like, "No one likes me" or "I won't be able to handle meeting my roommate's friends tomorrow," you're much more likely to treat them as true and get pulled into worrying mode or see them as a type of thinking that must be battled and purged. You'll never stop having undesirable thoughts, but with practice you can get better at not reacting to them.

The same approach can be applied to emotions. If a negative feeling such as nervousness or sadness comes on, the idea is not to fight it and inadvertently fan the flames. Your moods come and go, and if you let them run their course instead of overreacting, you'll usually feel different before long. For example, if you start to feel anxious, "be" with your anxiety, observe it with a detached curiosity, and let it do its thing; it will pass soon enough. It may not feel pleasant, but it can't truly hurt you. On the other hand, if you get freaked out by your nervous symptoms, you'll make them worse. A common analogy is that it's like being out in the ocean as a big wave approaches you. If you stay calm and tread water, it will pass under you. If you struggle and try to swim away from the wave, you'll stay with it until it slams into shore.

Practicing mindful meditation

You can cultivate your ability to experience your thoughts and feelings without overreacting to them by practicing mindful meditation. Unlike some other types of meditation, the idea isn't to achieve a state of relaxation, stop all thinking entirely, or come to some Zen insight about the universe that sweeps all of your problems away. The goal is to sit quietly and feel any number of feelings or think any number of thoughts, but not judge, label, or overreact to any of it. As with any skill, you can get better at it through consistent practice.

Here's a quick overview of how to mindfully meditate. Some books in the Further Reading section go into more detail if it's something that piques your interest.

Caution: If you have a type of anxiety that tends to get triggered by focusing on your physical symptoms, this exercise may not be for you, at least without a counselor who's familiar with the practice to guide you through it at first.

Set aside roughly fifteen minutes. The exact length of time it isn't critical. Sit or lie in a comfortable position. Feel free to use a chair or couch. Choose whether to open or close your eyes. Go with whichever you find easiest. Focus on your breathing. You don't need to breathe in any special way; just pay attention to it.

Sit or lie quietly. All kinds of thoughts will pass through your mind, from reminding yourself of errands you need to run to feeling insecure about yourself to thinking, "I'm bored. This isn't working." It doesn't matter what the thoughts are. Try to acknowledge them in a detached way and then set them aside and return your focus to your breathing. Allow yourself to feel a variety of sensations, like noticing your face is itchy, wanting to move your leg, or feeling pangs of nervousness. Whatever the sensation is, don't try to make it go away. Just sit with it and observe it with a gentle curiosity. Watch how it changes on its own and likely dissipates. If your mind wanders for minutes at a time, that's fine. The purpose of this type of meditation is to realize that your thinking can go in any number of directions, that it's all okay, and that you don't need to react to all of it.

When you're done meditating, sit or lie still for another minute or two, then simply get up and resume your day.

Try to mindfully meditate each day. If you'd like, gradually try to increase the length of your sessions, up to about an hour. However, don't feel you must. Short meditations are still beneficial.

As you become more proficient at being mindful while meditating, you'll find the skill will carry over into your day-to-day life. You'll have an easier time letting your thoughts and negative emotions happen and pass away without overreacting to them.

6

HANDS-ON STRATEGIES
FOR TAKING THE EDGE
OFF ANXIETY

THE LAST CHAPTER COVERED some ways you can reduce your anxiety by challenging it or rolling with it. This one gives you some more hands-on strategies to reduce its impact. It covers broad lifestyle changes you can make to turn down the volume on your negative emotions. You will also find many hands-on tips for reducing anxiety in the moment during various situations—when you're on your own, when you're anticipating a social interaction, and when you're in the middle of one.

Everything in this chapter should be a supplement to changing your overall relationship to your anxiety. As Chapter 4 explained, the best way to approach your anxiety is to make peace with the fact that it may appear and not rearrange your life to avoid it. However, from a practical standpoint, anxiety is still an unpleasant feeling, so it's okay to try to lower its volume. The strategies presented here won't be as useful if you let your anxiety have power over you by seeing it as something terrible you must prevent at all costs.

MAKE POSITIVE LIFESTYLE CHANGES
TO BOOST YOUR MOOD

Living a healthy lifestyle reduces the overall amount of stress and negative emotions you experience. If your day-to-day anxiety is mild, a few lifestyle changes may be all you need to reduce it to manageable levels. Even if the changes don't fully alter your mood, they can make a significant difference. Other emotional issues like depression also respond well to positive lifestyle adjustments.

The more of the following approaches you apply, the better. However, most people find that certain suggestions are more attractive than others, so use the ones that stand out the most to you. It's beyond the scope of this book to go into detail about each of them, but plenty of other sources cover that information. Here they are:

- Deal with the legitimate problems and stresses in your life (for example, being in debt, not liking your major in college, being bothered by memories of a childhood trauma). You likely can't fix the issues overnight, but just starting to tackle them should make you feel at least a little better.
- Talk to other people about your troubles and get their support (friends, family, a professional counselor, a therapy group).
- Exercise regularly.
- Purposely fit fun, rewarding activities into your day. (Do truly fun things that make life seem richer and fuller, not mainly time-killing pursuits like flipping through TV channels.)
- Consistently take time to relax.
- Meditate regularly (mindfulness meditation, described in Chapter 5, or another type).
- Practice healthy eating habits.
- Cut down on substances that can contribute to anxiety or depression, like caffeine and alcohol.
- Get enough quality sleep every night.
- Get enough sunlight every day, especially if you live somewhere with long, dark winters.

These suggestions can be extremely useful. Regular exercise alone can sometimes do as much to quell anxiety as months of therapy. However, because the ideas are so often suggested and easy to skim over, it's common to read them and go, "Yeah, yeah, yeah. Exercise more. Sleep better. Got it. What else do you have for me?" If you're not already doing them, give some serious thought to acting on several of these recommendations. You'll be pleasantly surprised at how effective they are.

SUGGESTIONS FOR COPING WITH ANXIETY IN THE MOMENT

No matter what approach you take to dealing with your anxiety, you'll be able to handle it better as you get more experience with it. Initially, intense anxiety is so scary and unfamiliar that it's easy to get swept up in it without stopping to think about what's happening or where it's taking you. The first few times you get unusually nervous, it will catch you off guard. In time, you'll develop a better understanding of your personal anxious tendencies and the course your anxiety takes when it comes on. You'll learn to step back, know what's coming, and apply a coping strategy. The following sections offer advice for dealing with anxiety when you're on your own, before an upcoming social event, during an event, and when you're in the middle of a social interaction.

Dealing with anxiety when you're on your own

You can use these approaches if nerves strike when you're, say, sitting at home and start thinking about an upcoming party you have to attend. You shouldn't use these strategies in the absence of shifting your overall attitude toward your anxiety, but as a spot treatment they're fine.

When you start to feel anxious, ride out the symptoms

If you can be with your anxiety and not overreact to it, it will often pass on its own (for more on this, see the previous chapter's section on mindfulness). Allowing your anxiety to play out may be uncomfortable, but it will fade. Intense bouts of anxiety often feel longer than they are, but they usually last only about five to fifteen minutes. Moderate nervous episodes of the pace-around-your-house-while-worrying variety can linger longer, maybe for an hour or two. That's more inconvenient, but ultimately only a small bit of the day.

Question the thoughts that are contributing to your anxiety

Sometimes you'll be too worked up to logically disarm your nerves, but at other moments, you'll be able to calm yourself if you question the thinking that's feeding your anxiety (see the beginning of Chapter 5 for pointers). For example, if an episode of nerves is getting more intense because you're thinking, "If I keep getting anxious like this, I'm going to go crazy," you could calm down by reminding yourself that real mental illness or "craziness" doesn't develop that way.

Distract yourself

You may feel too nervous to believe you can focus on something else enough to distract yourself, but if you force it, your attention will often move away from your anxiety, at least a little. You could put on some music or a movie, play a game, practice a skill, begin a text conversation with a family member, go for a walk, or throw yourself into a mentally demanding project. The breathing and relaxation techniques described in the next paragraph also have an element of distraction to them.

Calm yourself with deep breathing

Deep breathing puts your body into "relaxation mode," which will help counteract your anxiety because you can't physiologically be relaxed and keyed up at the same time. Breathing works best if you catch the anxiety early. The essence of deep breathing is to breathe slowly and from your abdomen.

One technique is called 4-7-8 Breathing. Breathe in through your nose for four seconds. Hold the breath for seven seconds. Exhale through your mouth for eight seconds. The exact numbers aren't super important. The key is that you're thinking about your breathing while taking time to do each step, instead of breathing rapidly, and that you're holding your breath and exhaling for twice as long as you're inhaling. This technique overrides your tendency to take quick, shallow breaths when you're nervous, which can make your physical symptoms worse by changing the ratio of carbon dioxide in the body.

Most people will find this exercise harmless and relaxing. However, you may want to be careful if your anxiety tends to get triggered whenever you focus too much on your breathing.

Calm yourself with progressive muscle relaxation

This works through the same principle as deep breathing. A loose, relaxed body is incompatible with a tense, nervous one. Set some time aside, make yourself comfortable, and lie down. Take deep, slow breaths. Work your way through each of your muscles, contracting them for about five seconds and then releasing them as you exhale. You can make the exercise more effective with some creative imagery. You could picture your stress and tension as a gas being squeezed out of your muscles, or imagine your body is melting into the bed or couch.

Put on soothing music or a recorded guided relaxation meditation

In a guided relaxation meditation, someone's voice guides you into a state of calm through instructions and soothing images ("You're floating down a warm, peaceful river on a sunny day. As you exhale you feel the tension leaving your face"). There are lots of free recordings online. Do a search for "relaxation meditation" or "rain sounds" or "relaxing music."

Exercise

Exercising regularly over the long term is a very effective way to reduce anxiety. It can also help in the short term by releasing mood-enhancing chemicals and letting you burn off some of your nervous energy. Any kind of exercise can do the job as long as it gets your blood pumping, even a brisk walk around your neighborhood. There's isn't a single correct length of time you need to exercise for. That will depend on how anxious you are and how intensely you're exerting yourself. Listen to your body and stop when you feel yourself calming down.

Channel your anxious energy into something useful

Sometimes you'll get really anxious and worked up, and even if you ultimately handle it well, you may still feel amped up and on edge for a little while. Getting nervous triggers chemicals in your body and puts it into an alert state; sometimes it takes a while for all systems to return to normal. Some people take the attitude of, "Well, if I have all this extra energy, I may as well use it," and then clean their bathroom or organize their apartment's storage locker.

Coping with nerves before an upcoming social event

Anticipating an upcoming social situation can cause you to feel anxious. The types that tend to be the scariest are the ones you know you can't back out of. You start feeling at least a little nervous as soon as you know the event will take place. The butterflies then build up more and more as the occasion gets closer. As always, you can try the previously suggested distraction and relaxation techniques or try to challenge or ride out your worries. Here are some other ideas:

Accept that you probably won't get rid of all your nerves

There are things you can do that may help you feel a little better, but in the lead-up to the event, you'll experience a degree of nerves that you'll have to manage as best you can. This is especially true if you're encountering a certain situation for the first time (like a get-together with your significant other's coworkers) or there's something unique about this particular event. Although you have only so many options for feeling better in the short term, in the long run you may be able to put yourself in that scenario often enough that it doesn't bother you as much.

Prepare and practice

You won't be as nervous if you're reasonably confident you're ready for the situation. Unfortunately, it's harder to prepare for loose, improvised social events like dates and parties than it is for predictable, performance-based ones like class presentations. You can semi-prepare for less structured events by coming up with questions or topics you could discuss. It may not make for the most ground-breaking few minutes of conversation, but it will help you get through an anxious patch.

You could also devise a general strategy for approaching the event. For example, when you're planning to attend a party, decide that first you'll catch up with your buddies, and then you'll ask them to introduce you to their friends so you won't have to do it yourself. Then you'll head to the backyard and try to join the people who are talking there.

These kinds of preparations will never be able to account for everything that may come up, but even planning ahead a little can make you feel more on top of things.

Another way to warm up for unstructured events is to socialize earlier in the day, ideally in a way that roughly parallels the situation you're anxious about. For example, if you're scheduled to hang out one-on-one with a new friend that evening, you could have coffee earlier in the day with a family member.

Coping with anxiety when you're at a social event, but not talking to anyone

When you're at an event, a bout of nerves may hit you as you're off to the side and not speaking to someone, or if you're in a group conversation but hanging back. Here's what you can do:

- **Ride out the symptoms:** They'll likely pass in a few minutes.
- **Use deep breathing:** With other people around, you won't be able to close your eyes and lie down, but you can still take some subtle calming breaths.
- **Put your attention on the current moment:** Get your focus out of your head. If you're in a group, really pay attention to the conversation. If you're on the edge of a party, really take in what's

going on around you—the music, the noises, what other people are doing.

- **Jump into an interaction:** It's counterintuitive, but if you're the kind of person who gets nervous before social interactions but is fine once you're in them, one of the best ways to take your mind off your jitters is to get into a casual conversation with someone. At the moment, this may be easier said than done, but it could become an option in the future.

Coping with anxiety when you're in the middle of talking to someone

Nerves are toughest to deal with when they occur as you're talking to someone. When anxiety hits, accept that it may interfere with that particular interaction and there's only so much you can do about it. Over the long run, you may get a better handle on your anxiety so you're less nervous in that situation, but when you're just starting to deal with your nerves, realize it won't go perfectly. Here are some approaches that have been covered earlier:

- Ride out the symptoms: When you're anxious around people, usually your nerves spike for a minute or two and then start to dissipate. If you can hang in there through the worst of it, they'll usually go away.
- Have some prepared questions and answers you can fall back on: When you're anxious, you aren't as fast at thinking on your feet. So prepare some standard getting-to-know-you questions. Likewise, practice the kinds of answers you've said a million times before and don't have to think too hard about (for example, a spiel about your job or a hobby).
- Accept that you may indeed look nervous. Accept your circumstances, and realize it doesn't have to ruin that conversation or the entire outing.
- Remove the pressure of trying to hide your anxiety by admitting you're nervous. You can do this by mentioning your nervousness in an offhand, self-assured way and then get on with the interaction. Any normal person won't care if you're a tad anxious, especially if the jitters only last for a few moments before you find your footing.

*Realize that your outward symptoms of anxiety
often aren't as obvious as it feels they are*

Symptoms like blushing are clearly visible, but others feel like they're more obvious than they are. Even when someone is fairly panicky, it often doesn't stand out that much to an observer. The person just looks a little tense and preoccupied. Knowing this can reassure you enough to calm down.

Be more of a listener or talker, whichever one you have an easier time with

You may be more comfortable listening when you're anxious. You can put on an interested face, place your attention on your conversation partner, avoid your worried thoughts, and buy yourself some time for your nerves to settle. For other people, anxiety and listening don't go well together; all that time when they should be listening allows them to retreat into their heads and zero in on how nervous they're feeling. Some people are actually better at riding out their anxiety when they're doing most of the talking, likely about something they can go on about without having to think too much.

Coping with nerves while trying to do optional social behaviors

You may find yourself anxiously on the sidelines contemplating a social move, one that makes you nervous and which you don't *have* to do. These usually involve approaching people under circumstances where they might reject you, like talking to a stranger at a party or inviting someone to hang out.

These situations create an *approach-avoidance conflict*. Certain factors make you want to do (approach) the behavior, like a desire to form meaningful relationships. Factors like a fear of being made fun of compel you to avoid doing the same thing. When you're at a distance, the approach factors are stronger. You don't feel as scared, and may even be eager to go ahead. As you get closer to doing the behavior, the avoidance factors kick in and often make you bail out at the last second. You may get stuck mentally when the two forces are in balance ("Okay, I'm feeling better.

I'm going to talk to them. Here I go… Ah! Still too nervous! Okay, let me regroup…"). Here are some ways you can make yourself act.

Give yourself time to calm down

If you arrive at an event where you have the option of doing a scary social action, it often helps to take time to collect yourself and let your anxiety fade somewhat. For example, when you show up at a party, you may feel too nervous to join any conversations right away. However, if you're not too hard on yourself for being hesitant and give yourself a moment, you may soon build up the gumption to do it. This may require several cycles of "beginning to approach and bailing out at the last moment" before you finally go ahead, but if you're patient, you'll get there.

Dive in before you have time to think

This is the opposite of the "give yourself time" suggestion and can work if the optional behavior is only a little bit anxiety-inducing for you. After you arrive at the venue, start socializing before you have time for the avoidance factors to really kick in. For example, at a party, jump into a conversation with an unfamiliar group as soon as you put your coat away, if not before. Maybe that one interaction won't go perfectly, but at least you'll have some momentum.

Warm up socially

Warming up socially allows you to mentally shift from hanging out by yourself to being in a social frame of mind where you're comfortable engaging with others. You can warm up ahead of the event by socializing earlier in the day. At the event, you can have a few quick, easy interactions before tackling the ones that make you more nervous. For example, at an Internet meet-up, you could start by chatting to the friendly organizer you already know before trying to talk to someone you've never met. You could continue the process by approaching some non-intimidating strangers and then moving on to more intimidating ones. (This is actually a condensed version of the gradual exposure process outlined in the next chapter.)

Force your hand a little

If you're close to being able to execute a behavior, this may be the final nudge you need. You could promise yourself a reward, like a nice meal, if you go through with it. You could tell a sympathetic friend you'll buy them a drink if you don't talk to anyone new at the pub that night. You could create a sense of urgency by telling yourself, "Okay, I have to leave this meet-up in half an hour, and I have to speak to at least one person before then." What will likely happen is that you'll still be scared for the next twenty-five minutes, but once you realize time is running out, you'll think, "Okay, it's now or never. I may as well just do it!" The time pressure takes away your ability to overthink things and not act.

Don't force yourself too much, however. You want to give yourself a gentle push, but still have it ultimately be your decision to act or not. A drink is one thing, but if you tell your friend with all seriousness that they can have your car if you don't start any conversations, it's not really a choice any longer. Any reasonable person would make themselves chat with someone new to save their car, even if they were a mess the entire time and could never do it on their own.

Build up some courage

You'll usually feel a bit rusty at the start of each event during which you want to perform the anxiety-producing behavior. Even if you've managed to do it in the past, some of your courage will have worn off, and you'll need to get the ball rolling again. The first few interactions you have will feel the creakiest, but then you'll settle back into your groove.

Don't be too tough on yourself

It's easy to beat yourself up for not being brave enough to follow through on an optional social behavior. You may feel like you're failing by hovering around a group at a pub, trying to work up the gumption to talk to them. It's not that big a deal. It's extremely typical for people to feel reluctant in these kinds of uncertain social situations.

Use the principles of gradual exposure to get comfortable
with your fears in the longer term

The previous suggestions address how to get past your nerves after you're already in the setting where you want to do the optional behavior and you just need to go for it. In the longer term, the best way to get used to the things that make you nervous is to expose yourself to them gradually. The next chapter goes into detail about this.

7

REDUCING FEARS
AND INSECURITIES
THROUGH REAL-WORLD
EXPERIENCES

THE IDEAS IN THE PREVIOUS CHAPTERS certainly help reduce counterproductive thinking. However, some beliefs are hardier and will start to fade only when they've been overwritten by contradictory real-world experiences. Sometimes you'll have a fear or belief that you logically know is inaccurate, but it still *feels* true and limits your behavior.

In these cases, analyzing and debunking your thoughts isn't enough. For one, your mind won't give much weight to the conclusions you come to. It responds much more strongly to real-life evidence, and wrong or not, as far as your mind is concerned, it has past experiences that show the belief is reasonable. You may feel like you've successfully disarmed a belief, but it will often return. The other problem is that when you have a fear or insecurity, it can generate a nearly endless supply of worried thoughts. If you debunk some of them, new ones will just take their place (for example, if you're scared to talk to people at parties and defuse your worries about being made fun of, you may develop new ones about accidentally making someone angry).

The bulk of this chapter covers how to get used to the social situations that make you nervous. But first, it explains how real-world experiences can affect your mind-set about socializing and reduce insecurities and limiting beliefs that don't necessarily have a big anxiety component to them.

KNOWING WHY YOU MUST GAIN
FIRSTHAND EXPERIENCES

Real-life feedback can overwrite unhelpful beliefs, but the process is gradual. Say you have the belief, "I'm boring and people don't enjoy my company." As you begin to polish your social skills, people will begin to show you that they like having you around. The first few times it happens, you'll probably dismiss it as a fluke. As it keeps happening, you'll tentatively start to accept that some people do like your company; you may adopt some more self-assured behaviors, but you'll largely remain skeptical. With enough time, the way you see yourself will stop lagging behind your actual progress, and you'll be able to see yourself in a more positive light. Some traces of the original insecurity may always remain, but should be easy enough to act against.

The process is the same for useful attitudes like "Don't care too much about what other people think." Again, you can't instantly take on that mentality because you've read it's good to have. On a deeper level, you may fear other people's opinion of you. However, over many small occasions, you can choose to do things you want to do, but may draw some negative responses (for example, speaking up with a less-popular belief, wearing unconventional clothes). As you continually experience firsthand that acting that way has benefits and that you can handle the consequences, it slowly reinforces the importance of not being overly concerned with what other people think of you. ("When I made that edgy joke, one or two people made mildly uncomfortable faces, but it wasn't so bad. Everyone else thought it was really funny. And it just felt good not to hold back my sense of humor like I always used to.")

A common piece of social advice in this vein is to "Fake it 'til you make it." That is, force yourself to act outwardly confident even though you don't feel that sure of yourself deep down; then let the positive reinforcement that comes from your self-assured behavior build true confidence. This suggestion has limits. You may feel comfortable outwardly faking some confident behaviors, but others will be too nerve-racking and too much of a leap from how you normally act. If you're really insecure, anxious, and socially inexperienced, you can't slip on the persona of someone who's highly confident just like that. However, you may be able to pull off smaller tasks, like introducing yourself to someone at your job when you otherwise would have taken a pass.

THE IMPORTANCE OF FACING YOUR FEARS

If a social situation really makes you nervous, you need to put yourself in it until you get comfortable with it. You may never be completely unfazed by the situation, but you can get to a point where your fear is low enough that it doesn't keep you from going after what you want.

Exposing yourself to a fear works because it overwrites your mind's association of *Situation → Cue to get nervous*. However, to do that, you need to be around your fear long enough that you calm down and experience firsthand you'll be okay. If you briefly put yourself in contact with something scary, then bolt while you're still feeling nervous, your brain hasn't learned anything new.

When it comes to situations that make you only mildly uneasy, just knowing this may be enough to get you to start changing your behavior. For example, inviting people to hang out may make you mildly anxious to the point that if you live on autopilot, you'll default to not extending invitations to anyone. Once you're aware it's important to offer invites, it may be easy enough for you to take a deep breath and go through with it.

If you have a fear that's more intense, you need to be more strategic about facing it. Psychologists have found the most effective way to face a fear is to gradually expose yourself to it; this is called *exposure therapy*. You start with a milder variation of your fear, face that until you're comfortable with it, and then work your way up to more nerve-racking scenarios. You do the exposure sessions frequently enough that you build up some courage momentum. For example, if you were afraid of standing on balconies, you would start on some lower floors and slowly work your way up (literally) to higher ones.

Facing your fears isn't as easy or tidy when it comes to social situations

It would be easy to face a fear of standing on high balconies in a way that's totally controlled and on your terms. Socializing is trickier. People aren't inanimate features of a building that you just have to be around to get used to. You have to interact with them, and their responses can be unpredictable. Your feelings toward them are more complex too. Most people's self-esteem isn't going to be affected that much if they don't like balconies, but your confidence can suffer if you can't socialize effectively.

It's also harder to design a tidy way to gradually face many social fears. The social situations you need to expose yourself to may not be available when you want them, or they may not last long enough or go well enough for you to experience the necessary relaxation and sense that things are under control. The progression from one step to the next may not be clear, creating unavoidable large increases in difficulty from one to the next. Real-life friends, classmates, and colleagues aren't robots that you can endlessly experiment with for your own purposes. This is not to say that facing your fears is pointless when it comes to socializing. The principles of gradual exposure are still very useful. The process of applying them is just messier, and it helps to know that going in.

HOW TO FACE YOUR BIGGER SOCIAL FEARS GRADUALLY

With the background theory out of the way, here's a practical step-by-step guide to how you can slowly get used to the social situations that make you uncomfortable.

Be at a point where you're really ready to make changes

The approach outlined below is the easiest way to face your fears, but even then the process won't be effortless. Facing a fear gradually with the aid of coping skills will make the task as pleasant as it can be, but you're still going to voluntarily put yourself in situations that make you feel anxious. It will take a few months of steady work. So you need to be at a place where you're really motivated to overcome your fear. It's not unusual for someone to have a fear for years, but do nothing more than avoid the situations that scare them. Even if they hate how much their fear restricts their life, they still prefer that to the work and discomfort of getting over it.

Before facing any fears, get a handle on the distorted beliefs and thinking that contribute to your anxiety in social situations

This point is extremely important. If you try to face your fears but leave all of your counterproductive beliefs intact, you're not going to get far. You'll go into every encounter feeling like it's life or death. If it doesn't go well, according to your unrealistic standards, you'll come away with the wrong conclusions and feel even more dejected and discouraged. If an interaction doesn't go smoothly, you need to be able to put it in the proper perspective. Learn and get some practice applying the concepts in Chapter 5 first.

FOLLOWING A PROCESS FOR FACING YOUR FEARS GRADUALLY

The general method for facing a fear is to break it down into a hierarchy from *Least Scary* to *Most Scary* variations, then regularly face the fears, beginning at the easiest tasks and working your way up to the tougher ones. You can use rewards and debriefing sessions to stay motivated and on track. Here's the process explained in detail:

Break your fear down into a hierarchy of Least Scary to Most Scary variations

Here's an example using a fear of talking to new people at parties:
1. Go to a party and briefly nod and smile at several people.
2. Go to a party and ask several people a quick question, politely listen to their answer, and then excuse yourself from the conversation.
3. Go to a party and ask a friend to introduce you to several people.

4. Go to a party and introduce yourself to one person who seems friendly and approachable, and who you're not particularly concerned with impressing.
5. Go to a party and join a group of approachable people. Don't put pressure on yourself to wow them or say too much. The idea is just to join them.
6. Go to a party, join a group, and try to talk to them a bit more.
7. Go to a party and talk to someone who intimidates you somewhat, but whom you'd still like to get to know.
8. Go to a party and join a more intimidating group.

It's all right if not every step in the hierarchy constitutes a "proper" way to expose yourself to your fears—that is, you face it long enough that you no longer feel nervous. As long as a step is leading up to that, it's okay. For example, if you're afraid of going to nightclubs, just setting foot in one for a minute may be all you can handle at first. That's fine as long as you're using it as a jumping-off point to stay longer next time.

Similar fears can be tackled similarly

Social fears come in many forms, and some of them need to be tackled on a case-by-case basis. However, some fears are similar and can be faced in similar ways, which is helpful if you experience variations of the same fear:

- Fears of being in a certain environment, like a party, a dance club, or a movie theater where you're seeing a film alone. In this case, your goal for each fear-facing session is to put yourself in that environment. Eventually you want to be able to stay there long enough that you start to calm down and realize that nothing bad is going to happen.
- Fears about certain types of interactions, like making conversation, approaching strangers, or inviting friends to hang out. The interactions themselves are often on the shorter side, so in each fear-facing session, you should try to carry them out multiple times. The first conversation you have might be nerve-racking, but the seventh may feel quite tolerable. Of course, this volume approach isn't always possible. If you shy away from inviting

people out, you may not have enough friends and acquaintances to invite every time you want to practice facing that particular fear.

Practice less scary variations of your fear in several ways

When creating a hierarchy, you can come up with many easier variations on the situation you're ultimately afraid of:

- Do the same basic action as your fear, but a simpler, less intense version (for example, talking to someone approachable vs. someone you're more on edge around, going to a club on a slow weekday night vs. on a busy weekend).
- Do the same action as your fear, but cut it off early (for example, asking someone a quick question and making an excuse to leave vs. sticking around to talk, like you hope to do eventually).
- Do something different from, and easier than, your fear, but that brings up similar feelings (for example, instead of chatting to strangers at a music festival, chatting to shop clerks or asking people on the street for directions).
- Practice the exact thing you fear, but in a controlled, artificial setting (for example, role-playing assertiveness techniques with a therapist or in a social skills training group).

If you're very afraid of something, initial steps may be imagining yourself facing your fear or looking at pictures related to it.

It can also help to start dealing with other non-social fears you may have so you can build your confidence in your ability to overcome your anxieties (for example, facing a milder hesitation toward learning to drive).

Here are a few more examples of fear-facing progressions:

Feeling uncomfortable in nightclubs

1. Go to a non-intimidating, low-key pub in the afternoon on a slow day.

2. Go to a non-intimidating pub in the evening on a slow day.
3. Go to a non-intimidating pub at night on a slightly busy night.
4. Go to a non-intimidating pub at night on a busier night.
5. Go to a somewhat intimidating nightclub early in the evening on a slow night.
6. Go to a somewhat intimidating nightclub at night on a somewhat busy night.
7. Go to a somewhat intimidating nightclub at night when it's busy.
8. Go to a quite intimidating nightclub early in the evening on a slow night.
9. Go to a quite intimidating nightclub at night on a somewhat busy night.
10. Go to a quite intimidating nightclub at night when it's busy.

Feeling uneasy with speaking up in groups

Have several hierarchies going at the same time:

- Start with short, simple contributions and then work your way up to more lengthy, involved, or controversial ones.
- Start by speaking up in smaller groups, and build up to sharing in bigger ones.
- Start with groups that are low key and easy to chime in to, and work up to rowdier discussions where you have to be assertive to be heard.
- Start with friendly groups that don't scare you, and work up to speaking in ones that intimidate you more.

Work up to dropping your safety behaviors

Safety behaviors (see Chapter 3) get in the way of overcoming fears. Even if you successfully face a situation, in the back of your mind you can always reason, "Well, X is still dangerous. It was just the safety behavior that got me through it." They keep you from realizing that your fear is manageable and that you can handle it without any help. If you use any safety behaviors and they seem to help you, by all means stick with them at first. But as you make more progress in facing your fears, try to drop them and go it alone.

Face the actual situation that scares you; doing
zany, gutsy stunts won't help much

Some people, when thinking about facing their social fears, say to themselves, "I'm generally afraid of rejection, so I'll get over that fear by doing a bunch of outrageous things to mess with strangers and get shot down as hard as possible. If I can get used to going up to random people and acting like a chicken, then anything else, like talking to guests at a party, will be a cakewalk."

It does take guts to act strangely around someone you don't know, and it may help build your courage, but the carryover to more low-key, day-to-day social situations isn't as big as you might think. When you're purposely being odd and screwing with people, you know deep down that it's just a lark. You'll probably never see that person again, and you're not putting the "real you" on the line. It's not the same as approaching someone to make genuine conversation and knowing the other person is going to respond to your true personality and interpersonal skills.

Start facing your fears, beginning with the least scary items

The item in your hierarchy you decide to start with has to feel manageable. It should push your limits, but only a little. It's okay if it makes you slightly hesitant and requires some willpower to face, but no more than that. If the thought of doing it makes you frozen and jittery, it's too much for you to handle right now. You need to begin with something simpler. People often quit when facing their fears and then declare that the process doesn't work because they jump straight to a step that's too overwhelming. Ideally your starter task should feel so simple that you think, "This is too easy. Do I even need to do this? Maybe I should start with something harder."

Only move up the ladder when you're fully used to the previous step. "Used to" means it only causes you mild anxiety, and is even starting to feel mundane and boring. You may reach this point for some steps in a day. You may have to stick to other steps for a few weeks. Don't be in a hurry to complete your hierarchy. There's no award for finishing quickly, especially if you rush so much that you don't really lock in your improvement.

The relevant thing is facing the fear, not the outcome of the interaction

When you're exposing yourself to a fear, your goal is to put yourself in a certain situation and get used to it. Don't worry about any other outcomes. If you want to get more comfortable chatting to people at parties, all that matters is that you're starting those interactions. For now, it's irrelevant if you weren't an enrapturing storyteller. If you want to get used to inviting people out, as long as you asked, it's unimportant whether they said yes or no.

Once you're on the scene, know some ways to get yourself to face your fear

When you've arrived at the situation where your fear is, you then have to take the step of actually confronting it. It's very common to get there and then hesitate for a good while before taking the plunge. The end of the previous chapter covered some ways to get yourself to act.

Once you're face-to-face with your fear, have ways to cope in the moment

Once you're facing your fear, you're going to feel anxious. You'll start to calm down if you stick around long enough, but until then, it helps to have some other ways to deal with your anxious symptoms. The previous chapter covered this as well.

Partial progress is an accomplishment too

It's important to give yourself credit for even partial progress toward facing a fear. For example, if you're fearful of talking to strangers at pubs, you may go out to several venues and not be able to talk to any-one for three outings in a row. However, on the first night you were only 40 percent of the way there. On the second night you were 70 percent close, and 90 percent on the third. Maybe on the fourth night you finally did it. That interaction wouldn't have been possible without those other three sessions, which may have appeared to be failures if you only looked at them in more simplistic "either I talked to someone or I didn't" terms.

Debrief yourself after each exposure session

Each time you face your fear, it may bring up some counterproductive thinking, such as "That person thought I was a creep when I said hi to them. Why do I even bother? I'll never get the hang of this." You must not unquestionably swallow these thoughts, or you may set yourself further back than where you began. Use the principles from Chapter 5 to address that thinking properly.

Don't dissect only the insecure thoughts you had. Remind yourself of what went well too. Did you face the fear with a lot less hesitation compared to last time? Did you find yourself thinking in any construc-tive ways that helped you feel more confident? Build up a written re-cord of your small and large successes.

Reward and congratulate yourself every step of the way

Every time you accomplish something listed in your hierarchy that you couldn't do before, you should give yourself a pat on the back and treat yourself. Your reward doesn't have to be anything big, just something that adds a little *oomph* to your day and caps off the sense of accomplishment you already feel. This is another effective behavioral psychology principle that makes the process easier. Something can seem less scary if you know a treat and sense of satisfaction are waiting for you on the other side.

You can also use rewards in different ways to motivate yourself: Specify something you like doing (for example, checking your favorite websites), and then tell yourself you can't do that until you meet your fear-facing goals for the day. This approach can be extremely effective if you pick the right carrot for yourself. You'll find yourself sitting around thinking, "Man, I really want to play more of that game I just bought. I guess I'd better get out there and try talking to people." When you meet your daily objective, you'll be proud of yourself and looking forward to the fun activity you've earned.

Face your fears on a regular basis and work up your hierarchy

Map out a schedule for how you'll work through each subfear. Not every fear lends itself to daily practice, but you can improvise. You may not be able to go to a party six days a week, but you could pledge to practice starting conversations by going to some Internet meet-ups.

The more often you work on exposing yourself to your fears, the better, because it keeps the momentum going. Building up your courage is like exercising to increase your physical fitness. You'll tend to lose your courage "gains" if you leave too much time between exposure sessions. You may not lose your gains completely, but you'll lose enough that you'll have to take some extra time to regain the few steps you lost.

Don't think you're cured after facing a scarier fear one time

The first time you successfully face one of your bigger fears, you'll probably be over the moon. In your excitement, you may feel like you've solved all of your problems, but you've really only taken the first step. It's common for people to face their fear during one session and then get discouraged when they go out a few days later and find they're nervous all over again.

Facing your fear for the first time is a huge accomplishment, but you need to repeatedly face it to solidify your progress. It's like lifting weights. If you want to be able to consistently move a certain amount, you have to regularly exercise with it. You'll often face your fear for the first time on a day when you're unusually confident, but then you'll find it takes more work to get to the point where you can reliably deal with it when your mood is more average. You have to face your fear again and again and again to overcome it.

You will hit snags

It's rare to plan out a fear hierarchy and effortlessly move up it. You have to be flexible and make adjustments as you go. You may find you have the order of the steps wrong. You could complete one rung and find the next step is too challenging, so you need to find a task to bridge the two.

It's also common to encounter an early step that is too hard to do once you're face-to-face with it, even if it seemed surmountable on paper. You'll need to add something more basic ahead of it. The key is not to get discouraged when these hiccups happen; just keep making tweaks so the overall project stays doable.

Finally, your progress may seem to slip at times. You may go out one day and face your fears easily, feel on top of the world, and then try again the next day but find you're nervous once more. When this happens, keep moving forward and focus on the overall improvements you're making. To use the exercise analogy again, when people take up strength training, they'll have the odd bad workout, even though they're getting stronger on the whole. This is completely normal.

If you conquer a fear and then go a long time
without facing it, you'll probably regress

If you do regress, it will take work to get your courage back, though it will come much quicker than the first time. Once more, it's like exercising. It's always easier to get back into shape than to get fit from scratch. A common scenario is for someone to work to overcome their social fear, go on to achieve their other interpersonal goals, and then "get out of shape" because they no longer need to deal with the old challenge. For example, someone with fears around initiating conversations and inviting people out gets comfortable with those skills, makes a bunch of friends, and no longer needs to meet anyone new. If they want to freshen up their social circle years down the road, they may find they're nervous about approaching people again.

8

INCREASING YOUR
SELF-ESTEEM AND CONFIDENCE

LOW SELF-CONFIDENCE LIES at the root of many people's shyness, social anxiety, and insecurities. This chapter addresses the most important points for improving your self-confidence (aside from the concepts
that have already been covered, like how to dispute counterproductive thoughts) by covering two concepts that both fall under the term
"self-confidence." The first is core self-esteem, which is your overall
assessment of your worth as a person. The second is how self-assured,
competent, and brave you feel in specific social situations—your situational confidence (for example, "I feel confident about how I'll do at
the party tonight").

Having high self-esteem gives you strengths that will override
aspects of shyness, anxiety, insecurity, and pessimism. People with
high self-esteem feel good about themselves and what they have to
offer, are more optimistic and more prepared to take risks, and are
better able to tolerate uncertainty, discomfort, and rejection. Their
positive feelings about themselves are stable and come from within,
and their emotions don't constantly go up and down based on outside factors, like whether enough people smiled at them in the hallway that day. Having a healthy level of self-esteem does not mean
being arrogant, boastful, and entitled. That mentality is damaging

and may be an indication of deeper feelings of inferiority; it's not true self-esteem at all.

Having situational confidence is similarly helpful. You'll feel calmer and surer of yourself, you'll perform better, you'll have an easier time putting yourself out there, and you'll tend to make a better impression on others.

WAYS TO INCREASE YOUR CORE SELF-ESTEEM

There's no one path to increasing your core self-esteem. Rather there are many things you can do that add up to feeling more sure of yourself.

Practice self-acceptance and realize it's okay to be a normal, less-than-perfect person

The foundation of good self-esteem is realizing you're okay the way you are. People sometimes imagine that if they had high self-esteem, they'd feel cocksure and amped up all the time, but having good self-esteem feels more like a deep, solid level of comfort with yourself. You're aware of your personality traits and quirks, your strengths and weaknesses, your successes and failures, and you're fine with the overall package they create. The following factors play into being self-accepting:

- **Realizing that it's all right to be a regular human who makes mistakes and isn't perfect.** Everyone gets things wrong sometimes, and it doesn't mean they're broken through and through.
- **Setting realistic standards for yourself and letting go of perfectionism.** People with low self-esteem sometimes believe they won't be able to feel good about themselves unless they become an overachieving superhuman who's the complete opposite of how they are now.
- **Being nice and compassionate to yourself.** Accepting yourself means being on your own side. If you mess up, you can look at the situation with an understanding eye, rather than tearing into yourself.

People are sometimes wary about the idea of being self-accepting. Being self-accepting doesn't mean you have to condone or approve of everything you do wrong or embrace all your flaws. However, when you do make a mistake, you don't need to disown everything about yourself. But don't think you need to abandon all desire to change or improve yourself either. Instead, acknowledge that there are areas in your life you'd benefit from working on. The well-known saying is "You're fine the way you are... and there's always room for improvement." When you accept yourself, personal development is something you choose to do because you see how it will add to your life, instead of viewing it as something you *have* to do to stay a few steps ahead of your supposed intrinsic shamefulness.

Similarly, being more self-accepting doesn't mean you'll become content in your rut and lose all desire to grow and achieve. If something is truly important to you, you'll still go after it. It's human nature to keep moving forward. However, you may find yourself losing interest in goals that were mostly a means of gaining faux self-esteem. For example, someone might retain their desire to become an artist because it makes them happy to develop their creative potential, but be less motivated to own an expensive wardrobe, because they didn't want it for anything other than to impress people.

Question the negative messages you've internalized about your value as a person

A core reason people develop low self-esteem is that at some point in their lives, they came to believe they were fundamentally defective. Usually this is because of messages they received and took to heart when they were young and impressionable. Kids can pick up these messages from the people they're closest to, either by hearing their words directly or through interpretations of their behavior (for example, a father has a horrible temper, and his children take it to mean there's something wrong with them).

The messages can also take the form of ubiquitous, taken-for-granted cultural values about what it means to be a worthwhile person. However, many of these messages are inaccurate and harmful. When several are taken together, they often suggest that there's something wrong with anyone who doesn't fit the standard mold. Here are a few cultural messages related to socializing:

- There's something wrong with you if you're not effortlessly socially savvy.
- There's something wrong with you if you're not naturally sociable and like spending time alone.
- There's something wrong with you if you feel shy or unsure of yourself in social situations.
- There's something wrong with you if you don't have a giant group of friends.
- There's something wrong with you if you have quirky, non-mainstream interests.
- There's something wrong with you if you don't always act like a traditional man or woman.

Here are few cultural messages not necessarily related to socializing that cause many people problems:

- You're not a worthwhile person unless you achieve a ton in your life.
- You're not worthwhile as a person unless you earn a certain salary.
- You're not a worthwhile person unless you have a professional, white-collar job.
- You're not worthwhile as a woman unless you get married and start a family.
- You're not worthwhile as a man unless you've had a lot of sexual conquests.

These messages are wrong and potentially damaging. No one's intrinsic worth is lower because they don't meet some random societal criteria. Someone isn't automatically inferior just because they don't have a lot of friends or the right job. Is a doctor who has devoted her life to operating on premature infants a "loser" just because she sometimes feels shy at parties? Of course, you may want to have more friends or a higher paying career, and you recognize the advantages they provide, but that's different from believing you're an inherent failure for not acquiring them.

Whatever negative messages they received, people with low self-esteem believe them in a very strong, unthinking way. You can bolster your self-esteem if you identify, question, discredit, and stop living by the negative statements you follow. Some of them will stop affecting you as soon as you stop and think about them for a few minutes. Others will be harder to shake.

Many socializing-related messages are so entrenched that they just *feel* right. If you had a particularly rough childhood, you may need to see a counselor or support group to dismantle the negative core beliefs about your value as a person that were instilled during your upbringing. If you're younger, you may also need to gain more life experience and perspective before you can accept that certain ideas aren't true (for example, when you're still in high school, it can seem like your life hinges on your social status. Once you're older, you can look back and see how overemphasized it was).

Gain self-esteem through your actions, behaviors, and accomplishments

A contradiction lies at the heart of self-esteem: On one hand, everyone has inherent value that doesn't depend on their actions or accomplishments. Self-esteem comes from within. It's not something other people bestow on you or a prize you earn after you've achieved enough to prove to the world that you're worthy.

On the other hand, self-esteem is partially affected by how you behave. It gauges whether you're living in a way that's important to you. If your life is not in a place you want it to be, your self-esteem will decrease. However, you can change your behaviors to boost it.

Make improvements in the areas where you're unhappy

Your self-esteem is affected negatively when you know you're missing something vital. One of these missing pieces could be poor social skills. They could also be problems in other spheres, like your finances, health, or career. Whatever your issues are, you should feel better about yourself once you get them under control. Doing so will take time because you can't make sweeping changes to your life in a few days. Though if you've been directionless and discouraged, just having a basic action plan for how you're going to start working on your problems may lift your self-esteem a bit.

It can be tricky to approach this point with the right mentality. Above all else, you should try to develop a foundation of core self-acceptance and a belief system that's reasonably free of harmful messages. Without a solid belief in yourself, you'll approach your weaker areas with the unconscious mentality of, "I'm worthless at my core. I'll cancel that truth by getting a lot of people to like me / succeeding in my field / making a lot of money." That mind-set may allow you to achieve a lot, and you may even temporarily feel better, but the confidence it creates is fragile and short-lived.

You need to directly address your core lack of self-esteem. You can't cover it up and compensate for it through outside sources of validation. This is not to say you should put all of your goals on hold until you become 100 percent self-accepting. Try to cultivate your goals at the same time as you work on accepting yourself.

Live a life based on core self-affirming practices

Your self-esteem monitors whether you're living a life based on certain key practices and then adjusts itself accordingly.

Practices that raise self-esteem:
- thinking and being responsible for yourself and choosing your own path through life
- living a life based on your own values, even when you encounter resistance
- showing the world your true self, even if not everyone responds well to it
- treating yourself with respect and standing up for your rights
- living constructively (for example, exercising regularly, trying to form meaningful social relationships, managing your finances)
- doing work and creating things that are meaningful and important to you

Opposing practices that will lower self-esteem:
- blindly following other people's ideas about how you should live
- breaking or selling out your deepest values (for example, valuing self-sufficiency, but purposely mooching off your family members)
- hiding your true self in order to gain approval from others
- letting others walk all over you
- living destructively (for example, abusing drugs, isolating yourself even though you want human contact, constantly wasting money)
- not doing work that feels meaningful to you

You could argue that principles like these are hardwired into people, though everyone varies in which ones they emphasize. For example, one person may feel a strong pull to have a personally fulfilling career and lose self-esteem if they're doing something just to pay the bills. Someone else may be happy to take any old job and put more importance on thinking for themselves. Living by these standards takes consistent work, and it's easy to unintentionally stray off course. Not perfectly fulfilling them doesn't mean you're a failure.

Work to develop positive traits

You'll feel a greater sense of self-esteem if you have some things going for you. Take time to develop your existing positive traits, or work to attain new ones. This could involve trying to cultivate certain aspects of your personality or learning a new skill. However, developing these characteristics only works if it's frosting on top of a deeper positive view of yourself. You can't just pile up a bunch of talents to smother a core sense of self-loathing.

Take on challenges and accomplish goals you set for yourself

You can't help but feel more confident if you've had some successes. The goals you choose to pursue will vary based on what's important to you. Challenging yourself also increases your feelings of self-efficacy, that is, the sense that you're generally competent and flexible, and can handle what life throws at you.

Create an environment that supports your self-esteem

All else being equal, who's likelier to have good self-esteem: someone who works a degrading job and whose "friends" and partner constantly belittle them, or someone who has supportive, encouraging people in their life? On one level, your self-esteem shouldn't depend on what other people think about you. You should be able to brush aside the inaccurate, hurtful things they say. On another level, you're human, and if you're constantly undermined and insulted, it can't help but drag you down. Try to improve or discard your toxic relationships, and seek out friends who make you feel good about yourself.

Use short-term self-esteem boosts when appropriate

Some suggestions for raising your self-esteem provide only a short-lived boost to your mood. Sometimes you just want to cheer yourself up, though, so there's nothing wrong with using them for the occasional pick-me-up. Here are some ideas:
* Take time to remind yourself of your positive
  traits and accomplishments.
* Say some positive affirmations (for example, "I love
  and approve of myself," "I have many strengths").
* Demonstrate happier, more confident body language.
* Dress up and make yourself look nice.
* Do something to treat yourself.

However, although quick mood-boosters help superficially, you can't just up the dosage to improve your core self-esteem, no more than swallowing more painkillers will heal a broken wrist. You have to use them in moderation. If you don't, the techniques will be a waste of time or become unhealthy habits. The methods above are harmless, but have diminishing returns if you do them too often.

There are two other techniques that are fine in small doses but unhealthy if taken too far. The first is comparing yourself to people who are worse off than you and realizing you don't have it so bad. Doing this frequently will get you in the habit of tearing others down in order to feel better about yourself. The second is seeking reassurance or compliments from others. Overuse will make you needy and dependent on others to shore you up.

INCREASING YOUR SELF-CONFIDENCE IN PARTICULAR SOCIAL SITUATIONS

If you have solid overall self-esteem, it can trickle down into your situational social confidence. The two don't always go together, though. Some people are very successful and confident at aspects of socializing, but don't think much of themselves deep down. Other people feel good about themselves on the whole, but still feel anxious and out of their depth in specific social situations.

Situational confidence comes in two flavors. When you're situationally confident, you're feeling one or both of two mental states. The first is a calm, logical knowledge that you have the ability to handle yourself in those circumstances. The second is a bold, psyched-up feeling.

Feeling calmly confident about your capabilities

When you're truly confident in your ability to succeed in a specific situation, you know you can perform well the same way you know the sky is blue. You have a well-tested skillset or some other reliable advantage. Your certainty comes from a string of past successes. This kind of confidence has to be earned.

When you feel confident in this way, you have a realistic sense of what you're capable of and believe your tools are good enough to complete the job. You don't necessarily think you're the best in the world; you're just as good as you need to be. If you've only been playing tennis for three years, you'd still feel calmly sure you could beat someone who's never held a racket. It doesn't mean you never feel nervous or unsure of yourself going into a situation. However, underneath those natural emotions is a current of "I'll be fine. I've done this sort of thing a million times before. It usually works out. And when it doesn't, I can bounce back."

You can build this confidence in an area you're weaker at through small successes. If you're a beginner, you can't skip to having the assuredness of an expert overnight. Instead, embrace your newbie status, learn the basics, and then feel confident that you know them, and that you'll know even more if you keep working at it. For example, if you're learning to make conversation with people at meet-up events, you may realize you can't have a long, engaging discussion with everyone you talk to, but you can feel confident that you've gotten the hang of introducing yourself and initiating interactions.

Feeling psyched

In contrast to feeling calmly assured about your abilities, the confidence that comes from feeling psyched is very emotion-based. When you're experiencing it, you feel charged up and notice how unusually confident you are. When you're certain you'll do well, you feel dry, logical confidence; if you know success is a given, there's no need to get emotional about it. Psyched-up confidence is more likely to show up ahead of events where you're not so sure of the outcome. An untested beginner could experience psyched-up confidence, but so could a veteran going into an unusually tough or high-stakes situation. It's like your mind is trying to amp you up so you can face the challenges ahead.

The big problem with this variety of confidence is that although it does improve your courage and performance, it's fleeting and unreliable. If it always appeared when needed, that would be great, but it usually doesn't happen that way. There's no consistent technique to bring out that psyched feeling on command. However, you may occasionally have success with the following methods:

- trying to psych yourself up physically, maybe by listening to driving music, jumping around, yelling, or pounding your chest
- listening to a passionate motivational speech or giving yourself a pep talk
- joking around with people to try to get yourself in a loose, playful mood
- trying to reframe the situation so it will seem easier or lower-stakes (for example, thinking of the situation as a potential

learning experience, not your one shot at making friends)
- trying to find a piece of practical information that will make you more likely to succeed, and therefore feel surer of yourself (for example, a conversation topic that you know will go over well with the crowd you'll be meeting)
- getting other people to pump up and encourage you

Even if these techniques work, they tend to have strong diminishing returns. What fires you up the first time never seems to work as well again. If a situation makes you unconfident, it makes you unconfident, and there's no foolproof short-term method to get around that.

Chasing psyched-up confidence often sidetracks people. They normally feel unsure and skittish in a situation and don't perform well in it, but every so often, for whatever reason, they get charged up and do much better than they normally would. They understandably begin to see that temporary emotional state as the key to their success, and they think there's no point in trying unless they're fired up. Because there's no way to conjure this feeling at will, they end up wasting their time and energy looking for that one surefire psych-up technique. If you want to become more consistently confident in an area, you have to put in the time and effort to build your skills. If you do find yourself feeling psyched up, by all means take advantage of it, but don't depend on it.

A COUPLE OF DISCLAIMERS ABOUT THE TASK OF BUILDING CONFIDENCE

When you're trying to build your confidence, whether it's of the self-esteem or situational variety, there are some things you should keep in mind:

Don't feel you have to get your confidence to a super-high level before you can work on anything else

Having confidence is undoubtedly useful. However, some people get sidetracked while working on their social skills by thinking they should solve their confidence issues first. You can do quite a lot to improve your social prospects without having rock-solid confidence. By all means, work on your self-esteem, but don't put everything else on hold.

Having confidence isn't the only thing you need to be socially successful

A lot of advice on self-confidence has the underlying message that having a better opinion of yourself is the key to success. At times, being more self-confident will improve how you act and come across around people. On other occasions, your success will depend more on having particular skills, like knowing how to make appropriate contributions to a conversation. When you have the ability or traits to get the job done, you often don't need to be especially confident. If you know how to organize a group outing, it won't matter if you're filled with self-doubt while you make a plan and invite everyone. Unless your insecurities are obvious and off-putting, they won't get in the way of your organizing efforts.

Your situational confidence can't jump too far ahead of your actual abilities

In that sense that social success is at least partially tied to confidence, people sometimes think they can increase their interpersonal skills by becoming as confident as possible first. That's not possible because your skills or previous track record and confidence in an area are tied together. If you know your skills rate a two out of ten, you can't make yourself feel eight-out-of-ten confidence in your ability to perform. Think of it as if you're building two small towers side by side, and you can only add to the height of one when you're working from the top of the other.

There's no quick or easy way to gain a lot of confidence

Sometimes when a person asks, "Can I just improve my self-confidence in order to be better with people?" they not only want the two to be connected, but they hope that gaining confidence is quicker and simpler than improving their interpersonal skills; by focusing on confidence, they hope to find a shortcut to changing their social situation. It doesn't work that way. Confidence has to grow slowly over time. Any attempt to increase it quickly will only result in a short-lived psyched-up feeling. We'd all be super-confident if all it took was reading a few inspirational quotes.

SECTION 2 DEVELOPING YOUR CONVERSATION SKILLS

IN THIS SECTION

- Some general strategies for making conversation
- Tips on how to succeed at the stages of a typical one-on-one conversation
- Advice on dealing with different types of conversation, such as group discussions and mingling at parties
- Three core skills that will improve your conversations: empathy, listening, and understanding nonverbal communication
- Suggestions on cultivating a few important broader personality traits that will make you more enjoyable to be around

9

GETTING A BASIC FEEL
FOR CONVERSATIONS

CONVERSATIONS TAKE WORK. Even people who are naturally outgoing and seemingly can talk to anyone occasionally get tongue-tied. So if you don't feel comfortable making conversation, you're not alone. Because they require you to think on the spot, your conversations are where the skills part of "social skills" really comes into play. How well your interactions go depends on three factors:

1. How comfortable and confident you feel in them: If you're anxious and insecure (the topic of Section 1), that can interfere with your conversations in all the ways outlined in Chapter 3. Shyness is many people's biggest obstacle to having good interactions. Their conversations are relaxed and flowing when they speak to someone they're used to, but when they get intimidated or self-conscious, their skills break down.

2. Your technical ability to make conversation: Technical ability includes your capacity to come up with things to say, your level in skills like listening and empathy, your body language, your knowledge of appropriate topics for a given situation, and so on. This section focuses on these skills and more.

3. Your overall personality, interests, values, and opinions: The choices you make in your interactions flow out of who you are

as a person. You could be very comfortable around people and always able to think of things to talk about, but if you're abrasive and condescending and have a bunch of offensive opinions, your interactions aren't going to go very well. The line between conversation skills and personality traits is fuzzy (if you're argumentative, that's a negative trait, but also a poor conversational style). Chapters 21 – 23 touch on some personality traits.

When people have trouble making conversation, one of their biggest complaints is that they "just don't know what to talk about" or that they "always run out of things to say." This chapter gives you some broad suggestions for keeping your interactions going.

A FEW REMINDERS ABOUT SOCIAL INTERACTIONS

As you work on improving your conversation skills, keep these points in mind:

- You can't make every interaction go well. You won't have enough in common with everyone you meet, and sometimes the other person will be in a grouchy mood. On occasion, you'll begin talking to someone who's initially unfriendly and win them over with your rapport-building skills, but it's not realistic to expect to do this every time. Even if you became the most charismatic person in the world, a percentage of your conversations would not go well because some people would feel jealous or intimidated around you. You can't win them all.
- There's no single right way to make conversation. Every person you talk to is different, and your conversations with them can go in any number of directions and still be a success. When someone asks you a question over coffee, it's not a test where you have to figure out the one "correct" response.
- Advice on interacting with people has to be general by nature. No book can tell you exactly what to say in every situation. You'll need to take the broad principles and fit them to the social culture and specific interaction you're in.

No matter what kind of conversation you find yourself having, the ideas in the rest of this chapter should give you a better idea of what to say in them. When you naturally get along with someone and the conversation flows effortlessly, many of the processes below happen automatically. Using them more deliberately will help you in the interactions where the words don't come as easily.

CLARIFY YOUR GOALS FOR THE CONVERSATION

If the average person was placed in the cockpit of a fighter jet and told to go through the start-up sequence and take off as quickly as possible, they'd sit there dumbly because they wouldn't have the first idea of where to begin. Some people go blank in conversations for the same reason. They find themselves speaking to someone and know they need to "make good conversation," but they aren't sure what to do beyond that. It's much easier to talk to people when you have a rough idea of where you should try to take the interaction. If you find yourself blanking, you can quickly remind yourself of one of the goals, and that should help you think of something to say.

Goals of day-to-day socializing

If someone says they have trouble making conversation, they usually mean they aren't good at the kinds of day-to-day interactions that are social for their own sake (if they have to give directions to their house, they're fine in that conversation). The quintessential example of this is having to make friendly chit-chat at a cocktail party. These kinds of interactions have one or more of the following broader unwritten goals:

Goal #1: Have an interaction that's rewarding for everyone involved

A conversation that engages everyone might include discussing a movie everyone is interested in, joking around about a series of silly topics, connecting over a shared experience, exchanging insights about a philosophical question, having a friendly debate about a political issue, or just enjoying one another's company for two minutes as you chat about nothing in particular. That doesn't mean every second has to be engrossing for each person, just that overall everyone is getting something out of the exchange. Sometimes you'll give the other person an opportunity to discuss a topic that's a bit more interesting for them, and they'll do the same for you.

This all seems obvious, but if you have trouble with conversations, you can forget they're supposed to be enjoyable and only see them as verbal obstacle courses. If your only concern is to keep an interaction going so you don't seem awkward, it can land you in discussions you don't get much out of ("Man, this topic is boring…but at least I haven't caused any awkward silences"). Don't passively drift along in your conversations. It's okay to push them in a direction you think you and your partners will enjoy.

Goal #2: Learn about the other person and try to find common ground

This is more clearly a goal when you've first met someone, but even if you've known someone forever, there's always more to discover about each other. Learning about someone shows your interest in getting to know them, and it allows you to get a sense of how much you have in common and if they could be compatible for a closer relationship. You'll also tend to grow that little bit closer to someone when you find out you have similarities.

Goal #3: Share things about yourself with the other person

You want to learn about the other person, but they also want to know what you're all about. You should share your interests, personality, sense of humor, values, and what you've been up to lately. As long as you're also allowing the other person to contribute to the discussion, it's not self-absorbed to reveal yourself this way. Your conversation partners want to know what makes you tick.

Goal #4: Show you're a reasonably friendly, sociable person

When you talk to someone, come across as if you like talking to them, not as if you're aloof and feel put upon for having to speak with them.

Here's an example of how being aware of broad goals can guide your conversations: Say you're talking to a new student in your art class. If the conversation hits a lull, you could think, "Okay, one general goal is to learn about them. I'll ask them what else they're interested in aside from drawing," or "I can share something about myself. I'll quickly explain how I've felt about the class," or "What would make for an interesting topic to discuss? I'll ask them if they've been to the new exhibit at the art gallery. Maybe after that we can talk about what kind of art we each like."

Aside from those general goals, many social conversations have more specific goals. Here are a few examples:
- If you know the person already, catch each other up on what you've been up to since you last saw each other (for example, events in your life, fun or interesting things you've done, current topics that are on your mind).
- If you run into a coworker in the break room, have a brief, pleasant interaction to show you're a friendly person and a team player.
- Talk about a topic predetermined by the situation, like discussing what else you've been reading before your book club meeting starts.

Tune in to what each person wants out of the interaction

Every individual brings their idiosyncratic goals to each conversation or to smaller sections of it. For example, maybe they're curious to hear the details of how your job interview went, they want you to be impressed with them as they recount their recent trip overseas, or they hope you'll validate their feelings as they tell you about a rough time they went through last week. If you can tune in to their objectives, it gives you more information about where you could steer the exchange. Chapter 16, which covers empathy, goes into detail about how to take on other people's perspectives.

Be aware of any personal goals you have that might harm the conversation

We sometimes want things out of conversations that serve our own needs, but getting them would make the interaction less enjoyable for everyone else. For example, "I want to make everyone feel dumber than me" or "I want my jokes to get a bunch of laughs, and that's more important than what anyone else has to say."

Another more innocuous personal goal to be wary of is "I want to keep this conversation going as long as possible." If you're just getting the hang of keeping interactions afloat, this is a reasonable thing to aim for, but it's not appropriate in every situation. Your social worth isn't based on being able to talk to anyone for the maximum length of time. If you met someone you had nothing in common with, maybe you could have a long interaction if you faked an interest in their hobbies and told them exactly what they wanted to hear about everything. But after the exchange was over you might look back and realize you go nothing out of it.

GO IN WITH AN OVERALL APPROACH FOR MAKING CONVERSATION

The approaches below often come naturally to good conversationalists. You can use the same strategies more deliberately. Having a broad game plan can help because it simplifies and clarifies what you have to think about, gives you the confidence that comes from knowing you're using a method that works, and provides some reliable, simple starting material so you can practice. It's good to have several approaches ready to go, and if one doesn't work, you can try another. You can also switch up broad approaches within a single conversation as it evolves. You don't have to apply only one strategy to every person or situation.

The broad conversation goals that were covered earlier in the chapter are one way to give yourself some direction ("I'm going to ask about their interests and try to find one we have in common," "My grandpa is interested to know what I've been up to lately, so I'll focus on telling him what's been new in my life since I last saw him"). Here are some other approaches you can use:

Approach #1: Be interested in and curious about other people, and make it your goal to find out what's fascinating and unique about them

This is the most popular general approach you'll hear people mention when it comes to making conversation. It comes up again and again, going back to classic books on people skills like *How to Win Friends and Influence People*. The idea is primarily to be someone who asks questions and listens to the answers, which leads to focusing the discussion on the other person. Your "mission" in the conversation is to discover what makes the other person interesting.

You don't need to only listen to or talk about the other person the entire time; you should bring up things about yourself and share your own opinions when relevant. Generally focus the conversation on your partner, but not to the point where you share nothing about yourself and become a forgettable nonentity that just helps other people talk.

The underlying assumption about this approach is that everyone's favorite subject is themselves, and that people like someone who takes a genuine interest in them and the things they have to say. People also tend to feel good about a conversation in which they can talk about aspects of themselves that they're proud of and passionate about. Another line you'll often hear in regard to this strategy is that you'll be more successful taking an interest in other people than you will be by trying to get them interested in you.

This approach predisposes you to adopt a positive, friendly frame of mind. Its basic premise implies that everyone is worth talking to if you dig past any preconceptions you may have of them. And because you're likely to find something interesting about the other person if you look for it, it ends up being a self-fulfilling prophecy.

Approach #2: Talk in terms of the other person's interests

Focusing on the other person's interests is similar to the approach above, in that you're mainly listening and the conversation is based around the other person and things they like discussing. This approach is not exactly the same. The approach above is more general and is about finding people's good traits, whatever they may be. This one is more about specifically trying to find out what the other person is interested in talking about, whether it's a hobby or a life decision they're wrestling with, and centering the conversation on that. You take an interest in their interest, ask thoughtful questions, and listen as they tell you about it.

The limitations of being an interested listener

Both of these listening / other-person-centric approaches can work very well and are essential to have in your toolbox. At the same time, their effectiveness is sometimes oversold. They're not the perfect, one-size-fits-all conversation cheat codes they can be portrayed as. Sometimes you'll run into people who

- don't want to do most of talking because they're shy, private, have been told it's rude to go on about themselves, or are bored of talking about their own lives;
- want to learn about you instead;
- like talking about their passions, but only with other knowledgeable enthusiasts, not anyone they have to explain the basics to;
- are self-absorbed and will use you as a prop that gives them permission to go on about themselves;
- are trying to use this strategy themselves and will be reluctant to take the spotlight; or
- will enjoy your interest and having a chance to talk about the things they like, but won't automatically want to befriend you just because of it.

Also, you can't use this approach as easily in group conversations because they're not about focusing on one person.

Approach #3: Figure out what topics you have an easy time talking about, and then try to steer the conversation in that direction

Having a conversation about your own interests is considered a more self-centered approach. It's generally thought of as better form to focus on the other person or have your contributions be equal. However, this strategy may help you organize your thoughts and simplify how you approach an interaction. If you're just starting to get the hang of conversation, you may be most comfortable expounding on a topic in your comfort zone. In reasonable doses, it's perfectly fine to try to talk about the things you enjoy. You just have to be sensitive to other people and take care not to bore them or monopolize the air space.

KNOW HOW TO ASK GOOD QUESTIONS AND MAKE GOOD STATEMENTS

To use a common analogy, having a conversation with someone is like working with them to rally a tennis ball back and forth. When it's your turn to hit the ball, you don't want to send them weak or difficult shots they have to scramble to return. When it's your turn to speak and you want to continue the conversation, you have to say something that will give the other person enough to work with. At the most basic level you can:

- Ask them a question, which directly calls on them to contribute.
- Make a statement of your own, which will hopefully lead them to think of something they want to say in response.

Questions

Questions can ask for new information ("So what are you taking in school?", "How was the show last night?") or ask for more details about something the other person has said ("You're studying business? What drew you to that field?", "No way! Then what did you do?"). Aside from allowing you to get more information, they also show your interest in the other person and let you direct where the conversation will go.

As much as you can, you want to ask open-ended questions rather than easy-to-answer closed-ended ones. Open-ended questions require an answer of a couple of sentences; closed-ended questions can be answered with one or two words. Closed-ended questions can stall a conversation because the other person may respond with only a yes or a no, or something like "It's good." A quick example of an open vs. closed question would be asking someone what they think of their college major (open), rather than asking if they simply like it (closed).

It's hardly a fatal error if you ask a close-ended question. Sometimes you'll want to know the answer to a question that's simple to reply to, or it will be all you can think to say at that moment. Just be aware that you may not get a good answer and will need to have another contribution ready to go (for example, "Did you have fun on vacation?", "Yep.", "Good to hear. What would you say was the highlight?").

Statements

A statement could be an answer to a question, an opinion, an observation, some information, or sharing something relevant that happened to you. The main guideline when making statements is that you want to say something with enough substance or "jumping-off points" to provide your conversation partner with plenty of ideas about what they could say next. If you're answering a question, provide enough details.

Rather than saying that you liked a movie, give a few reasons why. Rather than quickly replying that your weekend was fun, mention something you did. Let your interests, values, and personality show. You won't always know what to say, and it's fine if you sometimes have to give short, sparse answers. However, if you give too many, it puts too much pressure on the other person to keep the interaction alive. This isn't to say you need to go on for a full minute every time it's your turn to speak. You can offer your partner plenty of jumping-off points in a meaningful sentence or two.

Mini-questions, statements, or facial expressions that encourage the other person to keep talking

If the person is talking about something they're interested in, you don't necessarily have to come up with an elaborate reply when they pause to let you speak. You may just need to make a quick little utterance that tells them, "I'm listening. Keep going," or "Here's my reaction to what you just said. Continue." Some examples are "Hm", "Uh huh...

uh huh...", "Oh yeah?", "Go on...", "Ha ha, no way...", "Yep, that's something he'd do." Sometimes you don't even have to speak; you can just laugh, look sad, or look surprised at the appropriate moment and let the person continue what they were saying.

Mixing up questions and statements

In most conversations, you'll want to use a mix of questions and statements. If you ask someone question after question, it can create an interview or interrogation dynamic or cause a lopsided exchange where one person feels they're doing all of the sharing about themselves while the other remains a cipher. Sharing too many of your own statements may make you seem like you're not interested in the other person and their opinions, and simply want someone to talk at. Even if your responses have substance, if you only answer another person's questions but never ask any of your own, it can put too much pressure on them to keep driving the interaction forward. That too can make you seem like you're indifferent to learning anything about them.

Some types of discussions will naturally feature more questions or statements. If you're talking to someone about a mutual interest, you'll tend to make a lot of statements to each other as you share your opinions and information. If you're getting to know someone or listening and helping them work through a tricky issue, you may mostly be asking questions when it's your turn to speak.

GET BETTER AT NOTICING THE POSSIBLE JUMPING-OFF POINTS IN THE STATEMENTS PEOPLE MAKE

Not everything you say has to directly tie in to the sentence made right before. However, if you pay attention to what the other person says, their statements can give you a lot of ideas. For example, if someone says, "My weekend at the cottage was fun. I went jet skiing for the first time," some possible jumping off points are:

- **Weekend:** Talk about how your own weekend was. "Oh, that sounds fun. I stayed in town and went to a concert this weekend."

- **Cottage:** "Oh cool. Was the cottage more isolated, or on a busier lake? Whose cottage is it, your family's or a friend's?"
- **Jet skiing:** "Wow, I've never done that. How'd you find it?" or "I remember doing that as a kid. The newer models must be way more fun. How was it?"
- *First time* **jet skiing:** "I remember the first time I ever drove a boat up at the cottage..."

There's no single correct response in this example, so any of these statements or questions, or other ones, could be valid ways to continue the conversation. Sometimes people will set up obvious jumping-off points for you because they have something they want to talk about, but don't want to launch right into it without gauging your interest. For example, they'll say, "Man, the weirdest thing happened to me at the music festival..." You just have to say, "Oh yeah? What happened?" and they'll tell you.

ASK THE OTHER PERSON THEIR THOUGHTS ON THE QUESTION OR TOPIC YOU WERE JUST TALKING ABOUT

You can't build a whole conversation on this technique, but it's simple to use and can help you here and there if you're at a loss for words. Its most basic form is to ask someone the question they just asked you (for example, after telling them about your hobbies, you ask what they do for fun). If you give your opinion and observations on an issue first, then after you're done, you can ask them what their thoughts are.

REALIZE YOU HAVE MORE TO TALK ABOUT THAN YOU MAY THINK

People who have trouble with conversation sometimes say they have nothing to talk about and they know they're boring because all they do is work or play video games. Everyone has more topics they can talk about than they think. Even if most of your time is taken up by one activity, you still watch the odd movie, catch bits of the news, or have funny little things happen to you as you go about your day. You have your unique perspective and opinions on all of them. You have thoughts on your dreams for the future, your family, current events, larger philosophical questions, what it's like to live in your city, what type of cereal tastes the best, what cats are like as pets, and on and on and on. Don't unnecessarily dismiss an idea for conversation with, "Well, sure, I have an opinion on that, but no one wants to hear it, so it doesn't count." Any of them could potentially be interesting in the right context.

DON'T FILTER YOURSELF TOO MUCH WHEN TRYING TO THINK OF SOMETHING TO SAY

Often when you feel like you can't think of anything to say, there are actually lots of possible contributions passing through your mind. But instead of going with them, you nix them for one reason or another: "No, I can't say that. It's too boring." or "No, that's too out of the blue." Often this thought process is quick enough that you won't notice yourself doing it. Instead of censoring yourself too much, just toss out some of the ideas going through your head. It's better to say something than nothing. Even if you put something out there that didn't get a stellar response, at least you tried and did your part to keep the conversation going. There's always a chance to recover if something you say doesn't lead anywhere.

DON'T FRET ABOUT SAYING GENERIC THINGS

A lot of conversation advice tells you not to bore people with clichéd, unoriginal topics. Sometimes recalling this point can cause you to freeze in social situations. You'll meet someone new and not say anything to them because you think it's a huge faux pas to say something uninspired, like asking where they work. Don't put too much pressure on yourself by feeling that every statement that comes out of your mouth has to be sparklingly original, insightful, and entertaining, or that every question you ask has to get the other person thinking about things they've never thought about before. If you watch friends hang out, you'll see they often talk about pretty humdrum topics. If someone enjoys another person's company, they're more than happy to talk about day-to-day subjects with them.

If small talk makes you feel impatient, you may hesitate to bring up anything reminiscent of it. If you've just met someone, it may be a good play to ask them where they're from or what they're studying, but if you find that kind of conversation boring, you may say nothing, and the interaction might fizzle out. More on small talk coming up in Chapter 12.

DON'T FRET ABOUT CHANGING TOPICS

Sometimes you'll have something you want to say, but you'll abandon it because you can't think of a smooth way to segue into it. If you listen to friends talk, you'll see they bring up new topics all the time. When one conversation thread has come to an end, it's normal to jump to something unrelated. It's okay to change the subject as long as the transition isn't completely random and jarring, and you haven't cut the other person off from a topic they wanted to stay on. If you do want to switch topics, follow these pointers:

- If the other person is expecting a reply, give them one first. If they tell you about their winter holiday, comment on it or tell them about something you did with your own time off.
- Make a shift seem less abrupt by tacking on a phrase like, "Oh yeah…", "That reminds me…", "Speaking of…", "I'm not sure why, but that makes me think of…", or "This is going to sound random, but…".
- If you pause for a few seconds before changing topics, it often signals, "That subject is done, switching to something else."

PAY ATTENTION AND KEEP UP WITH THE CONVERSATION GOING ON AROUND YOU

This one applies to group conversations. It's always easier to come up with things to talk about when you really focus on what everyone else is saying. It's more likely you'll hear something that will trigger a contribution you could make. However, some people have a tendency to zone out and disappear into their heads. Group conversations can also be a bit annoying to follow at times, like if many people are talking at once or if the environment is loud. Sometimes it seems easier to give up and not devote your full attention to what the others are saying. With practice, you can get better at keeping focused during group conversations. If you tend to get distracted by anxious thoughts, Chapters 5 and 6 have suggestions on dealing with that.

PREPARE SOME TOPICS OR STATEMENTS AHEAD OF TIME

A standard piece of conversation advice is, "Before you go to a party, it's always good to catch up on the news so you'll have a few ready-to-go topics prepared or you'll have something to add if someone else brings those stories up." A similar suggestion is, "If you know you'll get asked a certain question a lot, it helps to have an interesting little blurb to give in response."

You can prepare for your interactions in a more general way by keeping a few topics in mind that you can bring out whenever the discussion hits a lull. This could be as simple as asking, "So has anyone seen any good movies lately?" It's hard to remember more than a handful of these conversation starters though. There's no need to try to memorize thirty different lines you could use at a party. In the moment, you'll probably blank on most of them anyway, or get stuck going through the huge mental list to pick out the best option. If you give yourself only three choices, it's easier to go with one of them.

A FEW LONGER-TERM APPROACHES FOR HAVING MORE THINGS TO SAY IN CONVERSATIONS

The suggestions above were more tactical and can be used right away. You can also work over a longer period to develop your conversation skills and give yourself more to talk about.

Have more experiences and develop your opinions

This chapter already argued that even if you think your life is sterile and one-dimensional, you still have much more to say than you think. That said, if you do the same things all the time, another way to have more to talk about is… to get more to talk about. Try new hobbies. Visit new places. If you find you don't have an opinion to share on some important topic, then do a little reading and develop one so you're prepared the next time the subject comes up. If you're really busy, even a small new experience here and there can go a long way. Eat at a new restaurant. Watch a few episodes of a new show. Listen to a few songs by a new band. Spend half an hour on a website about a subject you're interested in but not familiar with. Don't put unrealistic expectations on yourself to gain a whole new colorful life in a week. Just start small and let it add up.

Know facts and details about a range of topics

The more knowledge and experiences you have floating around in your head, the easier it is to chat with people. The likelihood increases that they could say something that will spark an interesting contribution from you. It's sometimes eerie how you can be reading about some seemingly obscure new topic earlier in the day, and it will come up in conversation that very evening.

This is a pragmatic piece of advice that you may not feel like using, but it never hurts to be at least somewhat familiar with the things other people tend to be interested in and are likely to bring up. Even if you can't have an in-depth conversation about a certain area, being able to share a little factoid or ask an intelligent question about it can keep the interaction flowing.

As practically useful as it is to have a lot of knowledge and experience, it has its limits. First, it's impossible to do and learn about everything. Second, everyone has areas that they're just not interested in, regardless of how practical it would be to know about them (for example, some women just don't care about fashion trends). That's fine. No one can be expected to make perfect conversation about every subject on the planet.

Learn to relate to a wider variety of people

You may sometimes find it tricky to make conversation with people who have different interests, priorities, and ways of looking at the world. At times their differences will intrigue you, but you can just as easily find yourself thinking, "I have nothing to say to this person. We don't think alike at all. We hardly have anything in common." You may find you can relate to these types of people better if you make an effort to put yourself in their shoes. Genuinely try to get a sense of why they think the way they do and like the things they like. Maybe try out some of the things they enjoy that you've dismissed up until now. Even if you don't share their exact worldview, you may realize you have some common ground after all, and they're not the caricatures you originally thought they were. Chapter 16 goes into more detail about this kind of empathy.

OVERCOMING CONVERSATION STUMBLING BLOCKS

Sometimes you may have a series of conversations, but you aren't getting good reactions from the people you're trying to talk to, and you're not sure why. It's hard to see outside yourself and get an objective sense of why you might not be making the best impression on people. There are a few ways things could be going wrong:

Reasons that lie with you

- You're not actually doing anything wrong at all, but you're insecure and seeing signs of rejection where there aren't any. You then give up too soon on interactions you "know" have gone south.

- Your conversation and shyness management skills aren't developed enough yet, and your interactions are stilted.
- You're expecting too much from various conversation techniques and think you just have to use them and everyone will instantly like you.
- Your nonverbal communication is putting people off (see Chapter 19).
- You make one of any number of possible mistakes when making conversation (see Chapter 20).

Reasons that lie with the people you're talking to

- You're trying to interact with people who wouldn't naturally click with someone like you.
- You're in a demographic that the people you're trying to talk to will unfairly dismiss (for example, if you have a Southeast Asian background and you're living in a small-minded mostly white town).

If you're consistently not getting good responses from others, the best thing you can do is ask a supportive person for some feedback on how you come across. Finding someone to do this can be tough because many people will be reluctant to be straightforward with you. They feel awkward about possibly hurting your feelings or worry you'll take their comments badly. And you may not want to ask because it's scary to willingly open yourself up to criticism and risk hearing something that may make you feel bad about yourself. This is another situation where a professional counselor can be useful. They'll be honest, and they'll word their critique in a sensitive and constructive way. They're also an impartial stranger, so their feedback will probably sting less than if it came from a friend or family member.

10

DEALING WITH
AWKWARD SILENCES

REGARDLESS OF HOW CLOSELY you follow all of the conversation tips in this section, eventually you're going to face the dreaded awkward silence while you're trying to talk to someone. If you fear silences, you likely imagine they'll be really uncomfortable and embarrassing in the moment. Furthermore, you may believe that if one happens, it "proves" you're incompetent in social situations. Nothing could be further from the truth. Read on to find out why awkward silences happen and what you can do about them.

SEEING WHY AWKWARD SILENCES OCCUR

Not every conversational lull or silence is due to a mistake on someone's part. Don't be too quick to blame yourself if the conversation hits a snag. Sometimes these lulls occur naturally, simply due to what was being talked about:

- You and your conversation partner(s) may have come to the end of a subject, and you both need time to figure out what to say next. When some topics end, it's fairly easy to think of the next direction to head in. With others, no immediate follow-up springs to mind.

- If someone makes a particularly profound or thought-provoking point, everyone may want to pause and reflect on it for a moment.
- Everyone may be in a somewhat tired, distracted, or laid-back mood and decide all at once they just want to relax and not talk for a bit.

KNOWING WHEN SILENCE IS OKAY

Silence is acceptable in some situations, and it's not necessary to try to fill it. If you've just introduced yourself to someone at a party, you both hope and expect that the conversation will flow easily. In other situations, it's natural to have quiet periods. Some cases are when you're riding with people in a car, bus, or plane; when you're chilling with a friend and watching a movie; when you're sitting at the beach or around a campfire; and when you're on a hike. If everyone goes quiet, you shouldn't consider these awkward silences that must be overcome at all costs. In fact, in these situations it's often the wrong play to try to keep the conversation going nonstop. It makes you look insecure and like you can't handle a second of peaceful reflection.

HANDLING A FEW SECONDS OF SILENCE WITH EASE

Silences happen. It's all about how you react to them. If you stay comfortable and in control, you'll send the message, to yourself and to everyone else, that what's happening is normal and not awkward at all. If you keep your cool and apply one of the suggestions below, it won't be long before the conversation is back on track.

Short silences happen all the time between good friends. Because they're comfortable in each other's company, they don't stress about it and are content when a few seconds of dead air happens. They may have as many silences in their conversations as two people who just met, but they don't really notice them, and they don't see the exchange as being awkward and halting.

DON'T WORRY ABOUT BRINGING UP A NEW SUBJECT

If a silence settles in, give yourself a few seconds to try to think of something that will continue the current topic. If you can't, maybe you could go back to a dangling thread from earlier in the conversation ("So, you were saying before that you were thinking of learning to knit?"). If nothing comes to mind, you'll have to come up with a new topic.

You may worry that it will seem clumsy to switch to a fresh topic so abruptly or that your choice will be boring or that by changing the subject, you'll reveal you didn't know how to keep the last thread going. It's fine to shift gears if the current subject has come to an end. It's also all in the delivery. If you change topics in an uncomfortable, stilted way, it might be awkward. But if you speak as if taking the discussion in a new direction is the most natural thing in the world, it won't seem out of the ordinary.

COMMENT ON THE SILENCE

When you comment on the silence, don't say something like, "Wow... this sure is uncomfortable. Can't think of anything to say...nope..." That usually makes the silence worse by drawing attention to it and putting people on the spot. Depending on why the silence occurred, you can make a casual observation about it before bringing up something new. Here are a few examples:

- If a lull settles in because everyone was kidding around and then one person made a funny but very random joke, you could say, "Ha ha, I guess there's not much anyone can say to continue off from that. Anyway..."
- If everyone has exhausted a particular topic, you could comment, "Um, looks like we've said everything we have to say about that. Um... so did you hear..."
- If you say something and it seems the other person can't think of anything to say in response, you could ease the silence with, "Ah, I guess you haven't thought about that. Oh, so the other week I..."

- If someone makes a statement that everyone needs time to digest, after a bit of silence you could say, "Yeah, that's an interesting point. My mind's mulling over it right now… I guess thinking about it more, I…"

BE OPEN WHEN YOU HAVE NOTHING TO CONTRIBUTE

Sometimes someone says something that gives you nothing to go on, and you can't think of anything to say in reply. For example, if you know or care nothing about cars and someone tells you the McLaren MP4-12C's engine produces 592 bhp, odds are your mind is going to go, "Uhh…." Rather than scrambling to try to come up with a relevant follow-up to their statement, you can say what you're thinking: "Ha, ha, sorry. I don't know much about that stuff."

Try not to leave the conversation hanging there, though. Some people are too quick to give up on a conversation when it turns to an area they don't have in common with the other person. Once you get your lack of familiarity about the topic out in the open, you'll often find a way to get the interaction going again. Maybe you'll decide to switch to a subject you can both talk about, or you could take an interest in their interest and stay on the current subject, but ask them to explain the basics and background details more so you can follow along and relate to it better.

BE PREPARED FOR SURPRISING STATEMENTS

Sometimes you experience a loss for words when the other person says something off-putting or unexpected. Imagine you're talking to a seemingly grounded, intelligent person, and then out of nowhere they say, "I think fashion is super important. I don't trust anyone who spends less than $2,000 a month on new clothes." It would stun you into silence. If you were thinking anything, it would probably be something like, "Wow…That is so out of touch. I have no idea how to reply." As a milder example, say you ask someone what their favorite shows are and they reply they don't watch TV. You may not have a problem with that, but it wasn't one of the answers you were anticipating, and you may be unsure how to reply.

Knowing you may face unexpected statements can help you respond better to them. Rather than beginning to panic because an awkward silence may be imminent, you can use a few fall-back responses. You could quickly acknowledge their opinion and change the subject. Or you could adopt a curious stance and question them about it. If you don't agree with them, you could respectfully say so, assuming you don't think you'll get pulled into a pointless, nasty argument.

TAKE THE OPPORTUNITY TO EXIT THE CONVERSATION

If you were planning on ending the conversation soon anyway, a quick silence can provide the opportunity to get going. Before the lull goes on for too long, take charge and say something like, "Anyway, I'll let you get back to what you were doing…" or "Anyway, it was good running into you. I'll catch you later…" Chapter 13 is all about ending conversations.

Even when you're not intending to leave, in situations like parties and networking events, there's nothing stopping you from exiting a conversation as soon as it starts feeling awkward by pretending you meant for it to be quick all along. Be careful, though, because bailing from conversations early too often can become a bad habit that reinforces avoidance behavior and prevents you from practicing how to recover from a lull and carry on.

11

STARTING ONE-ON-ONE CONVERSATIONS

THIS IS THE FIRST OF SEVERAL CHAPTERS on how to navigate the stages of a typical conversation. Of course, not every conversation will go through the same progression like clockwork, but thinking in terms of stages helps you know what's likely to come next.

The first stage of a conversation is obviously to start it. Beginning conversations, especially with someone they don't know, makes many people nervous. They worry that they'll say the wrong thing and get rejected, or that they won't be able to think of anything to talk about and the interaction will stall soon after it begins. When you're comfortable initiating interactions and handling their first few minutes, a lot more options open up to you.

THE TWO SUBSTAGES TO STARTING CONVERSATIONS

The beginnings of conversations have two parts, which often flow into each other.

The first is for one person to say something to the other to initiate the interaction. This could be as simple as a "hey." Sometimes the first step is taken care of for you: The other person approaches you, you're introduced to each other, or your circumstances force you to start talking. If none of those things happen, you'll have to start the conversation yourself if you want to chat with someone. An opening line may do nothing more than get the other person's attention and begin the interaction, so you'll need to follow up the opening with something else (introducing yourself is one example). Other openers can potentially lead to a full conversation (for example, going up to someone wearing a T-shirt of your favorite band and asking how they liked the latest album).

The second substage is navigating the conversation's first few, sometimes uncertain, minutes. When you're first talking to someone, you often don't know much about them or what you could talk about with each other. Although at this point the usual conversation goals (like learning about the other person and showing you're a friendly, interested person) come into play, your main priority is to find a topic you both have an easy, enjoyable time discussing and settle into a comfortable groove. After that, you may continue to talk for hours about any number of issues, or you may each have to run after five minutes, but still leave the conversation feeling you had a nice chat.

Again, this part will sometimes feel simple and you'll start gabbing about a mutually interesting subject right away. Your conversation starter may lead to an area you and the other person have in common. Or after initiating the conversation with another opening line, the first thing you think to ask about after that hits the mark. It's also possible someone else will introduce you to each other and set you up (for example, "This is Alison. She's studying to be a pharmacist too"). If a good topic doesn't fall into your lap, you'll have to look for one, and you may hit a dead end or two before finding something that works.

Things to keep in mind about initiating a conversation

Technically, initiating a conversation is simple. As long as it's not rude or totally out of left field, the exact opening line you use isn't that important. How the other person is likely to respond to you and how well the ensuing interaction goes will depend more on factors like whether the person you're talking to is in the mood to chat, what their initial impression of you is, how compatible the two of you are, and how good each person's conversation skills are.

However, your nerves may mislead you into seeing the task as more tricky and complicated than it is. Emotional reasoning may kick in and cause you to think, "This *feels* hard, therefore it must actually be difficult and require a lot of strategizing to find the perfect opener." If you're worried about getting rejected or offending someone, you may also hold out hope for a nonexistent magic line that will guarantee you won't get a bad response.

Things to keep in mind about getting through the first few minutes of conversation

There are good and bad sides to the first few minutes of an interaction. In the *Good* column is the fact that they're fairly predictable. It's also pretty easy to practice them. If you go to a big party or networking event, it wouldn't be unusual to chat with a dozen or more people over the evening. On the downside, if you're going to have trouble in a conversation, it's likely going to be in those first couple of minutes. There are two reasons for this: First, if someone doesn't feel like speaking to you or you don't have much to say to each other, that's going to become clear quickly. The other person won't give you much to work with, or you'll both struggle to find something to talk about. Remember, there's no way to ensure every interaction you have will go well. Second, you're usually feeling at your most nervous and on the spot when you're first talking to someone, and anxiety can cause you or your conversation partner to stall. If you can get past that point, the rest of the conversation is usually easier.

It's great when you find an interesting subject to talk about right away, but it's not at all unusual for a conversation to be a little stilted in its opening minutes. That's no reason to panic. This awkwardness isn't a sign that the interaction won't be enjoyable or that you have horrible people skills. It just means that each person hasn't found their footing yet. In a few minutes, everyone may be feeling more comfortable and have found something fun to talk about.

Sometimes a conversation you start may peter out soon after it begins. Knowing this takes some of the pressure away. Every time you talk to someone, realize that they may be preoccupied, have nothing in common with you, or be too shy to think of anything to say. Also accept that sometimes you just won't be on your game and able to do your part to keep the conversation moving. Have a plan for gracefully leaving a conversation that isn't going anywhere. Rather than panicking and blaming yourself, keep your cool and move on. (Chapter 13 covers how to end conversations.)

GENERAL GUIDELINES FOR STARTING CONVERSATIONS

The appropriate ways to initiate a conversation vary depending on the situation you're in. If you're at a friend's party, it's expected that people will talk to each other, and most of the guests are there to do just that. It's fine to start conversations in a more forward, familiar, casual way where you act as if you're already on good terms with everyone. In more formal settings, like a career networking event, you should be a little more reserved and mannered. Still be friendly, but don't be overly casual or chummy right off the bat.

Talking to strangers in public places during the day is on the other end of the spectrum. Some people are open to talking, but others are going about their day and have other priorities. Read their body language for clues about how open they may be to interacting with you (see Chapter 18). If they seem really preoccupied and closed off, it may be better to leave them alone. You need to respect that they may initially be wary and not know what you want from them or not be in the mood to talk. You may need to get their attention with a smile or an "excuse me" first. Still be friendly, but speak with them in a more pulled-back, noncommittal way to give them the sense that you'll back off if they don't want to chat.

Know your city and country's attitude about what's considered acceptable too. In some areas, people are constantly, cheerfully talking to each other in grocery store lines, while in other places, the culture is "Don't intrude on anyone's space." If your culture is less talkative, it doesn't mean you'll never be able to speak to anyone you don't know. If you try, you just need to be extra respectful and realize you won't always get a warm response.

Public places where people go specifically to socialize, like nightclubs, fall in between. You have implicit permission to try to strike up a conversation with people you don't know, and you can often be more casual; however, you also have to respect that not everyone goes to those places looking to chat with a bunch of strangers. If they don't seem like they want to talk and would rather stick with the friends they came with, then move on.

EXAMPLES OF TYPES OF CONVERSATION OPENERS AND EARLY THINGS TO TALK ABOUT

The following pages list several ways to initiate a one-on-one conversation and to try to find a good topic during its first few minutes. The two are together because many lines can pull double duty. Always have at least a few lines or topics ready to go. If you use one but the other person doesn't give you a response you can work with, be ready to try another.

Examples of many types of lines follow, but that's mainly to show you have lots of options. Don't feel you have to memorize every one. When you're in a situation where you want to talk to someone, go with one of the first lines that pop into your head because they could all work equally well. If you want to prepare ahead of time, settle on around half a dozen conversation starters that you'd feel comfortable using. In general, as you get better at thinking on your feet, you'll feel more comfortable using whatever type of conversation starter you want. Even if the other person doesn't answer in an ideal way, you know you can follow up and maybe recover the interaction.

Openers that will begin a conversation, but have to be followed up with something else

The only time these openers won't need to be followed up on is if the other person replies with a comment that naturally leads to a conversation. You can't count on that though, and should have another opener ready to use.

Introduce yourself

Try something simple like, "Hey, I'm Stephen." With new people, you don't always have to introduce yourself to begin speaking to them. You could start the interaction another way, and if all goes well, after a while it will feel natural to say, "Oh, I'm so-and-so, by the way. What's your name?"

Ask them a simple question about the situation you're in

For example, at a party you could ask them if they know the name of the song that's playing or if they can tell you what kind of sauce is being served with the hors d'oeuvres. Of all the ways to start a conversation, this is the one where people use white lies the most. They aren't interested in the answer and are just using the question as a pretense to talk. Some people think they can only use this type of conversation starter because it seems more spontaneous and natural. It also doesn't put them at risk of rejection as much because they have the face-saving explanation that they just wanted a question answered. There's no need to box yourself in by always needing a believable excuse to speak to someone. When you're chatting with people for friendly reasons, it's perfectly fine to start a conversation more directly.

Ask them to do something simple for you

For example, you could ask if they could save your chair while you get up for a second, if they have a lighter, or if they want to exchange email addresses so you can send each other your notes if one of you misses a class.

Say "Hello" or "Hey" or "What's up?" or "How's it going?"

This is a common way to get a conversation rolling, and it often does the job, but it can be confusing and cause the interaction to stall. The other person may think you're only greeting them, reply with something like, "Hey, I'm good, thanks," and move on. Using a "What's up?"-type opener works better in the following circumstances:

- You have some follow-up questions or statements prepared if the other person doesn't reply with anything substantial.
- The person looks friendly and like they want to talk to you. You sense that if you begin with "Hey" or "What's up?" they'll give you a more detailed response.
- Neither of you is rushing somewhere else, and it's clear that you can both stick around and talk to each other. For example, if you catch a coworker as they're walking past you in the hall, they may take your "Hey, what's up?" simply as a greeting. However, if they're sitting at a table in the break room and you join them and say, "What's up?", that sends the message that you want to have an actual conversation.

Lines that can be used to initiate a conversation or a few minutes in to try to keep it going

Some lines serve double duty. You can use them to initiate a conversation, or you can use them to keep a conversation going when it stalls or you finish talking about a topic.

Ask questions that are relevant to the setting

You and others in a social setting generally have something in common; otherwise you wouldn't be at the same place at the same time. With that in mind, ask an opening question that is built in to your common situation. This lets you exchange basic background information about each other or find out more about the setting you're in. Here are some examples:

- **At a party:** "How do you know everyone else here?"
- **At a gaming club:** "What games are you playing these days?", "How long have you been playing?"
- **Upon joining a recreational sports team:** "How long have you been on the team?", "Do you play any other sports?"
- **At a new class:** "Is this course part of your major, or just an elective?",

"I missed the first class. Did the prof hand out a course outline?"
- **At a meet-up:** "Is this your first time at one of these events?"
- **On your first day on the job:** "How long have you been working here?", "What's it like working here?"
- **While traveling:** "How long have you been here? What cities were you visiting before?"
- **At a dance club:** "Do you know if this place is normally good on this night?"

Comment on your shared situation

- "Man, there are a ton of customers in here today."
- "Today's class was pretty slow, huh?"

Make a statement about the other person or give them a compliment

- "You seem like you're really into this song."
- "I like your hat. Where did you get it?"
- (To the host of a party) "Wow, you've got a cool movie collection."

Lines that are more appropriate once you've already begun talking to someone

These can be used as an opening line, but will seem too out of the blue unless you already know the person or you're in a context, like a small, informal house party, where it's okay to approach people in a familiar way.

Ask typical getting-to-know-you questions

- "What kind of hobbies do you do in your spare time?"
- "Have you done anything really fun recently?"
- "What do you do for work?"
- "What are you taking in school?"
- "What do you think of (a popular interest you hope they share or a news story everyone is talking about)?"
- "Have you been able to travel this summer / winter?"

- "Are you from here?" If they reply no, ask, "How long have you lived in the area?"
- "Do you have any kids?" If they say yes, ask follow-up questions. "How old are they? How many? Girls or boys?"
- "How do you know Martin?" or "You went to the same school as Martin. Do you know Carmen and Justin?"

Ask a question or make a statement about an interesting outside topic

Question examples:
- "Have you seen (popular new movie)? What did you think of it?"
- "Did you read that article yesterday about...?

Statement examples:
- "I'm thinking of seeing (popular new movie). I saw the trailer for it, and it looks awesome..."
- "I read a really interesting article the other day. It was saying that..."

Make a statement about yourself

- "I'm so happy right now. I just handed in my last paper for this semester."
- "So I think I finally found a job teaching English in the Japanese city I want to visit."

If you already know the person, ask for an update about something that's been happening in their life

- "So how was your weekend out of town?"
- "How's your daughter doing? Has she gotten over her cold yet?"

Thoughts on asking more creative hypothetical questions

Some advice on starting conversations says you should avoid any standard lines and ask only unique, engaging questions. This suggestion is overrated. Sometimes it can work, but in your day-to-day life when you're talking to friends, coworkers, classmates, or friendly strangers at a party, saying more typical stuff is okay. Many people like a bit of predictability at the start of their conversations and may be caught off guard and draw a blank if you ask them something like, "If you could turn into any animal, what would you be?" Less is more when it comes to being creative in your conversations. The odd unique question can be fun, but it comes off as a bit random and gimmicky if you're constantly asking strangers at a party things like, "If there were no laws for a day, what would you do?"

How to respond if someone tries to start a conversation with you

If someone else has initiated an interaction and you're open to speaking to them, all you need to do is seem friendly and approachable. Use open, cheerful body language to show you're happy to talk (see Chapter 19). Give a good, full response to whatever their opening question or statement is. Even if it's something you've heard a lot and are a bit bored to talk about, still give a proper, amiable reply. Possibly end your reply by asking a question of your own.

BE WILLING TO TAKE THE LEAD TO HELP GET A NEW CONVERSATION OFF THE GROUND

Conversations sometimes die right away because each person is unsure how to act, doesn't want to seem too selfish or pushy, and is waiting for the other to direct where the exchange goes. If you're shy, directing the conversation may not be something you'll be comfortable with initially, but taking the lead can come with practice and experience. Here's how you can try to direct the exchange:

- Be the first to ask a getting-to-know-you question and pick the one you think will work best (for example, choosing to ask about their hobbies because you have a feeling you'll have some in common and they'll feel comfortable with that subject).
- Politely change the subject if you're on a topic that doesn't seem to be going anywhere.

- Say something to kick-start the exchange if it's petering out. For example, ask about their interests if talking about your jobs didn't lead anywhere.
- Ask general questions and make broad statements that take the discussion in that ever-important mutually interesting direction. (For example, you ask someone about their summer, and they mention working a part-time job, attending a wedding, and visiting Europe. You have a lot to say about traveling, so you choose to ask them about their trip or mention your trip to Spain.) It's selfish to always steer conversations to only what you want to talk about, but it's okay to do this occasionally, especially if it helps get or keep an interaction going.
- Do most of the talking until the other person gets more comfortable (again, this is a more advanced skill). For example, you ask them about their job, they don't say much, and you get a sense they're feeling on the spot. Rather than ask them more questions, you bring up your own job and tell a quick, funny story about something that happened to you at work. That gives them time to collect themselves.

12

HAVING DEEPER CONVERSATIONS

WHEN TWO PEOPLE FIRST MEET, their conversation usually starts on safe, surface-level topics, while the emotional tone stays neutral, or casual, fun, and positive. Once they get more comfortable and familiar with each other, they may click and start having a closer or deeper interactions. They may start sharing more personal, intimate information or really explore a philosophical subject. If you connect with someone, the discussion will naturally tend to move in a deeper direction, but this isn't to say you need to try to force all of your interactions along a lockstep template. Sometimes they're just as rewarding if they stay at a light-hearted, superficial level.

This chapter covers various ways conversations can feel "deeper"—by moving past small talk, connecting, opening up to each other, and discussing more intellectual topics. When you are able to comfortably have deeper, more intimate conversations, your interactions with people can become even more rewarding.

MOVING PAST SMALL TALK

When you're first talking to someone, you'll often cover general, well-worn topics like your career and education. Asking and answering common questions sometimes has a rote, uninspired feeling to it. This is one type of the dreaded small talk that many people say they dislike. In a perfect world, we'd never have to do it, but small talk serves some purposes:

- Routine questions are a reliable way to get a conversation going. They let each person cast around for a subject that's more engaging for both of them. A few lines of questioning may be repetitive and go nowhere, but the next one might be interesting.
- Standard chitchat helps ease your nerves when you're most likely to feel anxious. It gives you some safe, predictable, low-mental-energy topics to draw on.
- Small talk gives you a platform to show what kind of person you are, aside from the things you like to discuss. As you spend a few minutes covering familiar ground with someone, you can demonstrate that you're warm, confident, and glad to talk to them.
- Many people expect to start a conversation with some neutral small talk, so if you try too hard to barrel past it, you may seem like you lack social savvy.

Whether a conversation feels like small talk also depends on its context. If you're interested in getting to know someone, you usually won't have a problem telling them about what you do for work or where you grew up. However, if you're sure the relationship is never going to go anywhere, like if you're talking to a stranger in line at the bank, then the same topics can feel forced and like you're pointlessly going through the motions. You'll also tend to lose patience with any topic that comes up over and over in a short time (for example, being asked what you're taking in college during a family reunion).

Talking about unexciting, trivial topics

The term "small talk" also refers to conversations about mundane, trivial topics like the weather, often with someone you already know, at least casually. Many people aren't enthusiastic about this either and wish they could go into deeper, more meaningful subjects. This type of small talk also has some justifications:

- It allows you to socialize with people for its own sake, show your interest in them, and maintain your relationship.
- Often it lets you exchange pleasantries in situations where you don't have time to have a more intense conversation or the environment isn't conducive to it. If you run into a coworker in the parking lot, you want to acknowledge them and show you're friendly, but you may have only a minute before you have to head home. Some quick talk about the local news is better than nothing.
- It can keep relationships primed for more substantial socializing down the road. Maybe you make small talk with a neighbor in your dorm when you run into each other while getting your mail. Because you've been casually friendly to each other all semester, it seems natural to one day invite them to a party where you can get to know them better.
- Sometimes people truly want to chat about fluffy topics. We can't always be in the mood to talk about subjects like whether free will truly exists.

Ways to move past routine small talk

Small talk is always going to be a part of conversations. The way out of it is through it. If you refuse to engage in it because it makes you feel bored or impatient, many of your interactions will never get off the ground, and then you'll surely miss out on the possibility of having a deeper exchange. If you play along and know how to handle small talk, it shouldn't take more than a few minutes to move into more interesting territory. Here's what you can do to help the process be faster and less painful:

- Try to tap into the underlying friendly intent of the other person's communication, rather than the surface content. Realize they're trying to connect with you, not annoy you.
- Try not to simply see small talk as a deal breaker or an ordeal to endure. Reframe it as the opening round of a potentially good

conversation. Think, "If I have to do this, I may as well use it to set up the conversation to go in an enjoyable direction."

- Accept that even if you try to make the best of it, not every moment of every conversation is going to be fascinating for you. Sometimes it's necessary to get through those boring bits because it helps you meet other goals, like you want to be friendly, or the other person is enthusiastic about the topic and you want to let them share it with you.

- Whatever the other person says, even if you've heard it a million times before, treat it like a legitimate contribution, and try to answer with enough substance and jumping-off points to better topics. If they mention the weather, rather than thinking, "Ugh, do I have to talk about this?" and then answering with a flat "Yep... sure is nice out," you could cheerfully say, "Yeah, it's really warm out. I'm planning on going on a hike later today. How about you? Have any outdoorsy plans this weekend?"

- As soon as the other person mentions anything semi-interesting, grab on to that and use it to move away from the routine exchange. For example, if you ask them what they do for fun, and they say they like watching movies, ask them which ones they've seen recently and what they thought of them, or make a comment on a good film you've seen yourself.

By using these strategies, you'll hit on a more mentally stimulating subject before long. If you keep trying but don't find anything more substantial to say to each other, take that as a sign that this particular conversation may not be destined to go to a deeper level.

CONNECTING IN CONVERSATIONS

Conversations feel closer when you connect with the other person. It's hard to describe what connecting with someone means, but you'll know it when it happens. It's a combination of several things:

- generally feeling you like someone and
  sensing they feel the same way;

- bonding with them because you share an important commonality you can't find in just anyone; and
- seeing them as an ally or teammate, not a threat or competition.

You may connect with someone for many reasons: you both share a dry, sarcastic sense of humor; you're both going through a tough graduate program; you both had self-involved parents; or you share political values that are rare in your area. Sometimes you'll connect soon after you meet, but it's also possible to know someone for a while and only really click once you've learned a lot about each other. A connection may lead to nothing more than a warm, fuzzy feeling you share with a stranger you chat with on the bus for a few minutes, but it's often a sign that a closer friendship could develop.

Who we connect with is unpredictable. Sometimes you'll meet someone who's a perfect match for you on paper, but they'll rub you the wrong way, for a reason you can't put your finger on. Sometimes you'll meet someone who's very different from you on the surface, but you each recognize there's some indefinable commonality in how you approach the world, and you'll get along right away.

Encouraging connections

People who aren't where they want to be socially sometimes complain that they can't seem to connect with anyone. They make an effort to meet people and sometimes manage to carry on longer conversations, but they never click with anyone while they're talking to them. There isn't a way to create connections at will. You're not going to have enough in common with everyone. However, you can work on certain things that can increase the chances of possible connections happening:

- **Have your basic conversation skills and self-presentation at a reasonable level.** A connection will never have a chance to develop if people write you off before talking to you or you can't keep an interaction going with them.
- **Actually want to get to know and connect with people.** Don't just see others as puzzles to solve or props you can use to feel satisfied with yourself when you make a joke or share a clever fact.

- **Have at least a little in common with the people you're talking to.** People sometimes never seem to connect with anyone because they're an outlier in their community and don't have much shared ground with the individuals they usually meet. If they found and talked to more people in their niche, the connections would come a lot more easily.
- **Draw attention to any unique commonalities you share with the other person.** For example, "You like running? Me too. I'm the only one of my friends who's into it. They all think I'm crazy for jogging for an hour before I go to work." Pointing out a similarity or two you share with someone isn't a guarantee they'll suddenly like you, but it's better to let them know about these things than not.
- **Be comfortable letting people know you like them.** Get used to telling new friends you find them interesting to talk to or letting yourself show a warm smile when you see them.
- **Be comfortable with self-disclosure.** People often connect over aspects of themselves that they don't share with just anyone. It is possible to connect over a safer topic, like having the same favorite band, but you'll give yourself more opportunities to find a connection if certain subjects aren't off limits. The next section has advice on how and when to self-disclose appropriately.

FINDING VALUE IN SELF-DISCLOSURE

One significant way to take a conversation to deeper territory is to exchange information that's more personal. As two people get to know each other, they'll stop talking only about safe, superficial topics and slowly start sharing more of their vulnerabilities, blemishes, and "true selves."

Safe, surface-level topics include your job and education; your living situation; your hobbies and interests; your noncontroversial observations, opinions, and humor, who you're friends with; your family makeup; and your goals and plans for the future. People are generally comfortable sharing this information with anyone.

Somewhat personal topics include your milder insecurities, flaws, and doubts; your somewhat odder quirks; your mildly embarrassing or slightly emotionally heavy past experiences; your somewhat more controversial thoughts and humor; and your less conventional, more ambitious future goals. Because these details aren't overly damaging or private, most people are fine sharing them with someone who seems at least somewhat accepting and trustworthy. They may get to this point in a conversation within a few minutes.

Very personal topics include your deeper, more serious insecurities, flaws, and doubts; past experiences that you're very ashamed of, which most people wouldn't understand and which are quite emotionally heavy to talk about; and your opinions that are very controversial. In their day-to-day lives, most people only share these secrets with a select handful of very close, trustworthy friends. However, they may share a specific, highly private secret earlier than usual if they sense the other person has a similar one and won't judge them for it.

Overall, disclosing your emotions is seen as more vulnerable and revealing than sharing factual information. For example, telling someone that being constantly criticized by your parents made you feel sad and worthless will create more intimacy than just mentioning your mom was hard on you.

Seeing the balance in self-disclosure

As they open up to each other, people start with milder disclosures, and if they're met with acceptance and understanding, they gradually move on to bigger ones. The expectation is that if the person you're talking to reveals something about themselves, you'll match them and disclose something similar (for example, they describe how they were really stressed out during their last year of college. You didn't find college that stressful, but share how you had a tough time adjusting to your first real-world job). If someone shares with you and you don't disclose in kind, it disrupts the process of deepening the relationship. The person who opened up may feel unfulfilled, rebuffed, and perhaps a little unfairly exposed. If someone shares too many times and doesn't get anything back in return, they may decide they've hit a limit on how close that friendship can get.

Self-disclosure fosters intimacy, but sharing too much too soon puts people off. It puts them in an awkward spot. It's emotional work to take in a person's secrets and problems and be supportive in response. If someone barely knows you, they may not be ready to do that work yet, but feel obligated because you sprung it on them. Many people see early oversharing as a red flag that someone will be needy and draining in the relationship. It also communicates that you lack the common sense to be choosy about whom you share your private life with.

That's not to say you're always obligated to reciprocate when someone self-discloses to you. Maybe you're fine keeping them as a more surface-level friend or professional colleague. Maybe you've just met them, and they showed poor judgment by spilling their heaviest secrets too soon, and there's no way you're doing the same. Maybe you're particularly guarded about that one topic, but are fine opening up about other ones. Overall, though, if you've been getting to know someone, you're hitting it off, and they share a somewhat personal detail about themselves, you should self-disclose back.

Being overly guarded and secretive

Oversharing is a faux pas, but some shyer, less secure people lean in the opposite direction and are guarded and secretive beyond a regular, sensible level. Recognize any of these?

- You see your social issues, like a lack of friends or dating experience, as shameful failures that you must hide at all costs.
- In more extreme cases, you think everything about you is boring or "wrong" and would get a bad response if it came out. You may be reluctant to talk about safe, surface-level subjects like what kind of music you like.
- You're on edge in conversations because you can never be sure when those topics may come up and your secrets may inadvertently be outed.
- You're extra nervous in situations where your feared subjects are more likely to come up, like if everyone's drinking, getting loose-tongued, and talking about their love lives.
- You get touchy and defensive when people ask you innocuous questions related to your secrets (for example, "What are your friends up to this weekend?").

■ You use a variety of strategies to avoid sharing anything about your secret: changing the subject; giving vague, evasive answers; straight-up lying; hanging back in groups and not contributing; shifting the attention to someone else; or finding ways to leave the conversation just as you're about to be put on the spot.

Being overly guarded, for whatever reason, is a self-defeating strategy. It's stressful to carry around a bunch of supposedly shameful secrets and worry about what will happen if someone finds out about them. Ironically, secretiveness can create more problems than it helps avoid. If you have a secret, no one may think it's a big deal if they find out what it is, but they won't form the best impression of you if you're always closed-off and cagey. Their imagination may run wild and assume something worse about you than what you're actually hiding. Or they may simply think you're not interested in being friends with them when you continually rebuff their attempts to grow closer.

How to become less guarded and open up to people

You can find ways to be less guarded and more open with people. First, change your attitude about what it means to reveal your flaws. If you're guarded, you probably believe that others will reject you if they learn about your weaknesses. Similarly, you may think that the way to be liked is to come across as flawless and impressive. Actually, the opposite is true. When you reveal your vulnerabilities and rough edges, you seem endearingly human. When you act like you have no flaws, you become distant and unrelatable. It's cloying when someone seems too perfect and together.

Many secrets are only shameful and embarrassing if you feel they are. Maybe you don't have many friends at the moment. You could believe it's a sign you're a loser and dread being outed. Or you could adopt the perspective that being lonely isn't fun, but it happens to many people from time to time, and you're not defective just because you find it hard to meet people at the moment. Being at ease with your flaws creates a kind of self-fulfilling prophecy. If you tell someone about your vulnerabilities and display a calm, self-assured attitude about them, they'll often respond to your lead and feel they're fine as well.

The best thing to do is open up to trusted people and see that it's not so bad. You'll often get a positive response, and you can handle it if the odd person acts like a jerk or takes it badly.

Start by making milder disclosures to strangers or people like therapists or support-line workers who have to hold the information in confidence. Slowly work up to sharing bigger pieces of yourself with people who are more important to you. You don't want to become an open book to everyone on the planet; you just want to be able to self-disclose to the same degree most people can.

If one big secret is holding you back socially, consider getting it out in the open (for example, if you have trouble making friends because you're worried about everyone learning you've never dated anyone). Sharing the secret will take a huge weight off your shoulders, and more pragmatically, if people know you're struggling with the issue, they may be able to offer some practical help. You don't have to share it with everyone straight off the bat, but if the topic comes up, don't steer clear of it. Again, ease into things by telling the secret to people you're comfortable with and go from there.

HOW TO HAVE MORE INTELLECTUAL, PHILOSOPHICAL CONVERSATIONS

People also think of conversations as being "deep" when they go into depth on more cerebral or thought-provoking topics. A common complaint from more intellectual types is that they have a hard time getting people to have these kinds of interesting, meaningful conversations. They don't need to have deep, philosophical discussions all the time, but they start to feel frustrated and unfulfilled if they don't have any at all.

Unfortunately, there's no way have intellectual conversations on command. Some people are just more inclined toward them than others, and it's a trait that's not always connected to the factors you think it would be (you can meet PhDs who are surprisingly vacuous and factory workers who love to wax philosophical). All you can do is try to take your interactions in an intellectually deeper direction by bringing up the more cerebral ideas or topics you want to talk about. After that, it all depends on whether anyone else bites. With some people, if you mention the unemployment rate, it won't be long before you're both speculating about what a post-scarcity society would look like. With others, you'll just get some silence and a shrug before they change the topic.

If you want to have more brainy conversations, the easiest way to do that is to find some similarly minded friends. It's really the same with any interest. If you love talking about beekeeping, you can't expect everyone to care, and the simplest way to have more satisfying discussions about the topic is to find other beekeepers.

13

ENDING CONVERSATIONS

EVERY CONVERSATION has to come to an end eventually. Often it's easy enough to part ways, but sometimes you'll feel more unsure about how to wind down the interaction. This chapter gives you some options for doing that. As with the other stages, you'll feel more confident going into your conversations when you know you can end them smoothly.

Ending a conversation is a pretty straightforward skill, and once you have an idea of what to do, it's easy to put the concepts into practice. This chapter may also have the side effect of illustrating various ways that someone might to be trying to end a conversation with you, so you'll know if it's time to gracefully let them go.

Considering time limits to conversations

A general principle first: You can make ending many of your conversations a lot simpler if you go into them with an understanding of approximately how long you can talk so you can smoothly wind them down when the time comes. Many conversations are open-ended in length, but in the following situations, the other person may need to get going after about five minutes. They may want to talk longer, but it's always good to be considerate of their time:

- You run into a friend who's in the middle of getting groceries.
- You're chatting to someone at work while you're both grabbing coffee from the kitchen.
- You've called someone to quickly set up plans with them.
- You're chatting to someone at a party or networking event where everyone is doing a lot of circulating and mingling.
- You're sitting next to an acquaintance on a bus, who may want to get back to their book or headphones after catching up quickly.

It's okay to end a conversation quickly and cleanly

Sometimes people feel that they have to give a big, formal good-bye every time they stop talking to someone. Mostly this isn't called for, and you can finish the conversation in a to-the-point, casual way. Dragging out the end of the conversation can make it feel more awkward.

METHODS OF ENDING CONVERSATIONS

If you'd like to see or keep in touch with the person you've been talking to, you can use one of these approaches and exchange contact info, make future plans, and maybe promise to drop them a line in a few days.

Wrap it up without any window dressing

It's often fine to just pleasantly say you've got to go without any explanation, especially if you know the person already. They'll understand you have things you need to do and won't be offended.

- "I gotta run. Good talking to you."
- "All right" (to agree with what they just said). "Anyway, take it easy, man" (as you're heading off).
- (Speaking on the phone) "Well, I'm gonna go. I'll talk to you later."

**Say, "Anyway, I'll let you get back to it…" if
they were in the middle of something**

- "Anyway, it was good seeing you. I'll let
  you get back to your shopping."
- "Anyway, I'll talk to you more later. I'll
  let you get back to your work."

You can make up something for the other person to get back to.
Like if you're texting with someone on a Sunday evening, you could
say, "Well, I'll let you get back to getting ready for work tomorrow" or
"I'm sure you want to relax a bit before you go to sleep. I'll let you go."

**Use a reason, made up or not, for why you
have to leave the conversation**

Day to day

- "It was good running into you. I have to finish
  this shopping before I pick up my kids."
- "Sorry I can't talk longer. I'm actually on my
  way to meet my friend for coffee."
- "Let's talk more at lunch. I need to finish up this
  presentation before eleven o'clock."

At parties, bars, or networking events

- "I've got to go find my friends."
- "I'm going to go grab another drink."
- "If you'll excuse me, I just saw someone I've
  been meaning to catch up with."
- "I just have to head to the bathroom. I'll run into you later maybe."
- "I just got here. I'm going to look around
  a bit more. I'll see you in a bit."

**Make a statement to summarize and wrap up
the conversation, then say you have to go**

- "Yeah, that movie's going to be wicked. I'm really looking
  forward to it. Anyway, I should get going…"
- "Wow, a lot's been happening in our families, huh? We'll
  have to catch up about it more soon… I just noticed my
  friends have arrived. I'm going to say hi to them."

Use signals that show you're ready to end the conversation

While still being friendly and polite, you can start adjusting your body
language (more on that in Chapter 19) and your actions to indicate to
the other person that it's time for them to finish up the discussion or
that you're about to end it soon yourself. The idea isn't to be passive
and put responsibility for ending the interaction on them; it's just to
give them a heads-up. You could try one of the following tactics:

- Stand up if you've been sitting down.
- Start to give quicker, shorter responses: "Yep, yep,
  yep. Totally. Anyway, I should get going…"
- Look more frequently at the thing you need to get back to, for
  example, the direction you were walking in, the photocopier
  you needed to use before you started chatting to a coworker.
- Start angling your body away from them and perhaps
  toward something you need to get back to.
- If the conversation still hasn't wound down, actually get
  back to the thing you needed to do. For example, start
  to photocopy your documents or resume shopping.
- If you were about to leave and a conversation is holding you
  up, signal you're about to go by gathering up belongings
  like your coat, car keys, sunglasses, and purse.

**Introduce the person to someone else, or bring
them along as you join another conversation**

This is a party tactic. If you join another discussion, the conversation
you were having with the original person naturally dissolves. If you do
the introduction move, be subtle and genuine about pulling it off. If you
do it in an insincere, exaggerated way, the other person will be able to
tell you're blowing them off by trying to foist them on someone else.

Get back to your book, music, phone, laptop, or video game

If you're talking to someone on a bus, subway, or plane, you may not
feel like speaking the entire time you're forced to sit near each other.
In these cases, it's always handy to have something else you can turn
your attention to. To end the conversation, you could say, "Well, I'm
just gonna get back to my book now," or you could wait for a pause, not
make any effort to fill it, and then open a school assignment on your
laptop. The other person should figure out your intentions. On a bus or
plane, you can always pretend to take a nap as well.

**You can leave some group discussions
without saying much of anything**

If you're talking with a group at a party and after a few minutes you
decide you want to keep circulating, you can often just walk away. It's
understood that people are going to drop in and out of different discussions. You don't need to slink away silently. You can quietly indicate
you're leaving with a quick little nod or wave. You can sometimes do the
same thing at your job. If a bunch of coworkers are sitting around on
break at a table where many people are coming and going, you can join
them for a bit, then just get up when you have to go back to work. You
could say good-bye, and often you will, but they won't think it's rude if
you don't. They know they'll see you soon anyway.

Decoding those hard-to-read niceties that people sometimes use as they're wrapping up a conversation

One thing that confuses a lot of people is when they're talking to someone and as they're leaving, the person says something like, "We'll talk soon," or "I'll get back to you about it later," or "Let's do lunch." Sometimes they literally mean these things, and sometimes they're just saying them as niceties. They don't necessarily dislike you and are being deceptive to try to escape. They just want to end the conversation in a friendly way, and bringing up the possibility of future plans is a way to do that.

There's no reliable way to decipher what someone's intentions are here. You have to get a feel for what each person's style is and whether they tend to actually mean it when they say these things. Also, if someone ends a conversation by saying, "Let's have coffee soon," and you're interested but not sure if they really mean it, it doesn't do any harm to follow up and try to get a better sense of where they stand.

Extracting yourself from an uninteresting but determined conversation partner

If you find yourself speaking to someone who's boring you, you can usually use one of the above approaches to politely end the conversation. Sometimes it's not that easy. The worst-case scenario is when you're with someone who can seemingly talk at you forever, isn't being sensitive to your time or your nonverbal indications of losing interest or needing to go, and can smoothly transition from one subject to the next, so there's no natural break between topics where you can say you have to run.

With these people, you need to be more assertive in interrupting them so you can announce you need to get going. If you can, wait for even the smallest pause in their story or explanation, then jump on your chance. This moment may not always come, and sometimes you'll have to straight out cut them off (for example, "Sorry, I know you're in the middle of your story, but I have to go catch up with my friend"). They may get a bit offended, but you don't have anything to feel bad about. They forced your hand through their own mistakes.

14

NAVIGATING GROUP CONVERSATIONS

YOU'RE IN GOOD COMPANY if you're fine in one-on-one conversations but clam up or feel overwhelmed when more people are in the mix. Group conversations are different than one-on-one interactions in the following ways:

- Rather than two people sending communication back and forth to each other, each person in the group throws in their contribution for everyone else's benefit. That means many one-on-one conversation styles don't work as well. You can't ignore everyone else to lock onto one person and listen as they tell you about the graphic novel they're working on. You have to be able to chip in to the larger discussion.

- Their energy levels can vary because there are more people to influence it. One-on-one conversations are mostly conducted at a low-key level, but group discussions can range from calm and orderly to excited and rowdy.

- There's less pressure on you to keep the interaction alive because if you don't have something to say, someone else will. Unless every member in the group is feeling shy, a group conversation will keep going. The challenge becomes contributing enough. If you don't talk for a while, the interaction won't end, but you may be left sitting unhappily on the side or get the dreaded "Why are you so quiet?"

- Speaking in groups, such as if everyone's listening as you tell a funny story, can sometimes feel like you're giving a mini-performance because so many pairs of eyes are focused on you. When you're joking around or arguing a point, you may also have the sense that you have to play for the crowd.
- They can continually shift back and forth between a true group discussion, where everyone is talking together, and several smaller subconversations.

This chapter tells you what you need to know to handle group conversations. It lists some ways to join group discussions, be more talkative in them, and hold your own and not get too annoyed when they get more hectic and energetic.

WAYS TO JOIN GROUP CONVERSATIONS

Chapter 11 covered various ways to start conversations. A lot of what was said there applies here as well, like how your exact opening line is less important than your ability to get along with everyone once you're speaking to them. One new thing to keep in mind is that you should roughly try to match the group's energy level. If you're at a party and see a group that's boisterous and joking around, it won't work too well if you try to engage them in a calm, dry manner. Similarly, a subdued group that's talking about world affairs won't respond as well to an amped-up approach.

Try to read how open the group is to being approached (see Chapter 18). If a group is standing way off to the side, is formed in a tight circle, and seems to be having an intense, private conversation, it may be best to leave them alone.

You may worry that if the group isn't receptive, you'll be rejected in a harsh, humiliating way. Usually this doesn't happen, especially if you were just approaching them to be friendly and not aggressively hitting on anyone. Usually all that will happen is they'll respond to you in a token, noncommittal manner, then resume talking to each other and leave you standing on the sidelines. They might turn away from you or tighten their circle to box you out. At that point, you can quietly move on. It's a bit awkward when it happens, but hardly a scathing cut-down. To an outside viewer, it doesn't look like much happened.

Of course, this can be confused with when the group allows you to join but doesn't make a ton of effort to include you in the conversation because they expect you to use your own initiative. If you make several attempts to contribute and they make no effort to engage you, then it's likely they don't feel like speaking to you.

Introduce yourself to everyone

At parties, mixers, or networking events, it's okay to simply go up to a group and introduce yourself. A "Hey, how's it going, everyone? I'm ____" is all you need. After you introduce yourself, you could ask a standard discussion-promoting question like, "How do you all know the host?" or "Are you all criminology students too?" To join the conversation but also not interrupt too much, you can quickly give your name and then say, "Anyway, what you were guys talking about?" to get it back on track.

Sidle up to the group, listen to the conversation for a bit, and then make a contribution when it's appropriate

Sometimes joining a group conversation involves entering a circle of people who are talking. You may be able to do this silently, or it may be appropriate to give a quick "hi" or nod to everyone as you walk up to them. In other situations, like while sitting in a break room at work, you may not physically join the group, but be near them and able to hear their conversation. Either way, once you pick up on a chance to add something relevant, you can jump in with your contribution and then be part of the discussion. Make sure you wait for a small pause before you interject. You don't want to blatantly cut anyone off.

"Mind if I sit here?"

If you're already sort of friendly with a group who are sitting around, you can join their conversation by straightforwardly asking if you can sit down and join them. This may seem intrusive, but the idea is to do it only with people you're already pretty sure would be open to you joining them, like if you're at your school or work cafeteria and see a group you'd like to know better. Once you sit down, they'll either start chatting to you directly, or they'll continue with their current conversation, and you can try to chime in when an opportunity arises.

Start talking to one person in the group to get your foot in the door

If you see a larger group, there may be a member on the periphery who's focused on something else or who looks left out or uninterested in the topic. If you strike up a conversation with them, you may be able to transition to speaking to the larger group—they introduce you, they turn their attention back to the larger conversation, and they carry you along; or the group notices you talking to their friend, and then you introduce yourself. A similar strategy is to wait until one group member is on their own, like if they've gotten up at a party to grab a drink. You can start talking to them when they're alone and then join the rest of their friends with them soon after.

However, don't join a group discussion and then immediately try to steal one or more members away to have a side conversation. Respect that they want to talk to the group. If a smaller conversation splinters off a bit later, that's fine, but don't shoot for one right away.

Join the conversation by way of an activity

Activities can be used to start both one-on-one and group conversations. It's mentioned here because it often allows you to chat with several people at once. Parties often have group activities going on, like games of one kind or another. In pubs you can find pool, darts, Foosball, and maybe an arcade machine or two. You can easily get a conversation going by joining in and chatting with the other players. Even if you can't think of much to say, the ebb and flow of the game itself will provide some things to talk about.

Start a conversation with the group the same as you would with a single person

If you're taking a direct approach with groups you don't know, it's usually simpler and more courteous to begin the interaction by introducing yourself. However, you could also open with a typical conversation-starting question or statement. You'll need to size up the group and try to get a feeling for what type of opening line they may be receptive to. Some examples:

- **Ask about your common situation:** "Are you guys having a good night?", "So how do you guys know (the party's host)?"
- **Comment on the shared context:** "This apartment is decorated in such a neat way."
- **Ask them a question about themselves:** "Has anyone here been to any concerts lately?"
- **Make a statement about them:** "You guys seem like you're from out of town."
- **Ask a question or make a statement about an outside topic:** "Anyone here see the game last night?"
- **Make a statement about yourself:** (To a group of people you already know somewhat) "The craziest thing happened to me this weekend…"

HOW TO BE LESS QUIET IN GROUP CONVERSATIONS

As a loose guideline, in a group conversation you should aim to speak about as much as everyone else. So if there are four people in the group, you should talk roughly a quarter of the time. Of course, you don't need to hit that exact percentage. What you really want to avoid is being silent for long stretches. As Chapter 1 says, there's nothing inherently wrong with being less of a chatterbox. Many social circles have members who are on the quiet side and whom everyone likes just fine. However, there are times when you're being quieter than you'd like in a group conversation, and not by choice. Here are some suggestions about how to be more talkative:

Work on the anxiety or confidence issues that could be holding back your ability to contribute in groups

As with one-on-one interactions, it's often not a lack of conversation knowledge or technique that's to blame for quietness, but mental barriers like worrying about saying something lame or inappropriate, believing you have nothing worth sharing, feeling uncomfortable being in the spotlight, and feeling psyched out by certain types of people. If you believe this is your main barrier to talking more, focus on the advice in the previous section.

Accept that the topic won't always be one you can easily contribute to

When a pair is talking, the conversation needs to stay on topics they're both interested in. With several people involved, the discussion may shift to a subject most of the people want to talk about, but which the rest can't add to (for example, a job most of them share). Everyone finds themselves left out from time to time, and it's not a knock against you if you can't chip in. Just be a good sport and wait for the topic to change. If it doesn't switch after a few minutes, try bringing up a new one yourself. If you often find yourself in conversations about subjects you legitimately can't contribute to, that may be a sign you need to get more life experience or that a particular group isn't a good fit for you.

Make little contributions instead of remaining totally mute

You can still seem engaged and keep yourself in the middle of the action by adding small contributions like, "Yeah, I heard the same thing", "No way. Then what happened?", laughing when appropriate, or making little listening noises like "Oh" or "Hmm." These verbal tidbits are also a good way to speak a little here and there when another member has the spotlight for a longer period of time. If you're more inhibited about speaking up, smaller statements can also help you slowly ease yourself into saying more down the road.

Even if you're not talking, appear to be tuned into the conversation

If several friends are chatting at a pub, there's a big difference between someone who's not talking but is clearly attending to the discussion (by leaning in, looking at the speaker, making an effort to hear them over the background noise, nodding, and having an interested expression on their face) versus someone who's obviously bored or tuned out and trapped in their head. The first set of behaviors sends the message that even if you're not talking right that second, you're a part of the exchange. Even though you're not technically saying much, people will be less likely to consider you quiet. You're more prone to get that comment when your nonverbals show you're uncomfortable, uninterested, or checked out.

This point is also practical in the sense that if you make an effort to tune into the conversation, you'll have less mental energy to devote to fretting about how quiet you're being. You'll also be more likely to spot snippets of dialogue that could trigger a thought you could contribute.

Tell yourself that you have to say something every so often

If you want to talk in group conversations more, it's helpful to make an explicit rule in your head that you have to say something at least every few minutes. If the topic is changing constantly, you don't have to chime in on every one, but you should speak up often enough. If the discussion has been on one subject for a while, you'll want to give your two cents on it, assuming it's one you can add to. If you aren't conscious about needing to contribute, it's easy to settle back or zone out and go too long without saying anything.

The following rule trumps this one. If you find yourself getting more and more stressed out because you're too focused on monitoring your continually dropping "contribution percentage," give yourself permission to be quiet and take the pressure off yourself.

Give yourself permission to be quiet

A lot of people psych themselves out when they try to be less quiet. They put pressure on themselves to say something, and if they don't, they get more and more self-conscious and inhibited, which makes the problem worse. Take some of that burden away by permitting yourself to be quiet. If you can think of something to say, great, but if not, that's okay too. It's not that unusual for people to go silent during stretches of group conversations. Maybe in a few minutes the topic will change to one that suits you more, or you'll do better next time.

HOW TO HANDLE LOUD, LIVELY GROUP CONVERSATIONS

Many people don't have too much trouble with calm, orderly group conversations where everyone sticks to a topic, lets others finish their points, and listens respectfully. Shy, reserved types usually find group conversations more difficult and irritating when they get more hectic—when everyone is excited and trying to talk over one another, the topic keeps changing, and the overall vibe becomes more immature and show-off-ish. Your approach to these conversations should be a mix of accepting and adapting to them for what they are, while doing what little you can to try to turn their intensity down.

Accept these types of conversations for what they are and what they aren't

What sometimes bothers people about chaotic, boisterous group conversations is that they feel they could have been something else—polite, intellectual, easy-to-follow, courteous—but they aren't. By nature they're loud, scattered, inconsiderate, and "dog eat dog." They're for laughs, spirited debate, and enjoying the company and essence of all your friends at once. Aspects of them are an acquired taste. Being in the middle of all that noise and chaos can be energizing, and you may get a cheap thrill when trying to hold your own in it.

Try your best to tolerate the inherent annoyances of the situation

Hectic group conversations can create a maddening din as everyone talks at once. If the group is big enough, there may be several subdiscussions, and it can be confusing and overwhelming to try to follow them all. One or more people may be derailing every tangent with idiotic jokes. It's easy to become annoyed and exasperated, then give up and shut down. Do your best to put up with all the noise and stimulation so you can get what you can out of the interaction. It may be frustrating to try to keep your focus, but with time, you can improve your ability to follow along.

Realize if you want to get speaking time, you'll have to grab it for yourself

These conversations are more "every man for himself." They're not purposely heartless; it's just that everyone is excited and wants to talk, and they'd rather it be them than you. Waiting patiently for the others to recognize that you have something to say usually won't work. You have to treat these interactions like a game and find ways to get your fair share of the spotlight.

Below are some ways to become the speaker. All of these behaviors are more acceptable in wild group conversations than in standard day-to-day group conversations. You can still go overboard, but if you don't do them too obnoxiously, no one takes these behaviors too personally.

- Make it really, really obvious with your body language that you want to talk after the current speaker is finished by leaning forward, raising your hand slightly, and catching everyone's eye to let them know you want to speak next.
- Make a statement such as, "I've got something to say about that after she's done."
- Be the first one out of the gate when one person finishes talking.
- Interrupt someone or cut them off after they've spoken for a while.
- Raise your voice to overpower anyone else who's also trying to be the next to talk.
- Repeat the beginning of your statement several times until you're given the floor.

- Bring your point up again a minute later if you weren't able to become the speaker on your first try.

Once you've got the floor, here are some ways to defend it:
- Speak with enough volume that you can't be talked over.
- Talk quickly to get your point out before someone cuts you off.
- Make your statements to the point. You won't get away with rambling on.
- Use gestures to indicate to other people that you're not done talking so they shouldn't cut you off. For example, loosely hold your hand up to make a "stop, not yet" signal.
- Say things like, "Whoa, whoa, hold on, I'm not done, I'm not done."
- Don't be too dry. Zest up your statements with some humor or creative language so everyone will be more interested in hearing them.

Many people have painful memories of times they tried to chip in to a group discussion and got ignored or talked over, even if they repeated themselves several times. Reading about group dynamics may help put those experiences in perspective. Getting overlooked like this happens to everyone from time to time, and it's nothing personal. When people are really focused on following group conversations and are also busy strategizing about how they can talk next, they can inadvertently tune out the other members who are trying to jump in.

Ways to ease the madness and help other people be included

You have to accept that these conversations can get hairy and go along with their unwritten rules to a point, but you can do some things to try to rein them in too. Depending on how many people are in the group and how amped up they are, your efforts may not have a huge effect, but you can try.
- If you're good at getting your speech time, don't be selfish. Ease off a bit to give other people space to contribute.
- Help the quieter or less eager people in the group get a chance to talk by signaling to the others that they have something they'd like to say.

- If you can tell someone really wants to finish a point, and you're tempted to interrupt, try to resist that urge.
- If a less forceful person makes a point and it's falling on deaf ears, direct the conversation back towards them (for example, "Sorry, what's that Natasha? You were talking about...").
- If another group member keeps cutting people off, shift the discussion back to the person who got interrupted ("So anyway, before you got cut off you were saying...").

15

MAKING CONVERSATION IN PARTICULAR SITUATIONS

PEOPLE OFTEN SAY they have trouble making conversation in certain situations: when they're talking to people they know well, when they're first hanging around a group of friends who all know each other well, or when they have to mingle at parties. This chapter helps you navigate conversations in those situations.

TALKING TO PEOPLE YOU KNOW WELL

Some people are fine talking to someone new, when there's lots of unexplored ground to cover, but they feel like they're out of material with their closer friends. The good news is if you're already on fairly friendly terms with someone, they've unofficially signed off on being interested in you and what makes you tick. You may not have every last thing in common, and certain interests of yours may do nothing for them, but on the whole they're open to whatever you want to bring up. So don't hold back too much.

When you know someone, you can devote some of the conversation to catching up on what you've been doing since you last saw each other. The better you know someone, and the more often you talk to them, the more detail you can go into. If you haven't seen someone for three years, you'll answer, "What's new?" with a sweeping summary like, "Well, I started my own contracting business, and we have a second kid on the way." When you talk to someone all the time, you'll have a more detailed answer like, "I figured out what was making that noise in my car…" When you hang out with someone often, you'll also generate new events to discuss ("So I spoke more to that guy we met at the party last week…").

Finally, you can always find out more about each other. Even long-time friends don't know every detail about each other's childhood or their opinion on every topic. There's always more to learn.

HANGING OUT WITH NEW PEOPLE
WHO ALL KNOW EACH OTHER

A lot of us get nervous when we first hang around a group of people who know each other well, such as a friend's friends who all grew up together. Sometimes the initial meeting goes off without a hitch. You jell with the group right away and are welcomed into the fold. When it doesn't work out, the group members socialize among themselves, while making lots of inside jokes and references to past experiences, and you're left standing on the sidelines.

If that happens, it usually isn't because you did something wrong or the group is purposely being mean and exclusionary. They just all know each other, and it's easy and fun for them to stick to the familiar. They may also be a bit lazy and see getting to know someone new as work, when they could just hang out with their buddies instead. Some of the group members may be shy too, and feel inhibited about engaging someone unfamiliar.

If you don't have a good conversation with them, don't get too down on yourself. It's a trickier, more nerve-racking situation to navigate, and if the group isn't receptive to getting to know someone new, there's only so much you can do. Here's what you can try, alongside the general advice in the previous chapter on handling group conversations.

Take the initiative and throw yourself into the mix

Because it's easy for the group to benignly overlook you, take the initiative to try to get to know everyone. You can't wait and count on them to bring you in. Basically, whatever the group is doing, put yourself in there and attempt to join their conversation. If you're at someone's place and they're all playing video games, sit down and grab a controller. If you're all at a club and they're dancing or playing pool or talking on the patio, then that's where you should be.

Accept you won't be able to contribute to some topics

There's only so much you can do if the inside jokes start flying or everyone starts updating each other on what another friend has been up to lately. Maybe you'll have an opportunity to add something, but for the most part, you just have to wait out these stretches. You could also try getting in the loop by asking something like, "Who are you all laughing about? An old friend?" If the explanation is quick, the others may fill you in, but sometimes there will be too much backstory for them to cover.

Act as if you're a long-time group member instead of asking getting-to-know-you questions

When you're around a group of new people, your first instinct may be to ask them basic getting-to-know-you questions. Sometimes that works, but they won't always be receptive. Established groups already know one another's basic backgrounds and talk about other topics when they hang out. When they're speaking with you, they may not be in the mood to be interviewed about themselves. They want to talk with their buddies and want you to jump into the discussion and contribute as if you're familiar with everyone too. For example, if they're telling funny travel stories, they want you to pipe up and tell yours too. If they're talking about a popular TV show, they want you to share your opinion on it.

As the conversation moves along and hits on more topics, you'll get to know what they're like from what they add to it, and they'll learn the same about you. Chances to learn bits of everyone's life

history will come up organically. This isn't to say some members won't be open to a more standard getting-to-know-you exchange, especially if you get a chance to talk to them one on one. However, if you initially try that and they don't seem enthusiastic, switch to the other approach.

Don't feel like you're at an audition

Don't put too much pressure on yourself to show your best side and win everyone over the first few times you hang out with them. That can backfire. You can get a bit nervous, try too hard to be funny and interesting, and not make the best impression. Even though you do have to take the initiative to join the group's interactions, you don't have to go over the top and dazzle everyone either. Act the way you normally would around friends. If the group is going to like you, they're going to like you. Just do your thing and see how it all plays out.

MINGLING AT PARTIES

Parties are one of the top social situations people have trouble with. They know they're supposed to mingle, but they don't know how exactly, or it makes them too nervous. Depending on the type of party, there can also be an expectation to be "fun" and "on." Here are some tips for getting through parties and being able to talk to people (but not necessarily being the zaniest person there).

Acknowledging the outside forces at play

As with making conversation in general, some of your results at parties will be influenced by your interpersonal skills. The rest is out of your hands and determined by outside forces. Some factors that will affect your experience at a party are

- what kind of party it is and whether it suits your strengths and personality (that is, is it focused around cerebral group discussions or drunken antics?);

- the other guests and whether they're the type of people you get along with;
- how well everyone knows each other. Is it mainly friends who have known each other forever or people who are strangers to each other?
- how open everyone is to meeting new people. Are they there to make new friends, or do they plan to stick to the group they came with?

Don't place too much importance on how well you socialize at parties

Parties are just one way people get together. For the average person, they come up only occasionally. They can be fun and lively, but they're not the be-all and end-all of social interaction. Some people blow the significance of parties out of proportion and measure how well they get along with the strangers they meet as the ultimate test of their social worthiness. If it's important to you to be able to mingle, then you should work on it. But at the same time, know that plenty of people have great social lives even if working the room and being memorable at big gatherings isn't their strong point.

Regarding the expectation that you have to have a caaah-raaazy time, many people's idea of a good night at a party is to mainly hang out with the friends they came with in a low-key way, have a couple of drinks, and maybe chat with a person or two they don't know. They don't feel they've failed if they haven't done a bunch of keg stands, jumped off a roof into a pool, and made twenty new buddies.

Deciding the best time to arrive

How early or late you show up at a party can influence how comfortable you feel socializing with the other guests. Some people find it's good to arrive early (not overly early, of course, because that can inconvenience the host). Fewer guests will have arrived, and you can talk to everyone under more low-key circumstances and in smaller, more manageable groups. As the other guests trickle in, you can get to know them as they arrive. However, this doesn't work for everyone. Some people feel more exposed and on the spot if they're at a party early with hardly anyone else. It's also less of an option if you don't know the host(s) that well.

The other option is to arrive later, when you'll have lots of existing groups to join. You may also like that you can disappear into the crowd and not feel like you stand out. If you find a conversation awkward, you can quickly escape to someone else, rather than, say, being stuck having to chat with just the host and her two good friends for twenty minutes. There are downsides to this approach too. Some people find a room full of guests who are already talking to each other intimidating. Everyone may be into their conversations, and groups can feel harder to break into. Finally, as the night goes on, people get more rowdy, which may not be your style.

Ways to approach and chat with people at parties

Previous chapters covered how to feel comfortable approaching people and how to start and maintain conversations with them, so this section won't repeat all of that. Here are some party-specific ideas for getting into interactions:

- If you're going to mingle with strangers on your own, you can talk to whomever you want to. Pick a person who's close to you, or who seems interesting or approachable, or just go up to someone at random. That may sound too simple, but you really don't need to think about it more than that.
- Ask the person throwing the party to introduce you to everyone. (This isn't always an option, though.)
- Give yourself a role, like the person who takes people's coats and shows them where the snacks and drinks are.
- Join one of the activities that may be going on (for example, a card game, a group watching TV or playing video games in the basement).
- Initiate a new activity to get people talking, like playing a board game or drinking game (if it's the type of get-together where that would be appropriate).

Two approaches to mingling

The first approach to mingling is to be more mechanical and try to have at least a brief conversation with everyone at the event. The second is to go with the flow, talk to whoever catches your fancy, and see where the night takes you. You might end up in a bunch of short interactions, or you may hit it off with the second group you talk to and spend the rest of the party with them.

The try-to-talk-to-everyone approach is more appropriate if you're hosting the event; it's expected of you to be polite and say hello to everyone. You'd also use it if it's important for you to meet everyone there, or if the party has a business or networking component and you want to be sure to make the rounds and talk to everyone you need to. The more casual approach is best when you're attending a bigger, purely social party. In those situations, most of the guests won't try to speak to everyone else because it's often impractical and would get in the way of their spontaneous fun.

Leaving the party

Some people find leaving parties awkward. If you don't like seemingly being the center of attention as you announce you're heading out, that's simply something you can get used to in time. If you're not sure how to say your good-byes, it's polite to let at least the host(s) and your good friends know you're taking off. If you've met some new people you'd like to stay in touch with, you can track them down and get their contact info before you go. Don't feel you have to tell every last guest you're done for the night. Whoever you tell, just say you're heading off and don't think you have to have a five-minute going-away chat. There's no need to act sheepish if you're leaving early. Every party has guests who have to go before the others. If you get flak, stick to your guns, then quickly make your exit before you can get sucked into an argument.

16

BECOMING AWARE
OF EMPATHY

EMPATHY IS THE FIRST of four core conversation skills this stretch of the book is going to cover. You can technically interact with people without being empathetic, but you'll be at a big disadvantage. The chapter defines the two types of empathy and explains their benefits, then offers some suggestions on how to cultivate it in yourself.

EMPATHY DEFINED

Broadly speaking, empathy is the ability to put yourself in another person's shoes. There are two types:

- *Emotional empathy* is the ability to pick up on other people's emotions and have an appropriate feeling in response. For example, if your friend gets some upsetting news, you feel sympathetic for them and a bit sad yourself. Sometimes people refer to empathy as this ability to feel what another person is feeling. At other times what they mean by empathy is acting on those feelings and showing concern and support.
- *Cognitive empathy* is the ability to more logically get inside someone's head and take on their perspective. You don't necessarily feel what they're feeling, but you can rationally understand how they see the

world (for example, a certain book doesn't bother you, but you can grasp how it would be offensive to someone with more traditional values). Again, some people see this kind of empathy as simply being able to deduce what's going through another person's mind, while others don't think someone is being empathetic unless they effectively put their conclusions to use.

Of course, there's overlap between the two because you can often use one to give you information about the other (for example, knowing someone's worldview and history helps you emotionally empathize with why a certain event makes them so angry).

BENEFITS OF EMPATHY

Overall, empathy helps you to discern people's needs, emotions, values, interests, and overall personality. It doesn't take much effort to see how these skills could be useful in social situations:

- In conversations, it helps you answer questions like: What are they looking for from the exchange? What topics would they enjoy talking about? Which ones would make them uneasy, bored, or offended? Why are they telling this particular story, and what reaction do they hope to get from me? Having answers to questions like these doesn't mean you have to become a soulless chameleon or spineless people pleaser, but the information could help you make the interaction more mutually enjoyable and rewarding.
- In your day-to-day life, it helps you be considerate of others. Whether they're feeling cheerful or worried, you can show someone that you're tuned in and care about what they're going through. You can do thoughtful things for your friends, like being extra supportive to them on the day they have to give an important presentation or making sure to let them know you appreciate a favor they did for you.
- It helps you generally approach new people with a more open-minded, welcoming attitude. A core part of empathy is accepting that not everyone looks at the world the same way.

KNOWING THE MISTAKES THAT ARISE FROM NOT BEING EMPATHETIC

You can make social errors when aspects of your empathy aren't well developed and you unintentionally come off as thoughtless and insensitive. The errors fall into two categories that correspond with the two types of empathy:

Mistakes caused by less-developed cognitive empathy

When you're short on cognitive empathy, you don't always consider the other person's point of view, which may upset them. Here are some of the mistakes that arise:

- going on about a topic that bores your friend because you haven't thought, "Maybe they don't care about this subject as much as I do;"
- being offensive by making crass or edgy jokes to people who don't appreciate that kind of humor;
- bringing up topics that are inappropriate for the people you're talking to; for example, telling stories about your casual drug use to your conservative grandparents;
- being hurtfully blunt and casually critical; for example, "That shirt looks really bad on you. It looks too tight on your potbelly... What? Why are you getting mad?! I'm giving you useful feedback!"
- disregarding things that are important to other people; for example, forgetting an anniversary, or continuing to bring up a sensitive topic around a friend even after they've asked you to stop;
- seeming to take close friends for granted by always letting them do nice things for you, but not realizing they'd like you to show appreciation in return;
- getting annoyed at someone for not grasping something that's obvious to you because you don't consider that they may not have the same education, experience, or talents.

Mistakes caused by less-developed emotional empathy

When you haven't fully developed your emotional empathy, you don't always feel the emotions of the person you're speaking with. This creates a disconnect in the interaction. Consider these mistakes:

- not responding much at all when people are really upset or happy;
- giving invalidating, tone-deaf responses to people who are distressed; for example, "Why are you so upset your pet rat died? You knew it was only going to a live a few years when you bought it."
- seeming uncaring by not showing much reaction to bad news about other people; for example, looking unfazed upon learning a roommate's sister has been in a car accident.

Seeing why people may not show empathy

Sometimes people come across as unsympathetic and insensitive without meaning to. They often aren't aware that they're not responding in the most appropriate manner. Here are some reasons why people may not show empathy:

- They're socially inexperienced, and either it isn't on their radar that they should care about other people's feelings and perspectives, or they know they should, but they aren't very practiced at it. They may unconsciously have a mind-set of "This is how I would feel in this situation, so everyone else will be the same."
- They don't know how to show they're concerned or caring, or it makes them feel flustered and awkward. If a friend is upset, they're not sure what to do with themselves, so they say nothing. They may come off as emotionally blank because they're too stuck in their head worrying that they don't know how to respond properly.
- They have more logical, detached personalities and just don't get as emotional about things. News that may upset some people, like a child from across the country going missing, doesn't get to them because they think, "Well, I don't know them personally, so why should it affect me?" What someone else sees as an insult, they may see as a dry, rational critique.
- People with a more solitary, independent social style sometimes unintentionally become too focused on their own needs and forget to consider everyone else's. It's not that they're selfish monsters, just

that they develop some thoughtless habits as a side effect of spending most of their time in circumstances where they only have to worry about what's best for them.

- People who are going through a lot of stress and emotional turmoil will naturally focus on their own problems.
- When people are younger, especially in their teenage years, their empathy sometimes hasn't fully developed simply because they haven't had enough life experience. They haven't encountered enough hardship or been exposed to many contrasting worldviews, so they have a tougher time relating to people who are hurting or who see things differently than they do.

The above are benign, accidental reasons someone could seem insensitive, but the fact is, some people lack empathy because they have a selfish, self-absorbed, arrogant, or close-minded side to their personality. Those are clearly negative traits, which we all show bits of from time to time. If you realize you have more than the usual number of those traits, you can work on minimizing them.

HOW TO DEVELOP AND SHOW MORE EMPATHY

Your ability to emotionally and cognitively empathize with people can be improved. No one becomes a flawless mind reader, but even being moderately better at figuring out what others are thinking and feeling will make a big difference in your interactions.

Ways to develop your cognitive empathy

Generally learn about a variety of perspectives and worldviews and try to respect them

It's hard to be empathetic if you unconsciously assume your way of doing and thinking about things is the only correct one. Considering another point of view doesn't mean you have to condone everything about it, but you can at least try to see the reasons for it. For example, if you're careful with your money, try to learn about the benefits of spending it more freely. Don't look at a different perspective through the filter of "My default style of looking at the world is right, so I'm going to spot all the ways this other one is ignorant and misinformed." Aim to be nonjudgmental and open-minded, and try to consider how someone could come to think this way.

Practice actively considering particular points of view

You can consider another person's point of view while you're in the middle of talking to someone or as a solitary thought exercise. For example, if you're not a parent, try seeing things from the mind-set of your coworker who has two young children. What's important to them? What motivates them? How are they similar to you? How are they different? What types of things would they want to discuss? What wouldn't they want to hear about?

Learn people's basic needs

A component of empathy is figuring out what drives other people. Everyone has needs that are unique to them, but most people also share a set of basic ones. Most people want to
- be liked;
- be respected;
- feel like they're important to their friend;
- spend at least some time being social for its own sake;
- be kept in the loop about what their close
  friends and family are up to;
- feel like the things they have to say are interesting or entertaining;
- feel appreciated and acknowledged for the things they do for others;
- feel like their thoughts, emotions, and actions
  are healthy, reasonable, and normal;
- feel understood and supported when they're
  going through a tough time;
- be given the benefit of the doubt when they screw up;
- not be embarrassed or have their flaws or

failures thrown in their face;
- feel accomplished.

Once you start considering these basic needs, you'll feel much more confident about how you could act in various situations. For example, if a friend is telling you a funny story, odds are they want you to seem amused by it, not bored. If they share a mistake they made, they don't want you to tut-tut them.

Ways to develop your emotional empathy

Learn to respect the role of emotions

People with more logical, cerebral personalities sometimes look down on emotions and see them as irrational and unnecessary. When a friend or colleague is feeling a strong negative emotion, their first thought isn't "Oh no! They're so unhappy. How can I comfort them?" It's "This is so pointless. Why don't they pull themselves together and use their brain to work through their problem?" Emotions sometimes can lead people astray, but they can't be written off entirely. It's best to have a balance of emotion and logic.

Emotions are essential in making a lot of decisions. More logical individuals think dry facts are all people need, but without emotions, we're often left with two choices that have an equal number of pros and cons on each side. It's those gut feelings of "Mmm, this one makes me happy" or "Yech, I don't want that one" that break the tie. Emotions also motivate you to act. When you've been procrastinating on an assignment, the fear of failing finally gets you started. Emotions are also a part of being human. Even if you don't have much use for them yourself, you have to accept that they drive most people.

Learn to get in touch with your own emotions

People can have trouble with emotional empathy because they're cut off from their own feelings. If they see a family member looking depressed, they may feel sad for them deep down, but not be able to access it. Although some people are less baseline emotional than others, even the most logical, analytical person isn't a complete robot.

The idea of getting in touch with your feelings has a negative, touchy-feely connotation for some people, but it's hardly New Age fluff to have a basic awareness of what's going on in your own head and how your emotions are affecting your behavior.

Here are some starter, do-at-home suggestions for getting more in touch with your feelings. As a caution, if you've experienced a traumatic event and are suppressing your emotions as a coping mechanism, it may be best to do this kind of work with a counselor. Also be careful if you're prone to anxiety attacks that are triggered by noticing that things like your heart rate or breathing have changed.

- **Get into the habit of asking yourself, "How am I feeling right now?"** Do this randomly throughout the day and when you're vaguely emotionally charged up. Sometimes you'll be feeling a certain way and won't even be aware of it until you check in with yourself.

- **Try to add more nuance to the way you identify your emotions.** For example, instead of calling an emotion "sad," ask yourself if a more accurate label might be "disappointed," "regretful," or "dejected."

- **Think about whether you use any tactics to avoid or bypass your emotions.** Some common ones are distracting yourself with work or entertainment, immediately jumping into an intellectualizing problem-solving mode, making jokes about the situation, changing your mood with substances, or always being around other people so you're forced to hold it together.

- **In general, whenever you're having an emotion, see if there's another one beneath it.** It's not always the case, but one emotion can be masked by another. Sadder emotions tend to get covered up by ones like anger and worry.

- **Think about whether you have a default emotion that you feel whenever you're upset, which drowns out your other feelings.** Common go-to emotions are anger and anxiety.

- **When you're having an emotion, and you're in a safe place to do so, don't try to push it away.** Take your time and let yourself soak in it. Notice what's happening in your body. Is your jaw clenching?

Is your stomach upset? Do you want to make a glum face and slump your shoulders? Could you use any of these observations to let you know when you're feeling the same emotion in the future? Even if the emotion is on the stronger or more uncomfortable side, realize it won't hurt you or make you go crazy, and it will pass in time.

Practice feeling other people's emotions

Just as you can hone your skills in tuning in to other people's opinions and worldview, you can work on being able to tap in to their emotions. Start by watching a dramatic television show or movie. Pause during the emotional moments and try to imagine yourself as the characters and feel what they're feeling. Say the protagonist finds out her car has been stolen. Rather than continue on without giving it a second thought, take a few minutes to reflect on what that would be like, how confused and then angry and inconvenienced you'd feel. Next, think back on times people you know were being emotional and try to empathize with them. As you get the hang of that, empathize with people in the moment.

Practice in order to get more comfortable showing your support and concern

Maybe you aren't the best at seeming empathetic in the "showing concern" sense of the word because it makes you feel awkward and self-conscious. Even if you know exactly what to say and do to comfort a distraught friend, it feels forced and artificial. Through experience, you can get used to showing concern. Even if you're truly feeling com-passion for someone, the first few times you say something like, "Wow, that must be tough…" you may feel like an insincere bad actor, but it will become more natural.

Learn when it's appropriate to play along on the surface

You may find yourself in situations where someone else is upset about something that wouldn't bother you. Even when you make an effort to see things through other people's eyes, you're not always going to have the same emotional reactions they do. Sometimes the most sensitive move is to show the response that's expected in that situation. Acting supportive and understanding trumps getting to say everything that's on your mind right at that moment.

17

CORE LISTENING SKILLS

PRIOR CHAPTERS HAVE TOUCHED ON the usefulness of listening skills. Here they are covered in more detail with explanations about the benefits of listening well and how to improve your skills in this area.

UNDERSTANDING THE IMPORTANCE OF LISTENING

At the most basic level, listening well lets you take in the most information possible in a conversation. You'll have more to go on when deciding what to say next, and your interactions will flow better. If you don't listen well, you'll miss some of the information the other person is sharing.

More importantly, listening well makes other people feel respected, understood, and like you care what they have to say. If you're not a great listener, you can come across as uninterested, spacey, or self-absorbed. People may hang out with you casually, but feel they can't have a more serious, substantial conversation with you. Listening is more than parking yourself in front of someone and letting them make sounds at you. People don't need to feel that all of their conversation partners are fascinated by everything they say, but they do want a sense that the other person cares at least somewhat. Even if you just want to tell a corny joke to a coworker, it doesn't feel good when they're obviously tuned out.

Being able to pay attention to people and take in what they're saying, and not coming off as disengaged, are bare-minimum considerations when having a conversation. When people talk of "listening skills," they're often referring to *active listening*. When you engage in active listening, you listen in a more purposeful, focused, empathetic way; you really try to understand where someone is coming from, show your interest, and read between the lines of what's being said. You'd particularly need to use active listening if you were talking to someone about their problems, having a more philosophical discussion, or trying to see the other person's perspective during an argument. This skill helps you connect with people, make others feel accepted and supported, and resolve disagreements more easily.

While listening skills are extremely important to learn, you should have realistic expectations about the effect improving them will have on your social life. Some self-help sources oversell the significance of these skills and claim that good listeners are rare and that people appreciate nothing more than someone who truly listens to them. That's an exaggeration. Listening skills are really useful, but good listeners aren't *that* scarce, and being able to listen to people doesn't guarantee everyone will like you or that you'll easily be able to get through any conversation.

IDENTIFYING FACETS OF BASIC LISTENING SKILLS

More goes into listening than just hearing what the other person is saying. Your ears, mind, and body are all engaged when you listen well. Consider the following aspects that create a good listening experience, for you and the person you're talking to:

Intent

It sounds obvious, but one of the keys to listening properly is to want to do it. When people are poor listeners, they usually aren't that way on purpose. They unconsciously come into the conversation with another agenda or their own issues, which overrides their listening potential. For example, they may be too focused on what they want to talk about and trying to impress everyone. More on that at the end of the chapter.

When you interact with people, make a deliberate decision to try to listen well. That involves

- giving the other person space to say what they want to say, even if you're not entranced by every last word or they're struggling to make their point;
- seriously considering what they're saying, not just technically hearing it but not giving it a second thought;
- putting yourself in the other person's shoes and taking on their perspective;
- being as nonjudgmental as possible;
- avoiding any of the specific poor listening behaviors (covered in the last section in this chapter).

Adjust the intensity of your listening depending on the context. If a friend is telling you about a funny video his brother just sent him, you don't need to try to commune with his innermost being or worry about being open and accepting. Simply let him talk and don't interrupt.

Giving someone room to speak doesn't mean you to have to put all of your own conversation needs on the back burner. If someone's telling you an anecdote, you should listen respectfully, but if you have a story of your own you'd like to share, it's fine to bring it up at an appropriate time. If they say something you disagree with, you can tell them you see things differently, after you've respectfully heard them out. The good listener role also doesn't obligate you to stick in there with a long-winded monopolizer or someone who's inappropriately sharing the details of their recent trip to the doctor.

Engaged body language

This makes your listening clear. When you display engaged body language, you:

- Make good eye contact with the speaker.
- Face your body toward them.

- Tilt your head slightly to the side
- If you're sitting, lean slightly forward.
- Turn away from any distractions.
- Have an appropriate expression on your face, depending on what they're telling you and what they hope to convey; for example, concerned and understanding as they go over a problem, or interested and amused as they tell you about their eccentric neighbor.
- Nod and make little "uh huh" or "Mmm hmm" noises to show you're taking everything in and to encourage them to continue (mix up the noises you make and how often you make them, or you'll seem robotic).

Having a mind-set of wanting to listen is still the most important aspect of listening. Even if you nail all the nonverbals, people can usually tell if you're just going through the motions. Do each of these with a light touch. The idea is to appear interested, not act like a caricature of a therapist. Again, adjust this basic template based on the circumstances. If you're lounging on a couch and watching reality TV with your roommate while they casually tell you about something weird that happened at school, you don't need to full-on face and lean into them. You could show you're listening by turning your head toward them, making occasional eye contact, and saying "uh huh" and "yeah" every so often.

Responses

Responses in a conversation show that you're listening. Check out these pointers:
- Make appropriate responses to what the other person says; for example, replying, "Oh wow, that sucks..." in a compassionate voice when they tell you about a sad childhood memory, or laughing as they get to the funny part in a story.
- Show an interest in what they're saying. Ask for clarification if you don't understand a point, ask thoughtful questions to get more details, make it clear you really want to explore the topic, and make insightful

comments and help them think of things they never thought of.

- Make responses that show you heard and understood what they said. This can include agreeing they're going through a tough time, making a sympathetic murmur, sharing an experience of your own that tells them you're on the same page, and asking an intelligent follow-up question that only someone who was really paying attention would think of.
- If they shared some struggles or vulnerabilities, validate that their feelings are normal, and don't judge them for the way they feel.
- If they shared a lot with you, it may be appropriate to sum up what they told you to show you've taken it all in and maybe help clarify their thoughts for them. Paraphrase if you do this. Don't parrot back their exact words. Use this technique sparingly because doing it too much can *really* make you look like a cartoon psychoanalyst.
- If the speaker seems to want something from the interaction, like your thoughts on how to deal with an issue with their parents, don't be in a hurry to give it to them. Let them get it all out first. Give them room to explore on their own.

AVOIDING BEING A POOR LISTENER

A lot of being a good listener is avoiding the habits and behaviors that make you a poor one:

- Talking so much that you're hardly ever in the listener role
- Not seeming to pay attention to the other person or seeming like you'd rather be doing something else; for example, looking around the room, checking your phone every two seconds, not turning away from the TV, not putting down the magazine you're reading
- Having bored or distracted body language (see Chapters 18 and 19)
- Interrupting
- Being too eager to fill silences; not giving the other person space to form their thoughts
- Finishing the other person's sentences for them
- Cutting in with a premature summary of what you think the other person is going to say

- Cutting off the other person to respond to what you assume they're going to say
- Abruptly changing the subject right after the person you're talking to is done speaking without responding to what they said
- Giving a short, unsatisfying token response to what the other person said, then switching to a totally different topic

People can be poor listeners because they're self-centered, sure they're right, or not interested in a topic. There's often a non-malicious explanation. Someone could unintentionally come off as a bad listener because

- They're feeling shy and nervous and are too focused on their insecurities to pay attention.
- They have a naturally spacey, short-attention-span personality.
- They're in an energetic, overeager, talkative mood.
- They're legitimately distracted by stresses in their life.
- They misjudged the mood of the interaction (for example, they figured it was light and jokey, while the speaker thought they were having a more serious discussion).
- They thought the speaker had said all they needed to about a topic and that it was okay to change the subject.
- The environment is really loud or distracting.

You can't always get it right. Sometimes there will be a misunderstanding, and you'll be seen as a bad listener without meaning to. However, if you know you're prone to any of the issues above, working on them will indirectly help your listening skills.

18

RECOGNIZING AND ACTING ON OTHER PEOPLE'S NONVERBAL COMMUNICATION

NONVERBAL COMMUNICATION includes all the messages people are constantly sending out aside from their words. Someone's body language can tell you whether they're happy and energetic or tired and distracted. Their tone of voice can change a compliment from straightforward to playful teasing. They may tell you they're not annoyed, but their angry gestures and facial expression contradict their words.

You've probably heard that a huge 93 percent of all communication is nonverbal. That precise statistic is a misconception. How much of a message is nonverbal varies depending on the situation. However, the idea it captures is true. You need to have a grasp on nonverbal communication to socialize effectively. As with listening and empathy, being able to read nonverbal communication gives you useful information about the other person, which will help you make smart choices when you're talking to them. Managing your own nonverbal messages will let you present yourself more confidently and help you keep your communication clear and consistent; you won't say one thing and have your body language unintentionally say another. This chapter covers reading other people's signals. The next chapter goes into the ones you send out.

Reading nonverbal communication is a huge subject in and of itself, so this chapter covers only the core material. It focuses on reading people's signals in friendly social situations, rather than on more specialized topics like the body language clues that reveal someone is about to concede a negotiation. The chapter ends with some tips on how you can practice reading nonverbal cues. If you'd like to know more, the Further Reading section suggests some more in-depth books on the subject.

SOME OVERALL POINTS ABOUT READING NONVERBAL COMMUNICATION

Sometimes a person's nonverbals will reveal information they don't want to share through their words. However, reading nonverbal signals will never let you completely scan someone's mind. Tuning in to this type of communication is not fully reliable for a number of reasons:

- People know how to control and disguise the nonverbal signals they send in order to be polite. For example, they'll put a friendly attentive look on their face, even though they're not interested in the topic you're talking about. Sometimes their true intent will leak out, but they can often hide it successfully.
- People have different styles of communicating nonverbally, depending on their personality, mood, age, gender, and culture. Some are more cheery and animated; others always seem a bit flat and gloomy. Some use common gestures in idiosyncratic ways. If you've just met someone, you can't fully know what their nonverbal signals are telling you.
- A lot of nonverbal communication is quick and subtle. Most of the time, people don't feel the intense emotions that lead to obvious unspoken signals. For example, if you say something that mildly surprises them, their eyes may just go slightly wide for a split second. They won't do a cartoonish double take.
- Outside forces can interfere with the signals people would normally send. For example, if they find the room chilly, they might come across as more tense and closed off because they're distracted and hunching up to try to keep warm.

All in all, you should try to glean what information you can from people's nonverbal messages. At the same time, know you'll never have a perfect understanding of what they're thinking, so you should focus on going after your own social goals. For instance, if you want to talk to someone in your class but you can't tell if they're in the mood to chat, give it a shot and see what happens.

Any one nonverbal signal in isolation can be unreliable. Consider the overall picture when attempting to read people. For example, crossed arms can be a sign that someone is bored or guarded, but it could also mean they find the position comfortable. You need to weigh that one piece of information in light of everything else. If they've been smiling and eagerly talking to you the whole time they've had their arms crossed, it probably doesn't mean anything. If they suddenly cross their arms while turning away from you and making a disapproving face, that's another story.

Although it's vital to know how to read negative nonverbal cues, it can be nerve-racking territory if you have shy or insecure tendencies because you'll tend to overanalyze, assume the worst, and see unhappy signals where none exist. You can read negative meaning into ambiguous signals such as someone having a neutral facial expression. If you find yourself doing this, focus on dealing with those insecure thinking patterns.

SOME IMPORTANT CHANNELS OF NONVERBAL COMMUNICATION

When you think of nonverbal communication, you may think that the face, arms, and hands are the only sources of these signals. You can find out much about a person's thoughts through other means. Consider the following avenues of nonverbal communication:

Facial expression: This is a huge source of information because people's emotions are mainly communicated through their facial expressions. Sometimes a feeling only flashes across someone's face for a split second.

Tone of voice: You could consider tone of voice a part of verbal communication, but it's included with the other nonverbal signals because it can modify the meaning of someone's words. A simple "hi" can be injected with any number of emotions, like cheerfulness, tiredness, or polite obligation.

Use of eye contact: In Western cultures, people are seen as confident and interested in others when they maintain solid, though not overly intense, eye contact. Less use of eye contact can signal discomfort, distraction, or shiftiness.

Open or closed body language: When someone has open body language, their arms are at their sides, their legs are somewhat spread apart, they're facing you with their torso, and their body generally looks loose and relaxed. It's a sign they're feeling comfortable and accepting. Closed body language is tense and protective, with arms either stiffly held at the sides or crossed over the torso, and the legs close together. It could mean they're feeling guarded, nervous, or skeptical.

Leaning: If someone leans in toward you, it's a sign of their interest and attention. Leaning back is harder to read and can indicate anything from lower interest to just a casual, relaxed attitude.

Use of gestures and mannerisms: Individual gestures have their own meanings, like a nod to indicate interest. There are too many to list in this small chapter. Overall, when people are engaged and excited, they'll tend to gesture more. If they're tired, relaxed, or uninterested, they'll be less animated. Fidgety gestures can be a sign of boredom or anxiety.

Use of touch: Some people use touch more than others. Normally we're more touchy with people we like and are close to, and are hands-off when the relationship is more formal. With casual friends, we normally keep touching to the upper back and upper arms. Anything else is for more intimate contacts. You may give a friend a light clap on the shoulder when meeting them or playfully nudge them when they poke fun at you. If someone shrinks from your touch, they may not be sure of you yet or just not used to being touched in general.

Use of objects and the surroundings: If you're talking to someone and they're playing with their phone or absentmindedly ripping up a coaster, it's probably a sign they're not fully engaged with you. If you're not comfortable with someone, you may move until you've put a table between you.

Use of personal space: Distances vary between people and across cultures, but we all have a variety of personal space zones. Outside of a crowded subway or really noisy bar, you won't let a stranger get as close to you as you would your best friend. Closing the space with someone means you feel more familiar and comfortable with them. You tend to feel uneasy and back off if someone gets closer to you than you think the relationship justifies.

Body and feet direction: We often unconsciously point our body where we want to go. If you're interested in talking to someone, you'll face them. If you want to be somewhere else, you'll start angling away.

Positioning relative to others: In larger groups people can reveal aspects of their mental state based on where they place themselves compared to everyone else. For example, in a larger group discussion, if three people are standing together, it may mean they're especially close friends or they want to have a side conversation. If another person is standing slightly off to the side, it could mean they're feeling shy and left out or they're preoccupied or not interested in what the others have to say. If the entire group is standing away from everyone else at a party, it may mean they want to talk privately.

Fashion sense and grooming: The clothes people wear aren't completely reliable as a nonverbal signal, but people communicate a lot through their clothing choices. For example, they may be sending the message that they want to be seen as artsy and nonconforming, slick and wealthy, tough, or into a certain hobby. How well put together they are on any given day can also give you clues about someone's mental state (you'd know something was off if your normally well-dressed friend showed up to your house unshowered and wearing yesterday's outfit).

SOME IMPORTANT CLUSTERS OF NONVERBAL SIGNALS TO KNOW

When reading people's nonverbal messages, you want to be able to tune in to basic information like what emotions are showing on their face. People also make groups of signals to show their overall mood and comfort levels.

Approachability signals

You'll never fully be able to tell whether someone is open to talking to you. Sometimes the most unapproachable-looking person will happily chat to you once you break the ice. Here are some general guidelines:

Approachable

- friendly, happy facial expression
- open, relaxed body language
- looking around, as if scanning for people they could talk to
- standing near other people or in the middle of the room where all the action is
- smiling or nodding if you catch their eye
- (for groups) members are arranged loosely and are standing fairly far apart with plenty of room for someone new to join

Less approachable

- less happy or preoccupied facial expression
- closed body language
- in their own world, not paying attention to other people
- standing off to the side, away from everyone else
- clearly paying attention to something else, like their phone
- wearing headphones
- giving you a blank or unwelcoming expression if you catch their eye
- (for groups) members are standing in a tight, closed circle

Nonverbal signs of platonic, friendly interest, comfort, or happiness

- smiling
- solid eye contact
- eagerly nodding and agreeing with what you're saying
- learning forward
- open body language
- tendency to make more big, animated arm gestures

- body and feet facing toward you

If you're getting these signals, you can reasonably conclude everything is going well. Continue to watch the person's nonverbal signals to see if they change.

Signs of disinterest, discomfort, or being upset

There are a variety of ways someone may show that they're less than happy in an interaction with you. Again, any one signal is unreliable, but if you pick up a group of them, it's a sign something is off. You should think about what's happening in the interaction and whether you can do anything to change its course.

Boredom, lack of interest, or indifference

- glazed or tired expression in the other person's eyes
- tired, disengaged facial expression
- saying "Uh huh" and "Mmm hmm" and nodding along as you speak, but in a dry "going through the motions" way
- yawning
- looking around the room
- checking their phone
- fidgeting, shifting on their feet, or fiddling with nearby items
- leaning away from you
- crossed arms
- arms hanging leadenly at their side, lack of animation
- body and feet pointed away from you
- starting to edge away

If you're getting these signals, try one of these approaches to recapture the other person's attention:
- changing the topic to a more mutually interesting one
- your own energy and enthusiasm
- considering whether they've been talking too long and need a break

If you try one of those approaches and get the same result, it's likely that the other person doesn't feel like speaking to you, so you should end the conversation altogether.

Unease or not being sure about you yet

- strained, tight, polite smile
- mildly nervous or suspicious facial expression
- leaning away from you
- closed body language
- flinching or tensing up if you touch them
- standing away from you or increasing their bubble of personal space
- putting barriers up between them and you (for example, a table or a drink they're holding in front of themselves)

Here are some suggestions if you're getting these nonverbals:
- If you've just started talking to someone, give them time to get used to you.
- Back off a bit if you're being too touchy or animated, standing too close to them, acting too chummy and familiar, or asking them for personal information.
- If you're speaking about a controversial or emotionally charged subject, try switching to a more pleasant or neutral one.
- If you're mingling, consider finding someone else to talk to after a few minutes if their signals don't change much.

Nervousness

- stunned, deer-in-the-headlights facial expression
- tense, preoccupied facial expression
- tight or shaky voice
- struggling to get their words out
- sighing / exhaling noticeably
- nodding quickly and saying, "Yeah, yeah, yeah" much more than normal
- laughing too much at small jokes, laughing when someone

normally wouldn't (for example, "My name's Bill. Ha ha ha…")
- overall tense or closed, self-protective body language
- fidgeting
- self-soothing gestures like rubbing their upper arm
- twitchy, jumpy feet

To try to put someone else at ease, try one of these suggestions:
- Give the person time to calm down in your presence.
- Act pleasant and subdued, and stick to safe, routine topics that they can respond to easily.
- Consider whether you're doing anything that's making them feel off balance.

Offended or disagreeing with what you're saying

- look of anger or annoyance
- look of shock or incredulity ("Did they just say that?")
- suddenly closing off their body language
- suddenly leaning back
- partially turning away from you

If any of these signals arise during your interaction, think about the last thing you said or did. The other person must have found it disagreeable or insensitive. Consider changing the topic, backing off a strong opinion, or apologizing ("Sorry, that joke was tasteless").

HOW TO GET BETTER AT READING NONVERBAL COMMUNICATION

Humans have a built-in capacity to recognize each other's nonverbal communication, though some people aren't naturally skilled at reading it and need to work a little harder to get the hang of it. Here's what you can do to catch up.

Look up what different expressions and mannerisms look like if you have trouble recognizing them intuitively

It would be great if this book could include dozens upon dozens of photos of different types of nonverbal communication, but that's beyond its limits. Some books that contain this information are listed in the Further Reading section. You could also look up pictures of specific expressions online or ask a friend or family member to model particular ones for you.

Practice reading other people's body language

Here are some exercises you can try:

- Put on a movie or TV show and try to identify the emotions and nonverbal messages the actors are portraying. Of course, watch their facial expressions and body language, but also gather clues from the context they're in. Broad, exaggerated comedies or soap operas tend to be the easiest to read, while nuanced, understated dramas are the toughest. Muting the sound will make the exercise more difficult, because the dialogue won't give you hints.
- Do some inconspicuous people-watching in a busy public place like a food court or nightclub and try to read everyone's moods. Who's bored? Who's stressed out? Who's cheerful? Who's trying to be the center of attention? Who feels shy? Notice how some people have more expressive or restrained styles of communicating their feelings.
- Ask a friend or family member to act out various expressions and mannerisms for you to try to read. They can purposely exaggerate them at first, then gradually up the difficulty by making them more subtle.
- Try to read the nonverbals of people you're interacting with. If you're having a friendly chat with someone, they're not going to show you the wildest anger or the deepest sadness, but you can still try to look for changes in the more subdued expressions they'll make. Maybe they'll look a little more stressed as they talk about an upcoming assignment, or

seem mildly bored while you're talking about a topic they're only half-interested in, and then become livelier when the subject switches to one they're more passionate about.

19

IMPROVING YOUR OWN
NONVERBAL COMMUNICATION

YOUR OWN NONVERBAL COMMUNICATION affects how people see you. It's not the most flattering aspect of human nature, but we often size people up based on a quick surface impression. As much as possible, you want your nonverbal signals working for you. You'll also communicate more clearly and effectively if your words and nonverbal messages are lined up. This chapter shows you how to complement your words with your nonverbal communication.

SOME IMPORTANT ASPECTS OF YOUR
OWN NONVERBAL COMMUNICATION

Some of your nonverbal signals are beyond your conscious control. For instance, if you're scared your pupils will dilate. There's nothing you can do to override that. However, there are plenty of other nonverbal signals you can control. Here's a list:

Your use of eye contact: Are you making eye contact in a way that shows you're comfortable and attentive? Or do you give too little and seem nervous or checked-out, or make too much and come off as intense or combative?

Your resting facial expression: Does your neutral expression make you seem approachable and content, or does it unintentionally send the message that you're bored or angry?

Your voice volume: Do you speak at a volume that's easy to understand, or are you too quiet or loud?

Your voice tone: Is your voice pleasant to listen to, or does it have an odd quality to it? Does it convey confidence in what you're saying?

Your overall level of expressiveness: Are you able to reasonably convey your emotions, or do you come off as too blank and stiff or overly animated?

Your overall body language: Does it make you seem friendly and self-assured, or something less useful such as timid, overeager, aloof, or aggressive?

Your posture: Are you holding your body in a fairly confident, attractive way?

Your use of space: Are you maintaining a distance from people that fits your relationship with them?

Your use of touch: Are you reasonably comfortable touching people in a casual, social way? Do you shrink away when people do the same to you?

The way you dress and groom yourself: Are you styling yourself in a way that complements your appearance? Are you making any errors that could unnecessarily put people off?

GENERAL THOUGHTS ON IMPROVING YOUR NONVERBAL COMMUNICATION

Some of your nonverbal communication is influenced by your mental state. Your body language is naturally going to be different when you're feeling nervous and uncertain of yourself compared to when you're cheerful and self-assured. As your confidence and social skills get better, some of your nonverbals will improve automatically. Your body language may become more open and inviting, or you'll find it easier to hold eye contact. However, some nonverbals are ingrained bad habits. For example, even if you become more comfortable around people, you may still find you consistently fail to look them in the eye, and you'll have to try to correct this more directly.

It takes time to improve aspects of your nonverbal communication. When people realize they have poor posture, for example, they often consciously vow to carry themselves differently. They can typically only keep it up for a few days before it gets too physically and mentally draining, their focus, discipline, and enthusiasm wear off, and they move on to other things. If you really want to see improvements in an aspect of your nonverbal communication, you have to give it more time and make it a priority project, to the point where you schedule frequent practice sessions for a few months. It's not enough to just occasionally remember, "Oh yeah, I should stand up straighter." If you have several issues with your nonverbals, you should try to tackle them one or two at a time, not all at once.

It's often distracting to try to monitor and adjust your nonverbals while you're socializing. If you're working on your conversation skills, you can't exactly throw "practice using open body language" into the mix and expect to do either well. At first, try to work on your nonverbals in situations where you can put your spoken communication on auto-pilot (for example, while talking to a cashier). As your new nonverbals start to feel more effortless and automatic, you can push yourself to use them in situations where you have to think on your feet more.

WAYS TO IMPROVE SPECIFIC FACETS OF YOUR NONVERBAL COMMUNICATION

Eye contact

People are considered more confident, interested, and trustworthy when they maintain good eye contact with the person they're speaking with. That doesn't mean fixing your partner in a death stare. Instead, look them in the eyes for three seconds or so, then glance away for a moment before meeting their gaze again. In general, you should make more eye contact when you're listening, which is easier to do. When you're speaking, it's okay to look away more, which often happens naturally as you get distracted by trying to put together what you want to say. When talking to a group, spread your eye contact among everyone.

Poor eye contact can be nothing more than a bad habit, but people often avoid looking others in the eye because they find it too intense and intimidating. Having a tendency to get lost in your head during conversations can also hinder good eye contact. Here's what can help:

- If eye contact makes you nervous, start with social situations you can handle and build up to the harder ones (see Chapter 7 for more details). Maybe you can't look an attractive authority figure in the eye, but you can manage when you're interacting with a restaurant server or sales clerk. As mentioned, you'll likely find it easier to maintain eye contact when you're listening rather than talking.
- Two safe ways to practice are to watch TV and make eye contact with the characters on the screen, and to stand in front of a mirror and meet your own gaze.
- You don't have to look right into the center of people's eyes. Looking between or close by them will still register as eye contact from the other person's perspective.
- Give your eye muscles time to get into better shape. If you're used to always looking down and away in conversations, it can be tiring to continually look up at someone's face and hold your focus on it.

Resting facial expression

Ideally you want your neutral face to look relaxed, happy, and approachable. You don't need to walk around grinning like a clown at all times, but it's good if you can seem reasonably content. Some people create the wrong impression because their face unintentionally looks nervous, bored, angry, zoned out, or unfriendly. There are a few reasons this can happen:

- They actually are feeling that way and may not be aware of it (for example, they're more checked out than they realize at the office Christmas party).
- Their facial features naturally make them look that way (for example, someone with large eyes may seem more stunned and nervous; someone with a prominent brow may look angrier).

- Their overall look matches a stereotype (for example, if someone dresses in a stereotypical hippie or stoner style, people may read their neutral expression as zoned out and dopey).
- They don't always give off a misleading expression, but some of their moods can be mistaken for others ones (for example, they look annoyed when they're tired, or bored when they're deep in thought).

As with other facets of your nonverbal communication, your resting expression may shift as you change your mentality and social skills. If you tend to look nervous, that may go away as you become more comfortable around people. You may start to look more relaxed and happy at parties, rather than bored, when you know how to mingle and unlock their fun.

It's too draining to do all the time, but when it's important to do so, you can consciously try to wear a happy, approachable facial expression; simply smile slightly, open your eyes more, and relax your features. If you're tall, lower your chin so you don't accidentally look down your nose at people. You may also be able to adjust the impression you create with some tweaks to your grooming, style, and posture. For example, if your eyebrows are naturally downturned and grouchy looking, a little plucking may change the vibe they give off. If you're a big, imposing guy, some changes to your fashion may make you seem less intimidating. If you have a wide-eyed, fretful expression, better posture may help cancel out its effect and create a more confident overall look.

Voice

There are two aspects to having a decent speaking voice. The first is to be able to speak smoothly, pleasantly, and at a good volume. The second is being able to get your message out in a way that shows you're reasonably confident in yourself and what you're saying.

Voice volume

If you're shy and unsure of your opinions, you may speak with an overly quiet voice. The easiest way to talk with more volume and projection is to speak from down low in your abdomen, which is more resonant than when you use your throat to make higher-pitched sounds. Singing, acting, and public speaking lessons can teach you to use your voice more effectively. You may have to face a fear of making yourself heard and being the center of attention. If your voice is always quiet, not just in certain situations, there may be a physical cause, like weak vocal chords. See a speech therapist to rule that out.

Voice quality

Most people's voice quality is fine, but some have issues like stuttering or speaking with an unusual tone or cadence. Speech therapy can help in these cases too.

Voice conviction

The book has already mentioned the usefulness of bringing up your issues and insecurities in a "no-big-deal" tone a couple of times, so you already have a sense of how the way you say something can change the way it's received. A somewhat cynical observation is that if you watch popular people socialize, they often aren't saying anything that interesting or clever, but because they're speaking with conviction, everyone around them finds them compelling. It's too much to conclude, "As long as you seem sure of yourself, you can say whatever dumb things you want," but you do need to nonverbally package your statements.

When you're surer of yourself and your opinions, you'll naturally start to express yourself more confidently. Your statements will also seem more self-assured if other aspects of your nonverbals, like your eye contact and posture, are strong. Here are some more direct ways to speak with conviction:

- Purposely try to speak in a relaxed but assured tone that communicates, "This is a perfectly natural, acceptable, interesting thing to say right now."
- Speak with enough volume to be heard.
- Speak clearly. Don't mumble or talk into your chest.
- Don't speak too quickly in a rush to get your

point out or not take up too much time.

- Be reasonably concise. Know what you want
to get across, rather than rambling on.
- Try to cut down on filler words and sounds such as "Like"
or "Uh..." (if you need a moment to think, being silent
for a split second is better). Everyone uses filler words
sometimes, but overdoing it can make you seem ditzy.

Overall expressiveness

In addition to your facial expressions, expressiveness comes from varying your voice and the gestures you make. If your face is always a blank mask, you speak in a monotone, and you don't move your hands or body much, you'll seem flat and bored, and be hard to read. On the other hand, being overly expressive and animated can make you seem fake, flighty, or agitated.

Aim to hit whatever the typical level of expressiveness is for your culture. If you're under-expressive, you'll have to consciously force yourself to gesture more often and put on a smile when you want to seem cheerful. More than with many of these points, this feels very clunky and unnatural at first, but showing a wider range of emotion will feel more normal in time. Again, as you get more comfortable in your own skin, you'll likely naturally start to be more expressive. If you're over-expressive you'll need to do the opposite and tone down your gestures and facial expressions. This can also feel artificial and restrictive at first, but will become easier with time.

Body language

In day-to-day social situations, you want body language that makes you seem relatively confident, relaxed, friendly, approachable, and happy. This involves

- having open body language;
- holding yourself in a loose, non-tense, and non-rigid way;
- absence of nervous or fidgety gestures like rubbing
your hands on your pants or tapping your foot;

- absence of unintentionally bored or disrespectful-seeming actions, like looking around the room or fiddling with nearby objects.

You want your body language to seem self-assured, but casual and relaxed. If you come off as overly confident, you will seem like you belong at a sales convention, not a ho-hum social gathering. You also don't want to veer into confrontational or overly dominant territory (that is, standing with your chest puffed out, body too rigid and rooted in place, hands planted defiantly on your hips, invading other people's space, or resting your hands on people's shoulders). Sure, maybe you'll need to act like that if you're living in a rough neighborhood where only the strong survive. But in most social situations, that kind of body language will either make you look angry and unstable, or like you're a jerk who's trying too hard to be the top dog at the expense of connecting with people in a friendlier way.

Posture

The most attractive, confident posture is when you're standing upright with your head and shoulders back, though not in a standing-at-attention way. There are two main types of poor posture. The first is slouching—when your shoulders are hunched and rounded, and your head juts too far forward. The second is *anterior pelvic tilt*, which makes you look like you have a potbelly, even if you're thin. This poor posture occurs when your hips tilt too far downward and your lower back arches too far inward, causing your butt and stomach to stick out.

Posture problems are caused by muscle imbalances that pull your body out of alignment. In slouching, the chest muscles are tight, while the ones in the back are relatively weak. With the anterior pelvic tilt, the lower back and hip flexors (the muscles near your hips that raise your knee up) are too tight, while the abs and butt are weaker. These issues can develop due to factors like slumping in front of a computer too much, compensating for old injuries, or simply from entrenched habits. Some less-confident people slump their shoulders because they chronically feel defeated or don't believe in themselves enough to walk tall. Genetic differences in spine curvature can lead to posture issues as well.

To improve your posture, you need to strengthen your weaker muscles and increase flexibility in the tighter ones. If you slouch, you need to stretch your chest and work out your upper back. If your pelvic tilt is out of whack, you need to regularly stretch your hip flexors and lower back, and work your abs and gluteal muscles. If you log a lot of hours sitting at a computer, change the ergonomics of your work station so it encourages you to sit up straight.

Use of personal space

Confident people are comfortable taking up their reasonable share of personal space. To do this, stand with your feet shoulder-width apart and don't be afraid to use the occasional bigger arm gesture. Don't swing your hands around wildly and try to claim six feet in every direction, but don't be shrunken and huddled up either.

Avoid unintentionally getting too close to anyone. Some people default to speaking at a distance that's too close to the person they're talking to. Observe what distances people in your area talk at and try to do the same.

You may also have a larger need for personal space and tend to pull back when people try to talk to you at a distance that seems natural to them. If your space bubble is impractically large, it can make you seem like you're scared of or uninterested in people. Try to get used to standing closer to people. Don't force yourself to put up with someone who's standing too close and being too familiar, but if you're having a casual conversation with someone who's at a reasonable distance and you find yourself wanting to retreat, try to override the urge.

Your use and acceptance of touch

You don't need to touch others very often to do well in social situations. However, if you're uneasy touching people in even the most casual, friendly way—say, by giving a light hug good-bye or touching someone's shoulder to get their attention—you can get used to it through purposeful practice. Start with the types of touch that make you the least uncomfortable and then build up to the ones that you're more hesitant to do. If you notice people often retreat from your touch, it's a sign you may be doing it too much, too soon, and in too familiar a way.

Some people are uneasy with being casually touched and may flinch or show discomfort when someone else touches them. If that describes you, you can get more used to being touched by consciously being aware when it might be coming and forcing yourself not to react in a tense or jumpy way. With time, it won't faze you as much. Again, this does not mean you should put up with touching that's blatantly over the "casual and friendly" line.

Grooming and sense of style

How you dress or groom yourself affects how other people see you. If fashion isn't on your radar and you don't dress in the most flattering way, you may cause some people to unnecessarily write you off or assume negative things about you, like you're boring or don't take good care of yourself.

Don't worry, though. You don't need to become obsessed with clothes or completely overhaul your appearance to have a happy social life. The majority of people dress fine. They won't win any style awards, but the impression they make through their looks isn't holding them back either.

People can err two ways in their style and grooming:

1. The first, rarer one is when they make cut-and-dried errors like having bad breath, body odor, or unkempt facial hair; wearing clothes with holes or stains in them; or sporting classically unfashionable combinations like shorts, sandals, and pulled-up white socks. If you're making any mistakes at this level, then saying you should fix them is going to be this book's closest thing to mandatory advice. Fortunately, these are easy problems to fix once you're aware of them.

2. The second is when someone isn't making any flagrant mistakes, but their overall sense of style is below average for the town or city they live in. They dress and groom themselves in a bland, frumpy, or unflattering way. If you fall into this category, you don't *have* to change. Lots of people who are indifferent to fash-

ion have good social lives. However, polishing your appearance wouldn't hurt.

Maybe you're worried your fashion sense isn't good enough. However, just because you're reading a section on style and grooming mistakes doesn't mean you're necessarily making any. It's possible your appearance is okay as it is. If you want to know if there are any areas where you could improve, try asking some friends or acquaintances for their opinion. You can also upload some photos of yourself in typical outfits to fashion-related message boards online and get feedback.

Say you learn you could stand to polish your style. People often have stronger reactions to the idea of having to dress better than they do to things like improving their posture or speaking volume:

- Many people have been picked on in their youth for wearing the "wrong" clothes by peers who seemed overly concerned with the superficial parts of life. When these people are older, they carry baggage about dressing well. They see it as shallow and may even feel like they're letting the enemy "win" if they begin to focus on it themselves.

- More generally, someone may not personally care much about fashion and resent the fact that they're forced to devote energy to it because the rest of the world thinks it's important.

- Some shy, self-conscious people have a fear of standing out and making waves. One way they unconsciously manage it is by wearing very conservative, nondescript outfits. When they're told they should dress with a little more panache, it triggers their anxiety, and they react with a self-protective hostility.

- They have poor self-esteem and think they don't deserve to look nicer.

- They have an overly rigid self-image and equate dressing even slightly differently with giving up everything about who they are.

Developing your style

This subsection won't list a bunch of rudimentary fashion and grooming tips like "brush your teeth every day", "wear clothes that fit you well", or "regardless of your body type, you'll look better if you're fit." If you previously didn't give much thought to your hygiene or style, once you're tuned in to it it's easy enough to look up guides on those topics and figure out what to adjust. This chapter is also not going to give you any specific clothing suggestions, because what's considered good style varies immensely depending on your age, subculture, and the region of the world you're living in. Instead, here are some general guidelines on improving your style on your own:

- **Don't feel you have to become a fashion connoisseur to improve your look.** There are advantages to having above-average dress sense, but it takes time and effort to get to that point, and the typical person isn't going to think less of you if you don't look like you stepped off a fashion runway. You just need to dress on par with the other people in your city. That doesn't mean you have to mindlessly adopt the same uniform as them. You just need an average level of fashion knowledge.

- **You can't develop a better sense of style in a week.** You'll improve your instincts little by little as you read up on the topic, observe how other people dress, experiment with your own look, and get feedback from the people in your life about what suits you best. Practically, this means don't go out tomorrow and spend a bunch of money in an attempt to overhaul your wardrobe. Learn and buy a little at a time.

- **Changing your look, even for the better, may make you uncomfortable.** As you're trying on new clothes, you may think things like, "That's not me. I'm not the type of person who wears this stuff." When you first wear a new type of outfit, you may feel like everyone on the street notices how weird and different you look. Try to push your comfort zone. You may be surprised at how, within a few days, you'll feel comfortable in outfits that initially made you feel like you were playing dress-up.

- **Fashion-savvy friends can help you tweak your look, but any one person can be hit-or-miss, because their sense of what looks good may not match yours.** You can get better feedback by consulting a range of people. If everyone at your job or in your social circle says they like your new haircut, you know you're on the right track.

- **Try to get a sense of how people in your area and demographic are styling themselves**. You can do this by people watching. A less conventional but efficient way to check out a lot of people's styles at once is to join a free dating site, make a fake empty profile, and then look at who's in your city. Ask yourself: What are some of the broad style categories people fit into? What distinguishes the sharper-looking people from the more generic or poorly dressed ones?

- **Find a good-looking haircut for your face.** That might involve growing it out or cutting it much shorter. If you have hard-to-manage hair, take the time to learn how to properly handle it (for example, by changing your shampooing routine or using products to control frizz).

- **Glasses can look great if they're the right frames on the right person as the right accessory of a larger style package.** Glasses can just as easily send the signal of "stereotypical dork." If you wear glasses, consider whether you'd look better in contacts. They're not as expensive or high maintenance as you may think. If not, make sure to choose frames that look stylish on you and jell well with your overall look.

- **If you have a more bland style, you're at risk for two mistakes when buying clothes:** 1) Going too far and buying clothes that are overly flashy and gaudy; 2) Not going far enough and seeing run-of-the-mill clothes as too colorful for you. With experience you'll get better at finding that middle ground, but when you're just beginning to add pieces to your wardrobe, get a second opinion from a sales clerk or friend.

20

CONVERSATION MISTAKES

THE PREVIOUS CHAPTERS have mentioned some conversation mistakes when it made sense to bring them up. This one provides a more dedicated list of mistakes to try to avoid. It can't cover every mistake you could possibly make in a conversation, but it includes the most common ones. Mistakes can be one-off errors in judgment or be more habitual and stem from larger issues in a person's personality that they need to work on.

THE NO. 1 THING TO REMEMBER ABOUT CONVERSATION MISTAKES

Everyone makes mistakes while conversing from time to time. It's great to steer clear of as many bad habits as possible, but don't put too much strain on yourself to be flawless when you talk to people. No one gets it right 100 percent of the time. Also, even if you converse in a way that most people find acceptable, you'll encounter the occasional person who has a different perspective and sees something as a mistake on your part (for example, someone who's overly sensitive may take offense to normal affectionate teasing).

Don't let a fear of making a mistake paralyze you. Many so-called mistakes aren't ideal, but they're not *that* bad, and the conversation will often continue just fine. For example, it's not great to brag, but if you subtly talk yourself up one time, most people aren't instantly going to be turned off. They may not even see it as bragging to begin with, just you stating a fact about yourself.

If you're just getting the hang of making conversation and are anxious about getting rejected or making a bad impression, you can get so worried about all the behaviors you have to avoid that your mind goes blank. Saying something less-than-perfect is often better than saying nothing at all. At least that way you're keeping the conversation going and giving the other person something to react to. For example, if you mildly brag about how good you are at drawing, the other person may start talking about how they're into art as well.

If you catch yourself making a bigger mistake, you can usually smooth it over by apologizing for it. Don't say you're sorry in too serious a tone. Just quickly, casually acknowledge what you did wrong, then get on with the discussion. For example, "Whoops, I just cut you off. Sorry about that. So you were saying?"

KNOWING WHEN IT'S OKAY TO BREAK THE RULES

People get away with making errors in conversations all the time. An observation socially inexperienced people sometimes make is, "I've read about all these things that are supposedly bad conversation habits, but I see popular people doing them all the time. What gives?" There are a few explanations:

- **Some "bad" behaviors are okay in certain situations.** As Chapter 14 explained, it's acceptable in loud, rowdy group conversations for people to interrupt and talk over each other as they try to make their points heard.
- **Some "bad" behaviors are accepted in particular subcultures or social groups.** In a group of young, bro-ish guys, mild bragging may be common and acceptable. A circle of intellectual friends may be fine with members correcting each other.

- **Individuals vary in which social mistakes bother them.** Someone who's not a big talker themselves may have fewer issues with a monopolizer. Someone with a crasser sense of humor may not mind a less-sensitive friend. Our friendships are partially determined by what mistakes we don't mind, or even find endearing, in others.
- **People's personalities are somewhat defined by the minor, mostly tolerated mistakes they tend to make.** "Yep, that's Norm, always telling those meandering stories", "Mindy's just excitable. I used to get annoyed when she interrupted me, but now I'm used to it", "Ha ha, Dennis is a passionate guy. If you talk to him about politics, you're going to get into a debate with him. You've been warned."

MISTAKES

Mistakes fall into many categories and can creep into any conversation. You can't avoid all mistakes, but by being aware of potential missteps, you're more likely to sidestep or minimize the mistakes you'll make occasionally.

General

- **Interrupting:** Again, it's sometimes okay to cut people off in rowdy group conversations, but at any other time it's inconsiderate. Make an effort to let other people finish their thoughts and statements, even if you're eager to share what you have to say. The rare exception when it's okay to cut someone off is if they're obviously floundering, but can't get themselves to stop talking and would like someone to jump in and save them from themselves.
- **Not doing your fair share to keep the conversation going:** You don't want to make your conversation partner do all the work. Examples include giving short answers to their questions but not asking any of your own, or simply acknowledging their statements and not giving a fuller reaction. It's okay not to pull your weight at first if you're shy or initially getting the hang of conversation skills,

but after that, don't force the other person to do all the work of keeping the conversational ball in play.

- **Being unwilling to give the types of replies people reasonably expect to day-to-day questions:** When you reply with an unexpected answer to a standard question, you throw people off and force them to scramble to come up with something else to keep the interaction going. It may also make you seem negative or difficult. For example, someone asks you how your job is going, and rather than replying straightforwardly, you think, "Ugh, this question is so boring. They must be trying to annoy me on purpose" and give a curt, vague answer.
- **Trying too hard to force a particular dynamic:** By all means, try to start a certain dynamic if you think it will be enjoyable, but be willing to change course if the other person isn't biting. For example, trying to get a teasing vibe going is fine, but if the other person indicates they want to be more serious, you should respect their wishes.

Being self-absorbed

- **Being selfish, not looking out for the overall health of the conversation, and turning every subject back to what you want to talk about:** Within reason it's okay to steer a discussion to some of the things that interest you, but not at the expense of everyone else's needs. A good conversation has elements that every person in it enjoys.
- **Monopolizing the conversation by hogging too much of the spotlight and not letting others speak:** Although some people like talking more than others, in general everyone in the conversation should have equal time to contribute. The exception is when everyone has clearly shown interest in letting you take center stage to share a longer story or opinion. You can gauge this interest by throwing out a teaser sentence or two ("Did I tell you guys about the time I...?"), then seeing if they seem to want to hear more, rather than launching right into a longer spiel.
- **Being long-winded; going on and on when it's your turn to speak, rather than being more succinct:** Even if you have a longer point to

share, you should still aim to make it as concise as you can. People will get impatient if you ramble on too much. Continually check the other person's nonverbal signals (see Chapter 18). If they look interested, keep going, but if they seem bored, wrap it up.

Bragging

- **Straight-out gaudy bragging:** Simply put, most people find this obnoxious.
- **More subtly trying too hard to bring up your talents and accomplishments:** It's understandable that you'd want to make people aware of your strengths, but let them come up naturally. You may come across as insecure if you seem like you need to give people reasons to approve of you right away.
- **One-upping:** For example, "Yeah, zip lining's cool and all, but I've been skydiving about a dozen times, so I don't know how much I'd get out of it." One way people accidentally one-up is when they're trying to relate to someone by sharing a similar experience, but theirs is "better." If someone wants to share an accomplishment or experience, let them have it, and don't feel you lose something unless you can "beat" it.

Poor choice of topics

- **Bringing up inappropriate topics around people who won't appreciate them:** The topic could be too controversial, offensive, upsetting, disgusting, or overly personal and familiar. As Chapter 16 covered, try to consider other people's perspectives and potential reactions when choosing what subjects to discuss.
- **Not moving on from a topic that isn't going anywhere:** For example, you're trying to ask someone about their job, and they don't seem keen to talk about it, but you keep trying to get them to open up. Know when to switch gears, and don't assume someone would enjoy a particular topic if they just gave it a chance.
- **Changing topics too abruptly:** You don't always have to make perfect, artful segues, but switching topics too randomly can throw

people off. Chapter 9 gives some tips on segueing to a new subject.

■ **Over-relying on complaining, negative, or downer topics to keep your conversations going:** This simply injects too many negative vibes into the interaction, which wears most people down before long. Discussions about personal problems can feel "deep," but be careful not to always steer your interactions into that territory because it helps you get your fix of meaningful interactions.

■ **Over-relying on critiquing topics, like picking apart the plot holes in a movie you just saw with a friend:** In moderation this is okay, especially with other analyzer types, but it also adds some negative energy to your exchanges.

■ **Over-sharing by telling your heavy personal problems or foibles to someone you barely know:** Chapter 12 goes into more detail about appropriate ways to self-disclose.

Mistakes often made by people who consider themselves intellectual and logical

■ **Speaking in a way that's more blunt and direct than the other person is used to:** People and cultures vary in how to-the-point they are, but if you're more blunt than what your partner expects, it may offend them or hurt their feelings.

■ **Correcting people about minor things that aren't relevant to the overall point they were trying to make:** Doing so usually makes you look uptight and pedantic, and can throw the conversation off course.

■ **Being too quick to start debating people, especially if they weren't expecting it or don't enjoy that kind of verbal sparring:** For example, getting into an argument about politics when they offhandedly mention something funny about a politician. Most people find arguing emotionally unpleasant, especially if it's sprung on them suddenly. It's okay to disagree with people, but don't approach it from an adversarial stance where you think their view is stupid and you have to "win" with yours. Approach differences of opinion from the perspective that you're both on the same team and you're respectfully sharing ideas to help each other learn and grow.

- **Talking at people rather than with them:** That is, you're thinking out loud at someone about a subject that interests you, not having a back-and-forth interaction. The other person feels like they could be replaced with a cardboard cut-out, and it wouldn't make much difference. This is similar to hogging the spotlight, but it makes the other person feel especially unimportant. It also makes people who do it seem unaware.

Group conversation mistakes

- **Blatantly hogging the spotlight:** The bigger the group is, the more of a mistake it is to try to take all the airtime for yourself. However, you have a bigger audience, and that urge to try to capture everyone's attention can be stronger.
- **Trying to have a conversation with one other person in the group, rather than focusing on everyone:** That is, not breaking off into a side conversation, but just focusing on one person and ignoring the others. It's a group interaction. Every member deserves to be included.
- **Cutting people off, interrupting, and doing other things to fight to be heard when the interaction is low key:** These things are acceptable within reason during more hectic group discussions, but will seem domineering or attention-hogging if everyone else is interacting in a more restrained way.

21

BEING MORE LIKABLE

As the first chapter in this section said, your interactions will be influenced by your comfort levels, your specific conversation skills, and your broader personality. One trait that affects how much people enjoy your company is how likable you are. People know this and often ask how they can be more likable. The term seems vague, but this chapter lays out some well-known traits of likable people.

But first, some disclaimers to keep in mind as you work on your likability:

- A big factor in how people feel about each other is their compatibility. We typically like those who are similar to us. Even if you're warm and pleasant, someone may not like you if you have completely opposing views on the world. The traits covered below will affect your likability in addition to, or in spite of, how well matched you are to someone otherwise.

- The traits below will help you become more likable on average, but you can't reliably use any one of them to guarantee a specific individual will like you. As always, each person has their own tastes, and you can't win them all over.

- As a whole, the list may seem like a bunch of bare-minimum requirements to be a pleasant person, not someone outstandingly likable. Likable people don't operate using a set of secret techniques. They just do more of the things below and at a higher level.

* The traits below are pretty general. That means you can express them in a way that blends into your overall style and personality.

* There are many ways to be appealing. For every point listed, there are many people who don't have that trait who are still likable because they make up for it in other ways.

* Unless you have an especially off-putting personality, you're probably already likable to some people. You don't need to be in the top 1 percent of any of the points below to be liked; just being decent enough at them helps your interactions.

TWO WAYS TO BE MORE LIKABLE BEFORE ANYONE HAS EVEN TALKED TO YOU

People start to form an impression of your likability before you've even spoken. The first way you can seem more likable is if you make yourself more physically attractive: by dressing and grooming well, being in shape, and having self-assured body language. Even if you don't transform yourself into an Adonis, every little bit helps. People tend to see attractive, put-together individuals as having more appealing personalities. It's called the *halo effect*. Of course, attractiveness is somewhat subjective, and you'll need to adjust anything you do based on your social goals and the types of people you want to make a good impression on. An outfit or hairstyle that may be considered good-looking in an artsy neighborhood in a big city may not get the same response elsewhere.

Your reputation and accomplishments can also color people's perception of you. Have you ever seen someone from a distance and they seemed like nothing special, but then a friend told you about something they did that impressed you? It skews you toward seeing them in a more positive light when you talk to them. The opposite can happen if you know someone's a jerk. You can't actively control this point like the ones coming up, but when you become more accomplished, it may affect the way people view you.

BE ABLE TO PUT YOUR PERSONALITY OUT THERE

Obviously you don't want to seem unlikable. Another outcome that can be nearly as bad is when people meet you and don't form much of an impression at all. This can happen if you're extremely shy or quiet, or if you're so scared of saying the wrong thing that you discuss everything in a very safe, bland way. You don't have to become extremely outgoing or forceful with your opinions or humor, but you need to show enough of your personality that people have at least something to react to.

BE REASONABLY CONFIDENT

On the whole, people like confidence in others. However, this isn't to say you have to come across as an ultra-assured salesman type of person. That can be too much. Just be comfortable with yourself. Some people are even likable by being slightly shy or eccentric, but owning it, rather than acting ashamed and embarrassed.

BE REASONABLY CHEERFUL AND POSITIVE

Likable people are usually happy. They see the positives in things. They don't complain that often, and even when they talk about their problems, they don't let their energy get too negative. They can vent about their annoying boss but have it come across as an entertaining story. A cheerful emotional state feels good to be around and is somewhat contagious. Again, you don't have to be excessively chipper or never express a negative feeling or opinion. Just try to maintain a good ratio of positivity to negativity.

SEEM AS IF YOU LIKE PEOPLE

People generally find someone more likable if they seem as if they like us and people in general. Conversely, people usually dislike anyone who comes off as arrogant or aloof. The wording "seem as if" is used deliberately. Some people inwardly feel misanthropic, but they're seen as likable because they're outwardly friendly and personable. If you truly like most people you meet, that's great, but having that trait is easier said than done. Some of us are choosier than others about who we want to chat to or be friends with. You can still make it a point to be pleasant in your interactions:

- Show friendly and interested body language, like smiling, making pleasant eye contact, and giving people your full attention.
- Initiate conversations with people.
- Eagerly chat with anyone who starts a conversation with you.
- Take an interest in other people and what they have to say.
- If you don't have time to talk to someone, at least give them a cheerful greeting.

HELP PEOPLE FEEL GOOD ABOUT THEMSELVES

When it comes to this point, it's less about actively trying to make people feel good, and more about not saying anything that cuts them down. If you purposely try to build someone up by cooing over every little thing they do, it can seem very transparent, patronizing, and manipulative. It's more than enough to compliment someone or tell them you're impressed by something they've done when the opportunity comes up naturally. Being a decent, friendly person who's interested in others also makes people feel good about themselves.

If you want to work on this point, you should put most of your energy into not being petty and undermining. Perhaps you know someone who isn't a blatant jerk, but who's always peppering their interactions with cutting little comments. They'll make snarky remarks, downplay or dismiss their friends' accomplishments, and make "joking" insults that are a little too stinging. Maybe that person has social status and respect for another reason, but no one would call them *likable*. When you act this way yourself, you often won't even notice you're doing it. For example, a friend will tell you they just took up rock climbing, and before you know it, you feel threatened by the fact that they have more adventurous hobbies than you and are brushing it off with "Yeah, that is a popular fad these days." Likable people aren't immune to acting petty, but they do it much less often.

BRING SOMETHING TO THE TABLE IN YOUR INTERACTIONS

Aside from making others feel liked and good about themselves, likable people have traits that make them enjoyable to be around. They're genuinely funny, they have interesting things to say, they're fun to go out with, they're good listeners, and so on. Again, this is subjective. A sense of humor that's hilarious to one group may seem too dark or corny to another. One person may find a certain opinion interesting, while someone else thinks it's pretentious.

You can become more likable by developing your social strengths. Maybe you're fairly funny, but could refine your sense of humor. Or maybe being funny isn't your thing and you could focus on having intriguing things to talk about instead.

HAVE MORE POSITIVE THAN NEGATIVE PERSONALITY TRAITS

In a chapter full of general points, this one is even more general than the others. A likable person could be lazy at work and careless with money, but when it comes to interacting with others, they show mostly good personality traits. The socializing-related personality flaws they do have are often milder. They also tend to be aware of their irksome traits and can put a charming spin on them. For example, if they're a bit opinionated and temperamental, they can catch themselves at the start of a rant and poke fun at themselves about what a hothead they are. They don't randomly explode at people with no sense of how tedious they are to be around.

It's not practical for this book to list every possible good and bad character trait or tell you how to overhaul your entire personality. All you can do is tune in to your strengths and weaknesses, and work to change or eliminate the traits that may be annoying to other people.

AVOID BEING LABELED AS "NICE" IN THE BAD SENSE OF THE WORD

Likable people are often genuinely nice. They're pleasant, friendly, and helpful. Of course, that kind of true niceness is a positive trait. However, some people get told they're "nice" or "too nice" in a tone that makes it clear it's not meant as a compliment. What do people mean when they call someone "nice" and don't mean something entirely positive by it? The word is used to describe several interaction issues:

"Nice" = "I don't dislike them as a person, but they're not for me"

"Why didn't I invite Colin to the party? Uh, he's nice and all, but he's not really my style…" When "nice" is used this way, it means, "I don't hate them as an individual. They seem pleasant and like they have good intentions. They're just not someone I'd choose to be friends with." If you've been labeled "nice" for this reason, there's not a solution. It just means someone doesn't think you're a match for them.

"Nice" = Bland

Someone may refer to a person as "nice" when they see them as being boring and not showing much of their personality. "Nice" serves as a description that's used when someone can't think of anything else to say and they don't want to be negative. If people see you as nice in the bland sense, you should work on being a little more outgoing and forward about what drives and interests you.

"Nice" = "Not enough of an edge for my tastes"

People generally like to hang out with friends who have a similar level of "edge" to theirs. Someone may label a person who's less edgy as "nice"—too naive, wholesome, or innocent for their tastes ("She's one of those nice girls. I don't think she'd want to go to the bar with us"). By this book's definition, someone has an edge if they're willing to do "bad" things. Or if they don't do those "bad" things, they at least seem like they're knowledgeable about and not totally frightened by them.

Most people aren't edgy to the point of being dangerous criminals, but many have some edge because they sometimes do common, mostly harmless "bad" stuff like

- swearing
- telling tasteless jokes
- skipping classes
- drinking or smoking underage
- dressing in a way that's offensive or provocative to some people (for example, having lots of tattoos and piercings)
- casually hooking up with people
- coming across like they're tough and willing to get into a fight
- flaunting authority in small ways, like purposely skateboarding in an area where they know they'll get kicked out of
- committing petty crimes like tagging a mailbox with a marker or shoplifting some lip gloss at age fifteen for a cheap thrill

To be clear, you don't have to do any of these things to fit in. There's nothing wrong with being innocent or a bit naive. Friendship circles sort themselves based on edginess levels. The edgier folks find each other, as do the less-edgy ones, and everyone's happy. It's a whole other problem if someone has too much of an edge.

In general, though, it's good if you can find a nice middle ground. Practically speaking, if you're unfamiliar with commonplace "edgy" things or see them as more sketchy and dangerous than they are, it can socially hinder you:

- Even if you're open to hanging out with run-of-the-mill, mildly edgy people, they may unfairly dismiss you as a potential friend because they see you as being too wholesome for them.

- You may not get invited to slightly edgy events, like parties that you'd have no problem going to, because everyone assumes you wouldn't be interested or able to handle them.
- You may simply have the wrong idea about certain behaviors (for example, you may see every last person who smokes as depraved and evil).
- You may become scared of things that are mostly harmless (for example, seeing dance clubs as risky places).

Social issues aside, if you're overly naive scummy, unscrupulous people may use your innocence to take advantage of you.

To shed that naivety, you don't need to do any edgy things if you don't want to. You just need to become more knowledgeable about them. You can even do this by doing some at-home research. For example, if you're in college and know nothing about what goes on at parties, you could read a few articles on the rules of common drinking games. Try to get a more nuanced picture of behaviors you may initially have seen as completely bad.

You can also try some edgier activities yourself. Don't do anything that's so edgy it's illegal or could otherwise get you in trouble. However, some things that you may see as edgy are actually pretty harmless. For example, if you've been really sheltered, you may see going to a bar as a foolish, rebellious act. There's no reason not to give something like that a try.

"Nice" = "Too much of a people-pleaser"

People-pleasers are often told they're "too nice." They engage in outwardly nice behaviors, but their actions are motivated by a fear of being disliked, along with poor boundaries and assertiveness skills. They're nice when other people wouldn't be, and they show non-assertive behaviors, like putting other people's needs ahead of theirs, being overly agreeable, hiding their true feelings behind a cheery mask, and having a hard time saying no and standing up for themselves. Assertiveness is a big enough topic that Chapter 23 is devoted to it.

"Nice" = "Being overly giving, thoughtful, and considerate to get people to spend time with you"

Some people believe that being much nicer than average is a valuable social commodity that will pay off in the form of friendships, romantic relationships, promotions, appreciation, and respect. They're often not fully conscious that they're operating on this principle. They may do lots of unasked-for favors and always be available to provide practical or emotional support.

People who are nice in this way are often disappointed, and they may eventually become bitter when their giving style doesn't translate into the relationships and admiration they hoped it would. The fact is, most people don't place a huge amount of value on above-and-beyond niceness. It's not that they disregard niceness completely. It's just that the majority of humans are pretty nice (outside of rough dog-eat-dog environments). Being fairly nice is a bare-minimum social expectation, and once someone meets that standard, additional niceness isn't given too much credit. When they're choosing whom to be friends with, people place more importance on factors like having similar interests and values, sharing the same sense of humor, and whether they have fun together. If a "nice" person does something for them, they'll enjoy it in the moment, but it's not going to sway their overall opinion on whether the person is desirable as a friend.

Not only that, but above-average niceness can be a liability. Extremely nice, giving people may be taken advantage of. They may be looked down on as insecure suck-ups who feel they have to buy people's friendship because they have nothing else to offer. They may be seen as lacking judgment and common sense for being so loose with their time, money, and emotional energy. Many people feel uncomfortable when someone gives them too many unsolicited gifts and favors because it makes them feel obligated.

If you're "nice" in this way, realize that your preferred strategy for getting what you want in relationships isn't very effective. You don't need to do a one-eighty and become a complete jerk. Be as nice as the next person, or maybe slightly nicer, but nothing more. Learn to draw people to you through other aspects of your personality.

22

BEING MORE FUN

FUN PEOPLE ARE simply enjoyable to be around. But fun has a time and a place. If you're at a party or in a joking mood, you generally want to be around fun people and having fun yourself. If you're going on a quiet, contemplative walk with a friend, that same fun behavior probably won't fit the situation.

There are two aspects to being more fun. There are the behaviors that make you more fun, and there are the traits to avoid that make you less fun. This chapter covers both aspects.

BEING MORE FUN

As with likability, the traits that make people fun are general, and you can fit them to your personality style. You can be fun in a more subdued manner. There's more to it than standing on a table with a beer funnel. However, though everyone can be fun in their own way, this section uses the meaning of "fun" that involves having wacky, entertaining, funny times with people. If someone were to say, "My idea of having fun is to take an afternoon to quietly contemplate my garden," then what's written here won't line up with their use of the word. If the outgoing type of fun isn't all that important to you, then you can skip this section.

Understand people can be in different social modes

Sometimes people are in the mood to have a low-key, cerebral, logical conversation about politics, parenting philosophies, or their fears and insecurities. At other times they want to goof around, make dumb jokes, party, and blow off steam. Neither social mode is better or worse than the other. They both have their uses and drawbacks. It's the same as when you're not always in the mood for a heavy, depressing drama every time you pick a movie.

Some people are in their element in serious, logical social situations, but they don't know how to handle it when they find themselves in a more silly, party-focused one. They may feel out of their element or get annoyed that everyone isn't acting more refined. If you think like that, accept that not every situation has to be solemn and intellectual, and work to embrace your own carefree, immature side.

Some general ways to be fun

- **Purposely set out to have a fun time.** Don't approach the evening with the mentality of "We're just going to hang around and do nothing."
- **Joke around and be amusing.** Tell funny stories, make witty observations, do entertaining stunts.
- **Introduce people to fun new activities and situations.** For example, "Hey, instead of sitting around, let's sign up to sing karaoke," or "Let's check out the new stand-up comedy club."
- **Help people have more fun than they normally do.** Without being pushy, help them move beyond their default level of reserve. For example, "Hey, let's go talk to those people... Nah, don't worry. They seem friendly. Let's go."
- **Be a little more spontaneous and daring than usual.** Or to use a cliché, say yes to more things than you normally would.
- **Take things a little further than you normally would.** For

example, push your jokes into slightly more outrageous territory, or take your friend up on that stupid bet when you typically wouldn't.

- **Have little tricks and talents that make you more fun.** For example, knowing how to play darts or knowing a bunch of jokes or card games can help you and others enjoy your time together.

Be less "un-fun"

The traits that make you less fun are more concrete and straightforward than the abstract principles in the previous list. (Again, this section is based around a particular definition of fun, and these traits aren't necessarily bad in other circumstances.)

- **Don't be the person who never wants to do anything new or much of anything at all.**
- **Don't be the person who wants to quit everything halfway through.**
- **Wherever you are, don't just hang back and do nothing.** Sometimes you can't help this if you're shy or not interested in the activity everyone is doing, but as much as possible try to stay in the mix.
- **Don't be too picky about what you require to be entertained.** Make the best of the situation, and don't be someone who can only enjoy themselves when they're out in the perfect venue with the perfect music selection, crowd, and drink prices. Don't always think it's boring where you currently are and the fun must be at the next location.
- **Don't wait for the amusement to come to you.** Make your own fun. Don't expect your friends to be responsible for your having a good time. Don't think things like, "I'll only have fun once the band plays better songs."
- **Don't be a downer by complaining too much about what you're doing or by bringing up depressing or heavy topics on a fun night out.**
- **Don't be overly stingy with your money.** There's nothing wrong with being frugal, but accept that some activities require you spend at least a little cash to have a good time (for example, don't go to an amusement park then refuse to buy any ride tickets, play any games, or get anything to eat).

- **Don't see having fun as immature or beneath you.** Everyone can have fun. It's not something only dumb, vacuous people do.

OVERCOMING TRAITS THAT PREVENT FUN

Being too uptight or serious and having fun don't mix. You can hardly relax, goof around, and have a good time if you're irritated by everything or everyone. Here are the characteristics of someone who is uptight:

- having rigid, unrealistic standards about how you and other people should act and how the social world should be (for example, everyone should always follow the rules and be morally upright at all times)
- caring too much about whether people are acting in ways you view as inconsiderate and thoughtless
- getting irritated by everyday social annoyances that most people let slide
- thinking you always have to be controlled and proper and well-behaved
- seeing yourself as a refined, considerate, intellectual adult and looking down on what you see as silly, immature behavior
- not being able to laugh at yourself

Here are some ways you can lighten up:

Accept you can't control everything

At the root of some people's uptightness is a need to be in control and have everyone act the way they want them to. You can become more relaxed if you can let go of this need and accept that people are going to behave in a way you may not like or expect.

Develop a more realistic idea of what to expect in social situations

Lots of slightly irritating, but common and unavoidable, behaviors and events are going to come up when you're socializing. Friends will be flaky. Venues will be noisy and overcrowded. People will act crass and immature. Minor rules and laws will be ignored (for example, people will litter and play their music too loud at parties). Most people know these types of things come with the territory and don't let themselves be too bothered by them. If you're more socially inexperienced, the same things can really irk you, because you have the false expectation that a situation should go a certain way, and then feel upset when people "ruin" it.

Try not to take yourself too seriously

It's okay to be a normal dopey human, and it's fine do things like watch dumb movies with your friends while gossiping and making lowbrow jokes. It's okay to have light, brainless fun. You won't lose your Intellectual card. No one will care. In fact, they'll probably appreciate that they can let loose around you without feeling judged.

23

ASSERTIVENESS SKILLS

ASSERTIVE COMMUNICATION is when you look out for or stand up for your rights and needs in a self-assured, direct manner, while being respectful toward the person you're talking to. Assertiveness skills are often talked about in terms of intimate relationships or the workplace, but they're also needed in lots of day-to-day social situations:

- turning down drinks and letting people know you're not drinking at all, or any more for the night
- declining invitations you're being pushed to say yes to because the event isn't your style or you simply don't feel like attending
- leaving a party early when your friends want you to stay
- having an opinion about where you'd like to eat or go out
- turning down inconvenient requests for things like car rides, course notes, or free tech support
- excusing yourself from a conversation with someone who's full of themselves and not letting you get a word in edgewise
- telling someone you disagree with them, whether it's to express a minor difference in taste in movies, or to challenge them on an offensive view they hold
- telling a friend it annoys you when they're late all the time
- sticking up for yourself when people take

"joking" insults and teasing too far
- generally being able to put yourself out there, like inviting someone to hang out or sharing your views with a group of people you've just met

Knowing how to be assertive has many benefits. Your self-respect will naturally be higher if you're willing and able to look out for yourself, and refuse to be put down or cajoled into doing things you'll regret later. Knowing how to be assertive provides you with a sense of self-confidence and control. It makes your life more rewarding because you're able to get your needs met, go after what you want, and steer clear of situations and activities that you don't find enjoyable. It's a trait other people admire. Finally, if you want to live a less conventional social life, you're going to need to get the hang of standing up for what you want and resisting pressure from other people. This chapter goes into detail about what it means, and doesn't mean, to act assertively, then gives some suggestions on how to become more assertive.

BREAKING DOWN THE DEFINITION OF ASSERTIVENESS

As this chapter's opening sentence said, assertive communication is when you look out for or stand up for your rights and needs in a self-assured, direct manner, while being respectful toward the person you're talking to. Here's that definition broken down further:

...look out for or stand up for your rights and needs... You, and everyone else, have implicit rights in interpersonal situations, such as
- the right to be treated respectfully
- the right not to be used and taken advantage of
- the right to say no and not be coerced into doing things you don't want to do
- the right to feel what you feel, even if some people think your emotions or reactions are wrong or irrational
- the right to do things like form opinions, make decisions, set goals for yourself and take action, and not have

to justify any of your choices to anyone else

- the right to not be perfect, that is, you can make mistakes, say the wrong thing, change your mind, or not know how to do something

Everyone also has various needs and preferences, ranging from what they require from a friend to what type of restaurant they'd like to go to that night.

...in a self-assured, direct manner... When you communicate assertively, you're open about what you want and how you're feeling. That doesn't mean you have to spill your entire soul every time. You could be assertive just by saying, "Hey, cut it out" in a tone of voice that shows you're serious, or by ending a conversation with "Well, it was nice meeting you..." with a firmness that says, "I'm done talking with you now."

...while also being respectful toward the person you're talking to. Assertive communication allows you to protect your rights but respects those of the people you're talking to. It's different from aggressive communication, where you look out for your own rights but trample over someone else's by insulting, threatening, or badgering them.

CONSIDERING THE FLIP SIDE OF ASSERTIVENESS: PASSIVE COMMUNICATION

The opposite of assertiveness is a passive communication style. That's when you don't look out for your needs and rights, and people sometimes unintentionally or purposely disregard them.

Facets of passive communication

- having trouble saying no
- not speaking up to share an opinion or preference when it would be appropriate
- going along with what other people want, even though you're not on board
- being quick to say, "Whatever you guys want is fine with me"

- committing to things you'd rather not do, and then trying to get out of them later
- not defending yourself when people disrespect you
- easily caving into pressure to change your mind when you do speak up about what you want
- adopting a false easygoing, go-with-the-flow, helpful persona to make it seem like you're happy to put other people's needs ahead of yours

If you're passive too often, and subsequently get walked all over, other people's disregard for your thoughts and needs will eat away at your self-esteem and self-respect. A vicious cycle can start where people see you being unassertive around others, so they figure it's okay to treat you poorly themselves (it's not right or your fault, but it can still happen). Being taken advantage of can cause resentment to build, which can result in passive-aggressive behaviors where you act hostile toward people in indirect ways (for example, subtly trying to undermine them or purposely being undependable). Some people aren't even aware of when they're feeling resentful and being passive-aggressive, and continue to see themselves as laid back and giving. Chronic passivity can also cause you to try to get your needs met through indirect or manipulative means (for example, rather than telling your friends you don't feel like seeing a movie, you agree, then try to plant the idea of doing something else instead).

HOW TO IMPROVE YOUR ASSERTIVENESS SKILLS

You can improve your assertiveness through a combination of changing your attitude and learning practical, effective assertive behaviors.

Believe that your needs, rights, and worldview matter

One big reason people aren't assertive is that deep down they don't believe their needs are important or worth standing up for. They don't have faith in their own values, opinions, and preferences, and they let other people override them (for instance, they don't like nightclubs, but have swallowed the idea they're weird and antisocial for feeling that way, and let their friends talk them into going). You need to develop a mentality that your needs and worldview are valid and worth protecting. Here are some suggestions:

- Just hearing that your needs and views matter might be enough for the idea to take hold. If you've unintentionally gone through life assuming you deserve to put yourself second, learning about a better alternative may make you think, "Wow, that makes sense. Why haven't I been doing that all along?"
- Work on your overall sense of self-worth (see Chapter 8).
- Make a list of your personal needs and rights.
- Practice putting your needs and values first. Do fun activities that are solely a treat for you and no one else. Shamelessly indulge in interests that other people may see as lame or pointless. If you're not used to doing this, you may feel guilty or self-centered at first, but with time it will feel more natural.

Question your beliefs and fears about what being assertive means

Reason No. 2 people have trouble being assertive is they have the wrong idea about what it involves. If you have any of the thoughts below, you need to replace them with more adaptive alternatives:

"Being assertive means being selfish."

Alternative: Being assertive means prioritizing and looking out for your needs in a healthy way. It doesn't mean you have to become totally self-absorbed; you just can't let other people's interests run roughshod over yours. Even when you want to help other people, you can't do that to the best of your abilities if you're not taking care of yourself first.

"Being assertive means being rude and bossy and forcing my will on others."

Alternative: Forcing your will on others is aggressive, not assertive. A lot of assertive messages can be delivered with a smile. You don't need to be cold and abrupt to do so.

"If I become more assertive, I'm going to have to constantly get into battles."

Alternative: Having assertiveness skills doesn't mean you have to use them all the time. If someone slights you in a minor, unintentional way, it's often easier to let it slide. Assertiveness isn't the only tactic for handling certain situations either. For example, sometimes it's easier to get someone off your back by changing the subject.

"I'll hurt people's feelings if I always have to be open and speak my mind."

Alternative: Assertiveness is about being straightforward, but it doesn't mean you should pointlessly share every potentially upsetting detail. If a coworker invites you to see their band, which you don't think is very good, a quick "No, thanks. I'm into different kinds of music" is all it takes to decline the invitation without hurting the person's feelings. If you suspect even that will offend them, it may be simpler to go with another approach, like making a polite excuse.

"People won't like me if I'm assertive."

Alternative: Someone who's trying to walk all over you may not appreciate it when you stand your ground, but overall, people will tend to like and respect you more when they see you have a backbone and healthy boundaries.

"People may react badly if I'm assertive."

Alternative: Sometimes they will, but that doesn't automatically mean you did anything wrong. If someone has a tantrum because you don't agree with everything they think or they can't impose their will on you, that's their problem. Sometimes to get what you want in life, you're going to make other people unhappy through no fault of your own.

"I'll be more likely to get what I want with a more people-pleasing approach."

Alternative: Some people-pleasers tell themselves this, but deep down most of them know their strategy doesn't work and often leaves them feeling used and unappreciated.

Practice being assertive until you get comfortable with it

Reason No. 3 people have difficulty being assertive is that it can simply be scary and uncomfortable at first. To get used to being more assertive, start by role-playing scenarios with a friend, support group, or counselor. In real life, you can begin with situations you can handle and then move on to tougher ones.

Know some techniques for asserting yourself

Knowing some basic assertiveness techniques allows you to deliver and stick to your message in a calm, self-assured way. If you get push-back, you can also avoid getting flustered and giving in, or getting angry and having your communication slide into more aggressive, confrontational territory.

Say what you want in a confident, straightforward style

Once you've gathered up the nerve to do it, being assertive is pretty simple: Plainly state what you want in a composed, self-possessed manner. You don't need to add a ton of explanations and justifications. For example, if you're at a party and your friends are bugging you to drink more than you'd like, you can say, "No, thanks. I'm not drinking any more." If you're out with a friend and they're paying more attention to their phone than to you, you can say something like, "Can you please save that for when we're not in the middle of a conversation?" Again, you don't have to be exaggeratedly firm and forceful. If someone is really stepping over a line, that may be appropriate, but you can often be assertive in a friendly, casual manner.

Use "I" statements

A standard piece of assertiveness advice is that if you're asking someone to stop doing something that bothers you, you should phrase your message so it keeps the focus on you and how you're feeling. That's better than attacking the other person, which violates their rights, puts them on the defensive, and makes it more likely a pointless argument will break out. For example, if your friend sometimes gets a little too cutting and personal when they tease you, a textbook "I" statement could be "When you bring up my personal flaws to tease me, it hurts my feelings and makes me feel insecure about myself. I'd like you to stop."

However, a lot of people feel "I" statements come off as forced and unnatural. You don't always have to use them. As long as you're still being respectful to the other person, it's fine to make your message fit the communication style you'd normally use with them. For example, if you're a 17-year-old guy asserting yourself to your immature buddy, you could say something like, "Dude, knock it off. You go too far sometimes when you poke fun at me."

Employ the broken-record technique

A lot of the work of being assertive comes from having to hold your ground if people push back after you've delivered your initial statement. They may argue, pester you, question your character, get angry, lay on the guilt trips, subtly imply they'll stop hanging out with you if you don't give in, or insist you have no choice but to go along with them. It can be tough to resist all the social tension this creates. The *broken-record technique* is to keep repeating the same assertive phrase over and over again until they give up. You're giving them nothing to work with, so an argument can't break out. The best feature of this technique is that you don't have to do any thinking under pressure. You just need to repeat yourself.

Here's an example set at a bar:

"Here, I bought you a shot. You need a drink."

"No, thanks. I already told you I'm not drinking any more tonight."

"Come on, don't be so boring."

"I said, 'no, thanks'. I'm not drinking any more tonight."

"I bought you this shot. You have to drink it. It'd be rude not to."

"Feel free to drink it yourself or give it to someone else, but I already told you I'm not drinking any more tonight."

"You're no fun. You're dragging down my mood."

"I'm sorry you feel that way, but I already told you I'm not drinking any more tonight."

"Ugh, fine. Forget it."

Agree, but don't give in

When you agree but don't give in, you say you agree with the other person's arguments, but keep on point. Here's the bar example again:

"Here, I bought you a shot. You need a drink."

"No, thanks. I already told you I'm not drinking any more tonight."

"Come on, dude. Don't be so boring."

"You're right. I am being totally boring, but I'm not drinking any more tonight."

"I bought you this shot. You have to drink it. It'd be rude not to."

"Yeah, I am being totally rude for not drinking the shot, but I'm still not going to do it."

This technique and the last one also work if you're asking something of someone else. State what you want, and then keep repeating it if they argue against you. It won't guarantee they'll give you what you're asking for because there's no way to perfectly control other people, but at least from your end, you won't let yourself get pulled off course.

Have a plan for the odd cases where the other person won't drop the subject

Being assertive and standing your ground doesn't mean you have to calmly let someone debate your decision forever. If someone keeps pushing an issue, you'll need another response. If they're really being disrespectful of your wishes, you may need to leave or let them know they're acting out of line. If you have friends who repeatedly step on your rights even after you've asked them not to, the best call may be to end the relationship.

STICKING TO YOUR ASSERTIVENESS GUNS

You may get some resistance from people when you first start acting more assertive. If your friends, family, partner, or coworkers are used to getting what they want from you, they may not like it when you start sticking up for yourself. They might make remarks about how you've become selfish or rude, or ratchet up their pressure tactics. It's not necessarily that they're evil and liked it better when you were soft and timid; it's just that people are sometimes thrown off by change and will unconsciously try to force you back into behaving the way they expect. Although there may be a rough transition period, you'll eventually earn respect when you establish you're going to have more solid boundaries. If you lose the odd exploitive or disrespectful friend, it's not exactly a loss.

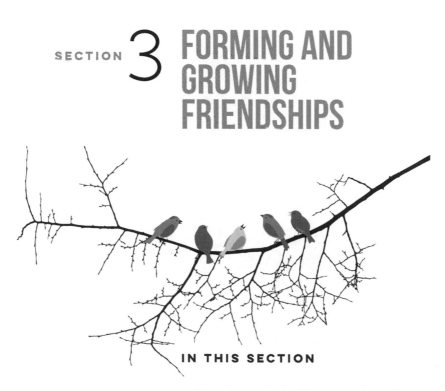

SECTION 3 # FORMING AND GROWING FRIENDSHIPS

IN THIS SECTION

- Details on the basic stages of meeting people and making friends
- How to make a group of friends
- How to make friends in specific situations
- Troubleshooting the process of making friends

24

INTRODUCTION
TO THE PROCESS OF
MAKING FRIENDS

HERE YOU ARE at the book's final section, which explains how to make friends, build a social life, and put any loneliness behind you. Even if you're the kind of person who's happy to spend time on your own, you'll still feel lonely if your lower need for social contact isn't met. Loneliness can really eat away at your happiness and sense of self-worth. It's demoralizing to unwillingly spend that fifth Friday night in a row by yourself. The good news is it's relatively straightforward to learn how to make friends, so much so that if you're lacking the knowledge of how to form friendships, you may see some results right away once you learn the skills and start applying them. If you're somewhat able to manage your shyness and carry on a conversation, then you should be able to use the ideas in this section to improve your social life.

When one source or another gives advice on "how to make friends," they approach it in one of two ways: The first is to focus on developing positive personality traits that would make you a more appealing friend (being a good listener, being loyal, etc.). The second is to explain the practical, actionable process of meeting people and forming relationships. This book's previous section on conversation skills covered the first approach, so this section focuses on the learnable, repeatable tactics. People who are good at making friends tend to unconsciously follow the concepts this section explicitly lays out.

THE BASIC STEPS TO MAKING FRIENDS

The basic steps for forming relationships are:
1. Find some potential friends (Chapter 25).
2. Invite and make plans with those potential friends to do something with you (Chapter 26).
3. Once you have some budding friendships, gradually take the relationships to a deeper level (Chapter 27).
4. Repeat the above steps until you've made as many friends as you'd like, whether it's a handful of close relationships or a giant group.

People who have trouble with their social lives usually stumble on one or more of these steps. This list seems simple, but each of the listed chapters goes into detail about it.

SOME THINGS TO KEEP IN MIND AS YOU TRY TO FORM A SOCIAL LIFE

As with tackling anything you're not yet good at, the process of making friends will be easier and more pleasant if you go into it with the right mentality and expectations. Know that...

Being lonely doesn't mean you're deeply flawed

Lonely people often see their sparse social lives as a sign of how broken and unlikable they are. Loneliness is usually just a symptom of a lifestyle and set of social habits that are not conducive to meeting people and forming relationships. Everyone has the potential to go through a lonely patch if they don't carry out the behaviors that will let them make friends. Someone who was well liked and socially connected in their hometown will be lonely in a new city if all they do is go to work and

THE SOCIAL SKILLS GUIDEBOOK

then head home to watch TV. Growing up, many people fell into their friendships without knowing how it happened, and they aren't sure how to deliberately create a new social circle from scratch when they're in a different environment.

Being lonely isn't automatically a sign that you have a horrible, off-putting personality either. There are plenty of annoying individuals who have big social circles because they're good and active at the specific skill of making friends. There are many pleasant, interesting people who are more isolated than they'd like to be because they're not as proficient at those same skills.

Trying to make friends doesn't make you lame, desperate, or needy

Many people want to make friends but worry that actively pursuing friendships means they're desperate or groveling. That's not true. It's more of that emotional reasoning: Because you *feel* desperate about something, you think it *is* desperate (see Chapter 5 for more about emotional reasoning). There's nothing pathetic about trying to make friends or taking an interest in others. It's an everyday activity that confident, sociable people do. Even if the rare person does see you as desperate, you have to take the attitude that it's all about you and you'll do what needs to be done to form the relationships you want. Who cares if a handful of people think you're a bit too eager along the way if it all eventually works out?

Don't handicap yourself by trying to hide your loneliness

Lonely people can get caught in a self-defeating cycle; they're ashamed of their loneliness and try to hide it, but that prevents them from doing the things that will let them make friends. They don't go to a meet-up because it might tip someone off that they want a better social life. They don't invite a classmate out for fear of revealing they don't already have plans. As their loneliness gets worse, so does their need to save face, and they get pushed further into isolation. In reality, no one can tell if you don't have any friends, and even if they know, they probably don't care that much. Everyone has times in their lives when they need to refresh their social circle—they're in a new city, they've grown apart from their old friends, or their previous group atrophied little by little as everyone moved away or got too busy with work and family.

If you want a social life, you have to make it happen for yourself

It's essential to take initiative. The quality of your social life depends on how much work you put into it. A key mistake lonely people make is they passively wait for others to do the work of befriending them, then conclude they're flawed when no one ever invites them out. Sometimes people will make the first move, but you can't count on it. If you want a group of friends, assume you'll have to put in all the effort.

Don't take it personally if people seem indifferent to you

This is related to the previous point. Lonely people often wonder what's wrong with them and why no one seems interested in hanging out. Usually it's nothing personal. Other people are often harmlessly thoughtless, preoccupied, and locked into their routines. They'd be happy if they hung out with you, but they wouldn't think to ask you themselves. Sometimes you have to take an interest in others and generally get the word out that you're open to new friendships before you appear on their radar.

There's always going to be some uncertainty in the process

When you're trying to form relationships with people, there are going to be times when you'll get unclear signals. For example:

- You've invited someone out twice, and they've had other plans both times. Are they truly busy, or are they just making excuses because they don't want to hang out?
- You texted someone, and they got back to you a few hours later with a one-word answer. Do they not want to hear from you, or is it just not their style to message back and forth with their friends all day?

▓ You always have to be the one to invite a new friend out. Are they hoping you'll eventually take the hint and leave them alone, or are they just used to you always getting in touch first because that's what you've been doing so far?

If you're prone to feeling insecure, it's easy to assume the worst. You can never fully know what someone else is thinking. All you can do is stay focused on your own goals and continue to take steps that move toward them. If you'd like to be friends with someone, invite them out a few times or contact them to chat. It's hard to draw conclusions from one or two incidents, but before long their behaviors will reveal whether they're going to help you meet your goals or whether you need to move on to other prospects.

Don't feel that making friends is super tricky

If you're inexperienced at making friends, you may see the process as being more drawn-out and complex than it really is. Often all you have to do to make a friend is meet someone you naturally get along with and spend time with them enough. You don't have to know them for months before applying the "friend" label either. One characteristic of more social people is that they'll throw the word "friend" around pretty loosely when describing their relationships, and it can become a self-fulfilling prophecy. If you've just met someone, it probably won't be a deep, intimate relationship, but you can still have a good time with them as you get to know them better.

Accept that it can take time

Under the right circumstances, you can build a new social life quickly, like if you've just moved to a new city to go to college or if you join the right club or team and instantly click with everyone there. At other times, it takes longer for your social life to fall into place. It may take a little searching before you meet some people you're compatible with, and then, if everyone is busy, it might be a few months before you're all hanging out regularly. Stick in there and don't give up on anything too quickly.

25

FINDING POTENTIAL FRIENDS

THE FIRST STEP IN MAKING FRIENDS is to look for some possible candidates. That's not a surprising place to start, but it's where some lonelier people get stuck. They don't put themselves around enough potential new friends. This chapter covers the two main ways to find prospects: drawing on your current contacts and meeting new people.

DRAW ON YOUR CURRENT CONTACTS

Drawing on your current contacts won't apply if you've just moved to a new area and don't know anyone, but often you'll already have the seeds of a social life around you. You don't necessarily have to go out and meet dozens of strangers. It's often easier to turn existing contacts into full-fledged friends than it is to scrounge up new ones. You might already know a handful of people who could end up becoming part of a new social circle:

- people from work or your classes who you get along with, but whom you've never hung out with;
- acquaintances you're friendly with when you run into each other, but who you never see otherwise;

- friends of people you know who you've clicked
  with when you met in the past;
- people who have shown an interest in being your friend
  in the past but you never took up the offer;
- people you very occasionally hang out with
  who you could see more often;
- friends you've fallen out of touch with;
- cousins who live nearby and are close to your age.

MEET SOME NEW PEOPLE

Getting more out of your current relationships can go a long way, but that isn't always an option. Fortunately there are countless possible places where you can meet new people. Before listing them, here are some points to keep in mind when starting the search for new friends:

- You'll likely have to force yourself out of your routine and make meeting new people a priority. Some lonely people fall into a rut where if they're not at work or school, they're comfortably settled in at home. If that describes you and you want to make friends, you have to shake things up and get out more. You may need to add some more social hobbies to your calendar or push yourself to get out and do things in the evenings when you'd normally be relaxing by yourself.
- You may have to try a few different spots for meeting people before one works. Finding new friends is often one of those situations where 20 percent of your efforts will get you 80 percent of the results. You may go to several meet-ups, classes, or events, and they're all busts, but then you easily meet a ton of fun people at the next one you go to. Don't get discouraged if you sign up for a club or two and don't see much potential in the other members. Definitely don't universally declare clubs "don't work" as a way to meet friends. Just try different ones.
- Realize lots of places where you can meet people aren't perfectly set up to facilitate connections, and sometimes you'll have to make the best of the so-so hand you've been dealt. Don't hamstring yourself by looking for the ideal set of circumstances. For example, you may sign

up for some art classes and feel there's not enough opportunity to get to know anyone because students are always coming and going and there aren't a lot of chances to talk during the lessons. You'll have to decide whether the situation is ultimately stacked against you and you should try elsewhere, or if you could make a few adjustments to make it work (for example, showing up earlier to give yourself more time to chat with your classmates).

Features of good places to meet people

Some places to meet new friends are better than others. The more of the following that apply to a place, the better:

- It allows you to meet people you have a lot in common with, naturally get along with, and are the types of possible friends you're looking for.
- It's somewhere where the situation breaks the ice for everyone and naturally gives them reasons to talk to each other.
- It allows you to be a long-time member or a regular and reliably see the same people several times so you can get to know them in a gradual, low-pressure way. It offers more than a five-minute chance to chat with people and then never see them again.
- It has a core of regulars, but new people continually enter the mix.

PLACES TO MEET PEOPLE

The following list offers suggestions of where to meet people, keeping in mind the features listed in the previous section. The easier places are roughly listed toward the top.

- through your current friends, significant other, and other people you already know
- your job
- school classes
- if you're religious, through your faith (for example, meeting people at your church, temple, or mosque; joining an association for Sikh students at your college)

- a club or organization
- a sports league
- a recreational / hobby class
- a volunteer position
- if you're a parent, through your kids (for example, meeting other parents at a playground; the parents of your child's friends)
- through your living situation (for example, hanging out with your roommates and meeting their buddies; inviting a neighbor over for dinner)
- your extended family (for example, hanging out with a cousin and meeting their friends)
- an individual sport where you can arrange to train with or compete against new people
- online, through sites like Meetup.com, or meeting up with members in a forum you frequent
- through a solitary hobby that you can make social (for example, forming a book discussion group)
- through having something to offer other people (for example, you're good at graphic design so you approach your student association and offer to do their event posters for them)
- a job where you get to be friendly with the public (for example, working in a gaming store)
- through any sport or hobby where people congregate at certain spots (for example, a skate park)
- bars or pubs (for example, showing up and playing some friendly games of pool with the other patrons)
- a part of town where people from your scene reliably hang out
- crowded places (for example, a small bar with music, comedy, or poetry readings, where someone may ask to sit at your table)
- various one-off events, like a multicultural food festival
- by chatting to strangers in public

How to find events and clubs to join in your community

If you're looking for places to meet people, an underappreciated skill is knowing how to find interesting events and clubs in your area. It's also useful when you're planning events with people and want to find something fresh to do. Most communities have more going on in them than you may realize. Even when you believe you've found everything there is to find, you'll continue to discover new activities and be surprised at how much you missed.

Change the range of your search area, depending on the size of your community. If you live in a gigantic city, you may want to limit yourself to just the downtown or your surrounding neighborhoods. If you live in a really small town, you should look within your several-town region. After you've established the area where you want to look for events, here are some ways to find out what's going on:

- search engines (for example, "[your city] event listings", "[your city] dance lessons", "[your city] softball league")
- event listings in newspapers, both mainstream and alternative weeklies
- event listings on classified ad sites
- event listings on community center or community agency websites
- event listing on your town's official website
- sites like Meetup.com
- websites and social media accounts of venues, like concert halls and artsy cafes, that hold events
- if you're in school, its listing of its clubs, teams, and organizations
- walking around your city and keeping an eye out for things to do (it's funny what new things you'll notice when you specifically look for them)
- flyers posted around the city
- bulletin boards in grocery stores, coffee shops, bookstores, and the like

- libraries (to find out about their own events and to check out any bulletin boards they have)
- a specific organization's website (for example, to find a listing of local Toastmasters groups in your area)
- travel guides for your own city
- people you know (sometimes you'll do all the searching in the world, and then a coworker will tell you about a festival you somehow missed)

APPROACHING AND GETTING TO KNOW PEOPLE

After you're in a place with some prospective friends around, you need to strike up conversations and try to get to know them (refer to the book's previous section for more advice on that area). Realistically, you won't hit it off with everyone you interact with, but if you're in an environment that contains enough of your type of people, you should get along with at least a few of them. Maybe you'll connect right away, or you may warm up to each other through smaller interactions spread over a few weeks. Either way, after you click with someone, you could say you're now friendly acquaintances or that they're context-specific "friends" (for example, work friends). The next step is to invite them out and make plans.

26

MAKING PLANS WITH
POTENTIAL FRIENDS

AFTER YOU'VE MET SOME PEOPLE you click with, the next step is to try to arrange to hang out with them outside of the situation where you met. This is an important step and another one where lonely people sometimes slip up. You can meet all the people you want, and they can think you're great, but if you don't make any moves to spend time with them, you won't form many lasting relationships. Your potential friends will stay as the girl you talk to in class, or the group you chat with at work on your lunch break, or the guy you joke around with at your rec league games. Even if you get to know them quite well in that environment, if you don't take the relationship to the outside world, it may vanish when the semester is over, they get a new job, or the season ends.

This chapter covers how to make plans with people so you can hang out with them and develop your relationship. It explains how to set up your own get-togethers—with individuals and groups—as well as how to get in on other people's activities. It also touches on some important habits and mentalities to keep in mind when it comes to making plans.

The ideas in this chapter are important for getting a new social life off the ground, but they are also really useful for maintaining or growing an existing one. When you're good at making plans, you can really take charge and create the kind of social life you want for yourself, instead of having to go along with whatever everyone else decides. Being able to coordinate plans is so powerful that even people who don't have particularly outstanding personalities can have busy social lives, just because they're constantly arranging one outing or another. Meanwhile, someone who is more fun or interesting, but lazy about setting up get-togethers, may not go out as much as they'd like.

TWO USEFUL HABITS

To up your odds that you'll be able to successfully make plans with people, get in the habit of doing two things.

Ask for people's contact information fairly soon after you've met them

You may meet someone interesting, but you often can't be sure you're going to see them again anytime soon. Ask for their phone number or email address, or see if they're on whatever social networking site people in your area and age group use. That way they'll be easy to reach if you want to try to get together. Also, if they have your info, they can get in touch with you if they want to chat or invite you somewhere.

Stay in the loop technology-wise

Events are often announced and planned through social networking sites, and sometimes only through them, so join whichever ones your peers are a part of. You don't necessarily have to enjoy or use them that much, but at least sign up for the social opportunities they facilitate.

KNOWING HOW QUICKLY YOU CAN EXTEND AN INVITATION

How long should you know someone for before inviting them out? There's no right answer. If you've quickly hit it off, it's fine to invite someone out right away. It's also okay to have an initial good feeling about them, but want to get to know them a little bit more before inviting them somewhere. You won't always have the option of taking it slow, though. If you've met someone you probably won't run into again, you can continue to get to know them better through texting or social media, but for the most part, you need to act on the lead before it goes cold. In these cases, you may have enjoyed initially talking to them, but be unsure how compatible you'd be if you spent a longer amount of time together. Again, there's no right answer about what to do. You could take a risk and ask them to do something, knowing the chemistry may not be there. Or you could extend an invitation only when you're fairly certain you'll have a good time.

STEPS TO ARRANGING YOUR OWN PLAN

There are only two steps to setting up a plan, though there are details to explain about each: 1) coming up with something to do, and 2) making the invitation.

Trying to set up one-on-one vs. group plans

For the most part, the process of setting up plans with people is the same whether you're inviting one person or a larger group. The main difference is that group plans usually take more work to coordinate because you have to find something that works for everyone. That will be covered later in the chapter.

Deciding whether to have a solid plan in mind or make a vague invitation and work out the details after

Either approach can work, though it's better to come up with a plan yourself and then see if everyone is interested. Friends take the loose, "We should do something this weekend" route all the time and still manage to see each other, but that method has more potential to peter out: You ask, they say, "Yeah, that sounds good…" and then no one takes it further.

If you come to people with a solid suggestion, they have something to react to. They'll do one of a couple of things: accept it, express interest but want to change some of the details, suggest an alternative, or turn it down. Even starting with one or two details is better than nothing. For example, "Want to see a movie next week?" is preferable to, "Want to hang out sometime?" The specific film, location, time, and day are still up in the air, but at least they can decide whether seeing a show seems like a good idea.

STEP 1: COME UP WITH SOMETHING TO DO

One early planning roadblock some people hit is they have someone in mind they want to hang out with, but they're not sure what to invite them to do. It's also not uncommon for socially inexperienced people to say they don't even know what people their age typically do when they spend time together.

Spending time with other people is always at the heart of hanging out with them

Don't think that spending time with someone is all about coming up with the perfect event to attend. Especially don't think that there's no point in being with them if you can't come up with something spectacular to do. When you choose to hang out with someone, the central reason you're there is to enjoy their company. Of course, it makes your time together more fun and memorable if you see a band or go on a hike or whatnot, but that's not strictly necessary.

Inviting people to get together is often more about doing variations on a few reliable activities than coming up with something incredibly original each time. If you really like your friend's company, then you can easily hang around their house several times a week or go to the same rotation of cafes or pubs with the just the occasional more exciting event thrown in to mix things up.

Examples of activities friends commonly do together

Hang out somewhere, mainly to talk
- chill at someone's house
- grab coffee
- eat at a restaurant
- get a drink at a pub
- hang around downtown
- sit around at a park

Wander around, also to talk
- go shopping
- go for a walk
- keep them company while they run errands

See a show
- see a movie
- see live music
- see a live comedy show
- see a play

Play something together
- play video games (possibly online and not even in the same room together)
- play cards
- play a board game
- play a pen-and-paper RPG
- play darts or pool
- go bowling
- play golf
- throw a ball or frisbee around

Do something sports-related
- watch a game at home or at a pub
- play a team sport together

- do an individual sport side by side (for example, rock climbing, skiing)
- compete against each other in an individual sport (for example, tennis)
- train or practice for a sport
- go to a game

Work on something together
- work on something artsy or crafty, like rehearsing with a band or knitting
- prepare a meal together
- work on a repair or building project

Get out in nature
- go for a hike or mountain bike ride
- go fishing
- go canoeing
- go boating

Party together
- go to a bar or dance club
- go to a house party
- hang around someone's place and have drinks

Try other one-off activities
- visit a local attraction like an art gallery, zoo, or aquarium
- go to a yearly festival or carnival
- check out a trade show or convention
- take a day trip out of the city
- go camping
- go on vacation together

How to narrow down what to ask them to do

What you ask someone to do will depend on what you figure they'd be interested in and, when you're first getting to know them, what you feel comfortable with. It may seem natural to invite a potential friend over to your place to watch a movie the first time you hang out. That may not feel as appropriate with someone else. As a general rule, if you think you'll be fine making conversation with someone, then invite them to do whatever you think will be fun. If you're worried the discussion may not flow that well, a more activity-focused outing is better. You won't be forced to chat with each other the entire time, and the activity will give you something to talk about. If you're not sure how well you'll click with them, a group outing is lower stakes. You're not stuck with them one on one if it turns out you don't have much chemistry. Also consider how convenient the plan will be for them, as well as their financial situation. For example, if you know they're broke and don't have a car, don't invite them to meet you at a pricey restaurant that they'll have to take the bus for an hour to get to.

STEP 2: MAKE THE INVITATION

After you've come up with something to do, you have to ask everyone if they're interested in doing it.

Methods of inviting people out

Whether someone accepts your invitation will depend on whether they want to spend time with you, whether the proposed activity interests them, and whether they're available. It doesn't matter if you asked in person, through a text, or over the phone. Go with whatever method is most convenient for you. However, group invitations are easier to organize through a single email that everyone can chime in on.

The tone of the invitation

However you invite people out, ask in a non-pressuring tone that suggests, "It'd be fun if you came, but if not, that's cool."

Examples of inviting a single person to do something

There are many ways you can phrase the invitation: specific; open-ended; open-ended but somewhat specific; and immediate / spontaneous. Here are examples of each:

Specific invitation

- "What are you up to this Thursday? Do you want to get something to eat after our evening class?"
- "I'm going to go see (band) when they come to town on the 17th. Tickets aren't that pricey. Want to come with me?"

Open-ended invitation

- "Do you want to grab a drink some time?"
- "We should go snowboarding sometime this season."

Open-ended, but a little more specific

- "Do you feel like getting coffee one day after class?"
- "Want to go hiking one Saturday fairly soon?"

If the person says yes to a more open-ended invitation, work out the details soon after. One mistake is to get a yes and then leave the other person hanging by not following through and arranging the rest of the plan.

Immediate / spontaneous

- At the end of the workday or as class is getting out: "What are you doing right now? Feel like grabbing a coffee?"

- To a dorm-mate you ran into in the hall: "Hey, I'm heading to the mall to get some stuff for my room if you want to join me."

It can feel a little less nerve-racking to invite someone out spontaneously. You know they may not be free right then, so it doesn't sting as much if they say no.

Examples of inviting a group to hang out

The group of people you're inviting out could know each other well already, and you're trying to join their clique. Or everyone could be fairly new to each other, and you're trying to turn them into a new social circle. Inviting a group out is similar to asking a single person to do something.

Some people find trying to organize a group event less scary, because if it doesn't work out, the rejection is more diffused. It feels like the suggestion itself fizzled, rather than one person specifically declining to spend time with you. Everyone wasn't just turning you down either; they were also saying they didn't want to spend time with the whole group (you can even phrase invitations as "We're doing X. Want to come?"). Alternatively, some people find extending an invitation to a group more stressful, because if their suggestion goes nowhere, they feel like a whole bunch of people are passing judgment on them.

Specific invitation

- "Do you guys want to hang out at my place this Friday? We could go out later if we feel like it."
- "Does everyone want to go to '80s Night at (nightclub) this Thursday?"
- "There's a fair coming to town this weekend. Who's up for it? I was thinking Saturday afternoon."

Open-ended invitation

- "Do you guys want to get together sometime soon?"
- "We should all hang out outside of work."

Open-ended, but a little more specific

- "What does everyone think of getting coffee after line dancing lessons one day?"
- "Maybe we could check out that new Korean restaurant before we all get busy with exams."

Immediate / spontaneous

- "Anyone feel like coming back to my place now? We could play some video games or watch a movie."
- "Do you guys want to go downtown after class gets out?"

What's different with group invitations is what happens after everyone starts considering the plan. When you invite one person out, they either say yes or no. If they say yes, then you only need to figure out the specifics with them. When you invite a group, more work goes into getting the plan fleshed out. Some people may say yes, some might say no. The plan may go through a few different permutations before everyone agrees on it.

Inviting one or more people to do something with your existing friends

When groups are involved, you can invite a potential new friend to do something with your current group of friends.
- "My friends and I are going out on Saturday. Want to join us if you're free?"
- "My buddies and I get together every Tuesday evening to play poker. You should come out one week."

If you don't have much of an existing social circle, you can't do this. However, if you have this option, it's probably the lowest-stakes way to extend an invitation. You're not inviting someone from a position of neediness. You're offering a social opportunity. If they say no, you can still hang out with your other friends.

What if you invite someone out and they turn you down?

If someone turns you down, you may get confused because you may not know where you stand with them. Most people find it uncomfortable to directly tell someone they're not keen on hanging out. They also don't want to make future interactions awkward by directly rejecting you. Instead, they'll make excuses, "forget" to reply to your written invitation, or vaguely agree that maybe the two of you could do something some time, but never follow up. Of course, these things could also just mean they're genuinely busy.

How many times should you ask someone to hang out before giving up?

Three times, maybe four if the invitations are spread out. You can ask a second time fairly soon, and if they say no again, give them some space before trying once or twice more. If you haven't gotten together after that, they're either politely brushing you off, or they've shown they're too busy to have new friends. On occasion, someone will genuinely want to be friends with you, but their life is hectic and they have to turn down your invitations for legitimate reasons. However, after three rejected invites with no effort on their part to arrange something, it's likely they just aren't interested, and it's better to put your energy elsewhere.

The exception to this guideline is when you're extending low-effort group activity invitations to someone you're on good terms with and who comes to your get-togethers, but only occasionally because they have hectic lives. In that case, it's fine to tell them, "We're all hanging out at Tina's this Friday" for several weeks in a row without them attending because you know they will show up every now and then.

Try to set up recurring plans

Usually once you've hung out with a person or group, you have to go through another round of making plans if you want to see them again. That's hardly a terrible amount of work, but it can make you feel like your social life is uncertain from week to week. You could try to set up a recurring plan, like watching a movie at someone's place every Wednesday night or going out for dinner once a month. Often everyone is too busy to establish an ongoing arrangement, but it's great when you can set up these reliable social activities for yourself. These arrangements take work to maintain, so don't take them for granted. Occasionally people will get distracted with other aspects of their lives, and it can take some effort to get everyone together each time, so be flexible about cancelling or rescheduling as needed. These plans also work better when a larger group is in on them, so that even if only half the members can make it each time, enough people still show up for them to be fun.

WAYS TO HANG OUT WITH PEOPLE, ASIDE FROM SETTING UP A PLAN YOURSELF

This chapter just went into how to set up your own plans, and it's the most important skill because you have direct control over it, but you can find other ways to hang out with people without doing much work yourself:

Be invited to hang out

It's great when other people ask you to spend time with them, though you should never count on it and always be prepared to take the initiative to make your own plans. But when it comes to hearing about plans made by other people…

Do your best to accept every invitation

If you're trying to get your social life off the ground and someone invites you to do something, do your best to go. Why turn down a chance to get out there? After you have more friends and invitations competing for your time, you can be choosier. If you're more of an anxious or solitary person, it's easy to overthink an invitation and come up with reasons why it won't be fun. Try to work past those worries and go anyway. You can never be sure how enjoyable something will be until you show up and see for yourself.

Sometimes you'll have to inconvenience yourself for the sake of your social life. You may get invited to a movie you're not particularly excited to see or be asked at the last minute to a party on a cold, rainy Friday night when you were planning to go to bed early. Again, being in a social setting outweighs these minor annoyances.

Most people will stop inviting you out if you decline too often. They may have nothing against you, but the next time they're planning an event, they'll think, "They've never come when I've asked before, so no point in letting them know this time." If you're interested in an invitation but can't attend for legitimate reasons, make it clear to the inviter you want to hang out with them and would if you could. The best way to show that is to extend an invitation of your own fairly soon after.

Figure out what other people's plans are and then hop on board

Many people consistently have things to do with their friends because they regularly ask around to see what everyone is up to. They don't try to initiate their own plan every single week. If they want to go out on the weekend, they'll start pinging their social circle around Thursday and ask what their plans are for Friday night and the weekend. If they hear something they like, they'll get on board. If no one has solid plans yet, but some people are interested in doing something, the "asking around" conversation provides a starting point for figuring out what they could do together (for example, "We could have a barbecue at the park like Morgan was talking about the other day"). Also, asking around is a good way to take initiative, show you're interested in spending time with people, and generally stay on a group's radar.

Inviting yourself to social events

A tricky aspect of getting on board with other people's plans is inviting yourself to a get-together when you're not sure if you'd be welcome. The key thing to know is that on occasion it is okay to invite yourself. Sometimes you won't get an invitation, but if you ask if you can come along, everyone will be fine with it. In the end, you'll have to use your judgment about whether you should try for an invite, but here are some broad guidelines:

- When you ask if you can come, always speak in a casual, non-pressuring way (for example, "You're going to a party tomorrow? Seems fun. Is that something I could show up to? No worries if you guys are trying to keep it small").
- Generally, don't invite yourself to events like dinner parties or cottage weekends where the host is putting in a lot of work and has limited space or resources. An extra person may inconvenience them.
- "The more, the merrier" drop-in-type plans like parties or pub nights are safer bets. Some get-togethers also have an unspoken open invitation, like a group of coworkers who go for drinks after work every Thursday.
- Consider the other people who are going. Are they are a loose, cheerful group of friends who are open to hanging out with anyone? Are they a pair of closed-off couples who want to spend quality time together?
- If you know who the organizer is, consider their personality. Are they a stickler for rules and etiquette, and protective of their social circle, or are they easygoing and eager to have new people around?

There's always a risk of coming off as rude, presumptuous, or needy when you try to invite yourself to an event. However, sometimes the risk is worth it. If you really, really want to attend a get-together, you may not mind if you're not entirely slick about how you get there.

Hear about someone else's plan, and then help build on it

This is similar to setting up a plan yourself, but some of the steps have already been taken care of for you. For example, someone in your gardening club suggests you all see a movie next weekend, and everyone expresses interest in the moment, but no one follows up. If you pick it up from there, it should be relatively easy to finish putting together the outing.

MENTALITIES TO KEEP IN MIND ABOUT MAKING PLANS

Now you know the basics of how to arrange to hang out with people. Here's yet another list of mentalities that will make the process go more smoothly for you.

Accept that making plans can take work at times

It's fairly easy and satisfying to get a text or call out of the blue asking if you want to go to dinner with six friends on a particular date at a particular time at a particular location. It's a lot harder to set up that get-together yourself. Making your own plans can be hard because you have to:

- Deal with any fear of rejection about inviting people out.
- Figure out what to do.
- Research the plan (for example, looking up restaurant menus or movie times, calling around to see what bars are showing a match on TV, staying on top of what attractions are coming to town).
- Ask everyone to attend.
- Adjust the plan so it works for everybody. This is often the lengthiest step. Sometimes no agreement is reached, and you have to try again later.
- Spend time persuading people to attend or not bail at the last second ("Ah, come on, you've studied for the exam all day. It's fine to come out and blow off some steam for a few hours").
- Set up things necessary for the plan to happen (for example, making reservations, buying food and drinks for a party, booking a camping site).

If coordinating plans seems like a big hassle, realize it also feels that way for everyone else. Other people shouldn't always have to step up and organize things for you. Do some of the lifting yourself when you need to.

After people have accepted your plan, be open to it changing

If you're arranging something with a bigger group and everyone's agreed to your plan, but they are still working out the details with each other, it's not yours any more. Don't get too hung up on it going in one particular direction. Be flexible and be prepared for the date, location, time, or even every last detail to change, possibly multiple times. Also, expect aspects of it to change up until the very last minute (they may even change on the cab ride there). Obviously there are times when you have to be more rigid than others, like if your favorite band is coming to town for one date this year. But if you just want to get together with some friends, what does it matter if you do it on Friday instead of Saturday? Or head out at seven instead of six?

Also keep in mind that until you're actually there with everyone, the plan could fall through at any time. It may never get off the ground because everyone's schedules conflict. Or it could be canceled at the last minute because two of the four people attending can't make it after all. These things come with the territory, and it does no good to be too tightly wound about them.

Be tolerant of some mild flakiness

It's annoying, but people can be flaky. They won't respond to your texts or email invites. They'll agree to come to your party and then bail at the last minute. They'll show up late. You'll drive yourself nuts, seem insecure, and run out of friends if you get overly annoyed every time these types of things happen. If a friend is consistently unreliable or they do something more serious like stand you up on a one-on-one outing, then you should say something or stop inviting them out. However, if you're planning a bigger get-together, it's usually a given that not everyone who says they'll show up will actually be there. Make the best of it with the people who do attend.

For larger activities, don't get too hung up on certain people attending

Once a certain number of people are involved, getting the event off the ground takes precedence over every last person being able to make it or guaranteeing certain people show up (unless it's for something like their own birthday party, of course). People have stuff going on in their lives, and it's not realistic to think every last person will be free on a certain date. If you try to set up the plan so everyone can show up, it will probably keep getting put off for a perfect time until it's eventually forgotten about.

27

DEEPENING
NEW FRIENDSHIPS

NOT EVERY FRIENDSHIP you have has to be really close. People are often happy to have some friends who are lighter activity or partying buddies. However, we usually need at least one of our friendships to be more deep and intimate. This chapter lays out the factors that lead to friendships becoming closer. The concepts described below often happen automatically as a friendship progresses, but you can take some control of your relationships by deliberately trying to use these points. They mainly apply to individual friends, but some of them also carry over to becoming tighter with a group. Some things to know going in:

**There's no formula to becoming better
friends with everybody you meet**

Not everyone you meet is going to want to hang out with you. And even if you get along on a surface level, not everyone you hang out with is going to become a closer friend. We're just not compatible with most people in terms of availability, interests, values, and what we're looking for in a friendship. Although you can try to apply the ideas below to your new friends, realize they're not all going to go the distance and become your soul mates. That's okay though, because people are often enjoyable to be around on a more casual basis.

On the same note, just because you may be able to successfully apply one or more of the ideas below to someone, that won't guarantee the friendship is going to go anywhere. For example, you may have a really intimate conversation with them, but overall they'll continue to think of you as someone they run into every now and then. If you're making an effort to become better friends with someone and you get the sense you're putting more energy into it than they are, consider backing off and adjusting your expectations.

Sometimes you'll become good friends with someone pretty quickly; at other times it takes a while

Many people have had the experience of meeting someone new and immediately starting to hang out with them nearly every day. Just as many have friendships where the bond grew more gradually. Neither progression is better than the other. Friendships can get off the ground quickly in the following situations:

- when you just click with a person unusually well;
- when you're both at a place in your lives where you're looking for new friends (for example, during the first weeks of college);
- when you're both available and easily accessible to each other (for example, you live in the same building and have lots of free time to hang out);
- when you fulfill an unmet need in each other's lives (for example, you absolutely love reading and discussing books, but none of your other friends care much about them);
- when you're in a situation where the usual standards for friendship progression don't apply, like when you meet people while traveling and feel like friends for life after knowing them for only five days.

Friendships can grow more slowly

- when one or both of you are pretty busy with your day-to-day lives and/or already have many friends who fill up your calendar;
- when you get along well enough, but there isn't that instant spark of

intense compatibility;

- when you're not actively trying to deepen your friendship with them. For example, they're on the periphery of your social circle, and you get to know them better here and there.

It's natural to feel a bit awkward and insecure as a new friendship begins

There are times when you'll hit it off with someone right away and never feel uncomfortable around them. There are also those times where your friendships will develop in a low-stakes, almost accidental way. However, sometimes the process is more nerve-racking, like if you meet someone at a one-off event and then actively try to start a friendship with them. Here it's understandable that things will feel uncertain because you're not sure how much they like you or if you'll continue to get along and have things to say to each other. It usually takes a month or so before you start to feel more relaxed and secure about the relationship.

WAYS TO DEVELOP A NEW FRIENDSHIP

Every friendship is different, and not every point will apply to every type equally. Some friendships are more about sharing and connecting, while others are based around hobbies, joking around, and going out at night.

Spend more time together

Simply spending more time with someone is the backbone of becoming better friends with them. A close relationship isn't something that happens in a few hours. You need space for all the relationship-enhancing things covered below to happen. Time is an important enough factor that we often become good friends with the people we naturally have a lot of contact with, like coworkers, friends of friends, classmates, and team members. With time, friendships can even develop between people who were initially indifferent to each other.

Make an effort to hang out with them regularly

The main way to spend enough time with someone is to hang out with them fairly often. Sometimes you'll be in a situation where you'll automatically put in those hours. If not, you should try to use the ideas in the previous chapter to organize get-togethers so you can continue seeing them. With some people, you'll quickly fall into a routine of hanging out all the time. With others, you may only be able to get together every three weeks for a quick bite to eat.

This step needs to be ongoing. It's not about coordinating a one-time hangout. It's about putting in the effort to keep seeing them continuously over a period of months. You might have trouble here because:

- You're a bit too busy or lazy, and don't put in the work to see your new friends regularly.
- You're shy and reluctant to invite someone to hang out because you fear rejection or an awkward moment. This most often comes up during the first few invites, but may subtly affect your actions later if you believe your friend is "above" you.
- You're insecure and prone to thinking you're not worth hanging around and your new friends must not really like you.
- You don't have the highest need to socialize, and it causes you to not initiate get-togethers as often as needed to keep your new friendships going.

Spend one-on-one time talking with them

People can get to know each other and bond in a group setting, but often the real opportunities to connect come when it's just you and one other person. Also, if you haven't hung out with someone on your own, how close is your friendship really? Many people have known someone through group outings, but have seen a different side of them when they started hanging out as a pair. They'll point to that as when their friendship really started to develop. You could get that one-on-one time by arranging to do something with them separately. You could also find moments to break off with them from the larger group. For example, the two of you may be able to retreat to the backyard to talk at a party.

Keep up with them in between hanging out

One thing that distinguishes closer friends from more casual ones is how much they stay in contact between times when they hang out in person. Good friends often keep in touch. More casual buddies think along the lines of, "I'll be happy to see them when we run into each other in person, but I don't need to keep up with them otherwise." Especially if you're not hanging out with your new friends all the time, keep up with them in between get-togethers. Send them a text making a joke or asking how their week was, email them a link they may like, or call them on the phone to catch up.

Take their response rate and their own efforts to reach out to you as a gauge of how often you should be in touch with them. Some people are happy to text back and forth all day. Others are more of a weekly contact type. Of course, after you've established a certain level of friendship, you can often get away with going weeks at a time without talking, then picking up where you left off. However, you'll only maintain the relationship this way, not actively grow it. The problems listed as hindrances to hanging out with a friend regularly—laziness, shyness, insecurity, fear of rejection—can also crop up when it comes to keeping in touch (for example, you start composing a text and then think, "Ah, I'm probably bugging her. She doesn't want to hear from me").

If you do go a few months without talking to someone you know well, it's usually not a huge deal to get back in touch and catch up. There's nothing odd about dropping someone a line after being out of contact for a while. It's another one of those emotional reasoning moments where if you feel awkward about doing it, you believe it's an inappropriate thing to do. Never feel you have to throw a relationship away because you went too long without speaking and now it would be weird to get in touch. When you contact them, just say you've been busy lately and ask what they've been up to. If they don't want to reconnect, you can handle it. It's not like you were regularly spending time with them anyway.

Have a good time together when you hang out

What a "good time" entails depends on what you're looking for. It could be an intellectual conversation over coffee, an afternoon working on a car together, or a night out at the bars. You can help grow a relationship by going out of your way to do things you know your new friend will enjoy. As the last chapter mentioned, you don't have to do something incredibly novel each time. On the other hand, don't fall into a rut where all you ever do is sit around and be bored.

Learn more about each other and expand the range of topics you talk about

When you're not particularly close to someone, you only know their standard biographical info, and your conversations often stay on a handful of topics, like your shared workplace and a sport you both follow. We feel closer to people when we know more details about them and can discuss any number of subjects.

Open up to each other

Not every friendship has to include tons of intimate sharing, but in general, people see their relationships as deeper and more rewarding when they can talk to each other about weighty or personal topics that they don't feel comfortable bringing up with just anyone. It also feels good to know you've shown someone pieces of your "real self" and they accept you for it, or to connect when you realize you both share the same hidden quirk or past experience. You should consciously try to steer your conversations with your new friend to deeper territory if they aren't heading that way on their own over time. If your friend is the first to head in a more intimate direction, don't shy away. Check out Chapter 12 to refresh your memory on self-disclosure.

Be a good friend in all the usual ways

Being a good friend is a broad concept that's hard to sum up in a few paragraphs. A friendship will grow closer if each person comes to see the other as someone they can count on and who makes them feel good about themselves. That means showing the standard traits of a good friend and a likable person, including

- generally showing that you like the other person and want to hang out with them;
- being positive and fun to be around;
- being dependable;
- being emotionally supportive;
- being willing to go out of your way for them;
- not gossiping or complaining about them behind their back;
- not blabbing to everyone about things they told you in confidence;
- not using them or taking them for granted;
- not freaking out at them over little things or taking out your frustrations on them;
- showing good character on the whole. You can act awesome around them, but if they hear that you're a scumbag otherwise, they may not want anything to do with you.

No one's perfect, and no one expects their buddies to be, either. Everyone's also different regarding traits they think are important and the flaws they're willing to overlook. One person may primarily look for friends who are entertaining to go out with and not care if they're unreliable. Another may see flakiness as a deal breaker and put a premium on someone who will be honest with them and keep their secrets.

Have some adventures or crazy times together

Having a shared history increases the sense that you have a strong relationship with someone. Even better is a history with some truly memorable experiences. It gives you that ability to say, "Ha ha, remember the time when we...?" Lots of people have memories of seeing someone, or a group, as casual friends until they took that one legendary camping trip together and started to think of each other as a tightly knit unit. An adventure is some sort of excursion or experience that's fun and out of the ordinary. It doesn't have to be a ridiculous drunken night if that's not your style.

Be there for them during their difficult times

People can bond when one of them helps the other. They can also grow closer when they support each other through a shared challenge, whether it's being in a demanding graduate program, working under an annoying boss, or living together as broke aspiring entrepreneurs. They can look back over the relationship and think, "We're pretty close. We've gotten each other through some rough patches." It's harder to see someone as just a casual friend when you've seen their vulnerable side, had them lean on you, and empathized with their struggles.

As always, this isn't a guarantee you'll become closer, and you could even come to feel used and unappreciated. But if the friendship is going in a good direction, helping each other can strengthen it further. Although larger, emotionally heavy life events lead to stronger bonds, helping a new friend could be as simple as offering to give them a ride to the mechanic to pick up their car or letting them vent over something inconsiderate their mom said.

28

MAKING A
GROUP OF FRIENDS

MAYBE YOU HAVE NO PROBLEM making individual friends who you can do things with one-on-one, but you also want a group of buddies to hang out with. This chapter covers how to do that. It goes over the three main ways to make a group of friends: 1) merging your individual friends into a group; 2) making one friend and then falling in with their social circle; and 3) making a new group of friends all at once. The second and third methods involve joining an existing group, so the second half of the chapter gives some pointers on how to do that.

Once more, keep in mind the social world is unpredictable, and over the short term, you'll only have so much power to create the exact type of friend circle you want. Even if you set out to become part of a group, it may not happen right away. Here are more details on the three ways to make a group of friends:

MERGE YOUR INDIVIDUAL FRIENDS INTO A GROUP

If you have several individual friends, how can you get them to start hanging out with each other? First, you'll need to arrange some way for them to meet. You could try introducing them to each other one or two at a time, perhaps by seeing a movie or going out to eat together, or you could organize a bigger get-together and have them all meet at once. However, there's no foolproof way to ensure your individual friends will like each other. Everyone hangs out with a variety of people, and they're not always compatible with each other, even though they all share the commonality of getting along with you. You just have to put them together and see if it works out.

One basic tip is to mention things they have in common to break the ice between your friends to get them talking ("Bob, David used to work at the same nonprofit you did"). If you're introducing one friend to a small group, don't leave them to fend for themselves. To allow for the best chance of your friends clicking, try to hang out with everyone on several occasions. People often don't have enough time to really learn much about each other during one meeting. Spending time with each other over multiple outings also gets everyone thinking along the lines of, "We're a group that often hangs out together."

MAKE ONE FRIEND, MEET THEIR BUDDIES, AND TRY TO FALL IN WITH THAT GROUP

If you've made an individual friend or two already, you can try to meet their friends and see if you can join that social circle. If you hang out with someone enough, these opportunities will likely come up naturally. If not, you can take the initiative to meet your friend's friends. If you catch wind that they do any kind of group activity regularly, you can ask to come along. You could also try to meet them by planning some sort of party or larger get-together. Here it's also a good play to try to meet your friend's friends more than once so they have more time to get to know you and get adjusted to the idea of having you around.

MAKE A GROUP OF NEW FRIENDS ALL AT ONCE

There are two ways you can do this. The first is when you join a pre-existing social circle at a class, job, or club. For example, you start volunteering at an animal shelter and quickly fall in with a group of fellow volunteers you see often. The second is when outside circumstances force you and several other people, who don't know each other either, to spend a lot of time together (for example, you all moved into the same floor of a dorm, or you've all started a job at the same time).

When you're in these situations, try to organize a get-together that brings everyone together outside of the context where you've all met. If you want to make a group of friends in a work, school, or club setting, it's also important to be friendly with many of the people and existing groups there. You can hardly create a larger circle at your job if you only talk to two coworkers.

MORE ADVICE ON HOW TO JOIN AN EXISTING GROUP OF FRIENDS

When people talk of wanting to join groups, they usually mean one of two things:
- They've identified a group they think they want to join, haven't talked to any of the members much, if at all, and don't know how to approach them.
- They interact with the group at least somewhat regularly, but still feel like an occasional guest; they'd prefer to be a full-fledged member.

Just like you can't form a group of friends to order, there's no way to guarantee you can join any specific group. This subsection covers how to join groups that you have some things in common with and who are open to having you, not how to sneak into that one super-snobby clique. Some groups are just going to be difficult to join because the members have known each other a while and are reluctant to include new members. Whatever the group you're trying to get in with, try not to put them on a pedestal. They're just a social circle, not gods with the power to determine your happiness. If you don't become closer with them, it may be disappointing, but there are always other prospects.

Depending on your particular situation and the group you want to join, you may not need to use every one of the following steps:

Step 1: Make initial contact

This step may be taken care of automatically if you've been introduced by a friend or your circumstances. If not, your options for making the initial contact depend on the access you have to the group. Here are the two main possibilities:

Approach 1: Introduce yourself to everyone at once

For example:
- You work at a big company. In the cafeteria you notice a group of coworkers from another department who seem right up your alley. One day you ask if you can sit with them.
- There's a gaming store on your campus, and every time you've walked by, you've seen a bunch of regulars hanging out and playing a game you're into. You walk in one day, introduce yourself, and explain how you're a fan of the game too and looking for a group to play with.

It takes a certain amount of guts to go up to a group of people and insert yourself into their conversation. You may worry it will come off as lame or overeager. If you've seen them around for a while without approaching them, you may also think they'll see you as strange for only coming over now. But if you're their type and you come off as reasonably likable and confident, it can all go quite smoothly. If it makes you too nervous, you can always try the next option.

Approach 2: Get to know a few members, then meet the rest of the group through them

Again, these are situations where you have to go out of your way to make contact with the group. A few examples:
- You've noticed a group you want to join in one of your university classes. In a second class, it's just you and one of the members. You get to know her in that class, and after the two of you are on friendly terms, you start sitting with the whole group in the other course.

■ You play in a rec softball league and have noticed one of the other teams is made up of a group of friends whom you seem to have a lot in common with. A few weeks later at a league-wide end-of-season party, you start talking to one of them and seem to get along. You ask them to introduce you to their teammates, which they happily do.

However you first make contact with a group, if you're a good fit, this step may be the only point of struggle. After you've broken the ice, the rest will easily fall into place.

Step 2: Find a way to hang out with the group consistently and become closer with everyone

Assuming you didn't effortlessly become accepted as soon as you met everybody, the work will then be in moving from "The group now knows I exist and seems okay with me" to "I spend time with them regularly, and they consider me a friend."

Don't get discouraged if things don't go perfectly the first time

The first time you spend time with a group usually doesn't make or break you. People may form a rough idea of what you're like after talking to you once, but they don't decide then and there if they want to be friends. They usually have to hang out with someone a few times before they know how the relationship is going to develop. Occasionally, your first meeting with everyone isn't super encouraging. Your interactions may have been a little strained or inhibited, or you may have felt stuck on the sidelines despite your best efforts to stay in the mix. It can be tempting to throw in the towel, but give it a few more chances. Sometimes people get off to an iffy start and then realize they're more compatible than they first assumed.

Figure out how to get in on the group's get-togethers

Sometimes people successfully make initial contact with a group and become friendly with the members in a light, casual way. However, they're not getting in on the fun group activities that are one of the reasons they want to join the group in the first place. For example, they may be able to chat with a group of people in one of their classes, but not see them on the weekends when they all hang out. If you're in this situation, there are a few things you can try:

- As with making friends in general, you may just need to get on the group's radar as someone they could hang out with outside of the situation where you all met. After you let them know you enjoy the same activities they do, they may get the picture and start keeping you in the loop (for example, "You all go out and try new restaurants every week? I'm into trying new places too, and I'd be down to join. I can even suggest some good spots").
- You could ask about more specific future plans and then politely ask if you can take part.
- You could try arranging a get-together yourself (see Chapter 26). Even if everyone can't make it, your invitation sends the message that you're interested in hanging out with them. For this suggestion, you have to use your judgment about whether planning something for the group would be appropriate. Some groups are fine with newer members trying to make plans. Others are more established and set in their ways and will tune out ideas from anyone they don't know well enough.

If you got into the group through one or two people, get connected to the other members

Another problem people have when joining a group is they'll start hanging out with a group regularly, but even if everyone is nice to them, it's still like they're perpetual guests of the friend or friends who initially introduced them. Aside from spending more time with the group, here are some ways to move beyond that situation:

- When you're all hanging out, take time to break away from your original friend(s) and get to know the other members. Make it clear you want to get to know everyone better and not just accompany your buddy to the odd get-together.
- Get the other group members' contact info. Aside from allowing you to get in touch with them and sending another signal that you want

to get to know the whole group, it also frees you from having to rely on your original connection as your sole means of hearing about the group's plans.

You don't have to become equally close to everyone or have them all like you to the same degree. Although you want to get away from being seen as the guest of one or two members, you don't have to become best friends with every last person in the group. As long as a group on the whole wants you around, it's okay if your connection with a few members is a little undeveloped. In most social circles, even though everyone gets along, some members are closer than others. If the group is big enough, there will be subgroups within the larger one. When you're new to a group, try to be on fairly good terms with everyone, but also look for the handful of members you get along with best. As long as one of the subgroups takes you in, you'll be seen as part of the bigger crowd.

Step 3: Put in your time with the group and deepen your relationship with everyone

After you're hanging out with the group consistently, becoming more enmeshed in it is mostly a matter of time. If you put in enough hours with them, they'll naturally start to think of you as a member. You'll get to know everyone better, even if it's only a group that gets together to party, rather than have lots of intimate discussions. You'll share some memorable experiences. You'll become familiar with their private jokes and get in on the ground floor for new ones that develop. Mostly this will all happen automatically, but you can speed the process along by consciously adapting and applying the ideas in the previous chapter on growing relationships.

Understand that you may not feel like a full-fledged member for a while

Sometimes when you join a group, you'll feel like a full-on member right away. Alternatively, you might feel like a hanger-on for a few months. That doesn't necessarily mean the group doesn't like you; if some members have known each other for years and years, they'll be more drawn toward each other and might unintentionally leave you out. Once you're hanging out with the group on a regular basis, you're in. Don't discount that and convince yourself you're still an outsider. Just keep showing up and doing what you're doing; over time you'll get to know everyone better and become more of a core member.

Accept that becoming part of a group doesn't always work out

Exposure and familiarity generally increase bonds between people, but it's not guaranteed. Sometimes you'll join a group, feel on thin ice the whole time, and then eventually leave when you realize you'll never be fully included. You need to be willing to go through this uncertain, risky period. Any feelings of being a second-tier member may only be temporary. If you really feel yourself struggling, it may be a sign the group isn't a good match for you.

29

MAKING FRIENDS IN PARTICULAR SITUATIONS

UP TO THIS POINT, this section has covered a general structure for how to make friends. Here are some additional suggestions for two situations that people commonly have trouble with: making friends in college, and making friends as an adult, after university, or when you're in a new city.

MAKING FRIENDS IN COLLEGE

The college environment is one of the easiest places to make friends. You're surrounded by thousands of peers, most of whom are open to meeting people. Of course, that statement can seem like a slap in the face if you're at university and struggling with your social life. Students have two main problems with making friends in college:

- They fell into their friendships in high school and don't know how to deliberately make new ones.
- They feel like everyone effortlessly made friends during the first few weeks of school, but they didn't, and they don't know how to form a social circle after missing that window.

Making friends during day-to-day college life is mostly a matter of following the concepts laid out in the previous chapters. Meet people in your classes, at your dorm, through clubs and student associations, and at any part-time jobs you may have. Take the initiative to invite possible friends out, then try to continue to see them so the relationship can develop. Of course, if you have problems with shyness or making conversation, you need to put some time into tackling those issues too.

Suggestions for making friends during your first few weeks of college

When you begin university, you aren't the only person who doesn't know anyone. Most of the other students have left their friends and family behind too, and need to make new friends. Here's how to more easily meet and get to know them:

- Realize pretty much everyone feels a little nervous, unsure of themselves, and overwhelmed when starting college. Most people are just putting on a brave face because they mistakenly assume everyone else has their act together.
- Get to know some people before the school year starts. If you go to an information session in the months leading up to the first semester, get people's contact info and keep in touch with them. If your major has a group on a social network, reach out to some of your soon-to-be classmates through it. If you're in town a few days before school starts, arrange to meet up with anyone who's also around.
- If it's feasible, try to get familiar with the campus and surrounding area ahead of time. You'll feel more comfortable once school starts, and you'll be able to start a few conversations by offering to help other students find their way around.
- If it's a realistic option for you and you really want to get some practice with the university experience, go backpacking in another country beforehand and stay in hostels. The hostel life is similar to living in a dorm, both practically and socially.
- Go to as many Orientation Week events as you can. You'll meet a lot of people, especially ones from your faculty. The rowdy, party-centric atmosphere of the first week isn't for everyone, but there should be

some non–drinking-related events. If you're not into partying, you won't be the only one, and you can seek out other students who are on the same page.

- If you live in a residence hall, get to know the people on your floor. Go door to door and introduce yourself, or hang around the lounge and talk to whoever comes in. Drop in to visit your neighbors on the floors above and below you too.
- If you live at home or off-campus, hang around school as much as you can. You can't meet new people if you're always holed up in your own place.
- Chat to whoever you want to. The first few weeks are a social free-for-all, and no one is going to look sideways at someone who's being outgoing and trying to meet people.
- Realize it's okay to tag along with groups of people or to go to Orientation Week events alone. The group you're going with probably just met a few days ago, so it's not like you're intruding on their clique. If you head to an event alone, you can start conversations with whomever you want because the whole point of them is for people to mingle.
- One or two of your fellow students may be vague acquaintances from your high school. If you weren't that close to them back then, chances are it's not going to be any different now. You have many other prospects, and it's better to put your energy into pursuing them instead.

Don't give up if you haven't found a group of friends after the first few weeks

After the first few weeks of school have passed, you may think that everyone's social circles are solidified, so it will be harder to make friends. Yes, the atmosphere where everyone is open to making friends with everyone else dies down after the first month. However, that doesn't mean that every new social circle is completely locked. Groups are usually open to new members who are likable and who bring something to the table.

More important, the social circles that people fall into during the first few weeks of university sometimes don't last that long. They can form because everyone is antsy get into some sort of group and will link up with the first batch of people they meet. In the months that follow, these circles can drift apart as everyone realizes they aren't that well matched.

MAKING FRIENDS AS AN ADULT, AFTER UNIVERSITY, OR WHEN YOU'VE MOVED TO A NEW CITY FOR A REASON OTHER THAN TO GO TO COLLEGE

These circumstances are lumped together because they're similar and the advice for dealing with them is the same. In each case, it's no longer as easy to meet people as it was in school. You're no longer surrounded by classmates who have lots of time to devote to socializing. As people get older, they become busier with their careers, families, and homes, and they have less time to spend hanging out with their current friends or meeting new ones. They also have higher standards and a clearer idea of what they're looking for in a new friend. This isn't to say it's impossible to make friends when you're new in town or when you're in your forties. You just need to work harder at it, and you shouldn't get too discouraged if everything doesn't slide into place after a few weeks.

Get what you can from your job or existing contacts

If you're lucky enough to have a job that's a source of potential friends, take advantage of that as much as possible. Do you have coworkers you get along with, but whom you don't hang out with outside of work? Maybe they'd be up for doing something one weekend. Just because you're out of school, new to town, or older doesn't necessarily mean you have no existing social connections. Even if you've moved somewhere far away, you may have a past acquaintance or relative in the area. Maybe you could meet that old buddy for lunch and be introduced to their friends soon after.

Pursue your hobbies as a way to meet people

When you're in university, you can meet lots of friends through your classes, living arrangements, and part-time jobs. If you meet anyone through a hobby, it's almost a bonus. After college is over, your interests become a lot more central to your social life. People who have a lot of social hobbies have an easier time making friends. If they're settling down in a new city, it's natural for them to join a bunch of teams, get involved with a theater group, or start volunteering somewhere. Before long, they have a social circle. It's harder for people who have more solitary interests like reading, watching movies, or going for long hikes by themselves.

Consider getting some more social hobbies if you don't already have any. You don't need to totally overhaul your personality or all of your pastimes, but tweak how you spend your time so you can meet as many friends as you'd like. Do more activities outside of the house. Find a way to use your existing hobbies to put you in contact with more people. For example, if you normally exercise at home, join a class or running club. If you like reading about new ideas, attend some free talks or seminars, or join a book discussion club. If you like stand-up comedy, see if there are any Internet meet-ups where fans can arrange to go to shows together.

Be more active about seizing opportunities with potential friends

When you're in college, you can afford to be a bit lazy about making friends. If you meet someone you get along with in one of your classes but don't pursue the relationship as hard as you could have, it's not the end of the world. You'll probably see them again in the next eight weeks. And if it doesn't work out with them, there are tons of other prospects. When you're no longer in college, the opportunities don't pop up as often. You have to be a little more on top of things when it comes to following up with people you hit it off with.

Sure, at your job or at the start of a league's season, you can drag your feet, but there will often be times when you'll meet a possible friend only once or twice, and if you don't jump on the chance, you'll lose it. A lot of hobby-related venues like dance classes or rock-climbing gyms have people who only drop in a handful of times and then move on. When you meet a person you could imagine yourself being friends with and there's a chance you may not cross paths with them again, be more active about getting their contact information. Then follow up on the lead fairly quickly.

Expand the range of people you could possibly be friends with

When you're still in high school and college, you mostly form friendships with people around your age and from a similar background. As you move through adulthood, the range of people you meet and could hang out with increases. Don't be too quick to dismiss someone who's older or younger because they don't fit what you imagined your social circle would look like. Just because someone's age is a decade up or down from yours doesn't automatically mean you have nothing in common, or that they're silly and immature, or stodgy and out of touch. Don't assume someone with a different background is from a totally different world and could never be into the same things you are. Look at everyone on a case-by-case basis.

30

TROUBLESHOOTING
THE PROCESS
OF MAKING FRIENDS

Aside from being unsure of how to handle specific situations like being new in a city and not knowing anyone, other mental and practical issues can hinder people from making friends: having various worries about trying to make friends; experiencing life circumstances, like a lack of money, that interfere with your social life; getting poor reactions to your friendly overtures; and feeling iffy about many of the potential friends you meet. This chapter gives suggestions for handling all of them.

COMMON WORRIES PEOPLE HAVE
ABOUT MAKING FRIENDS

Chapter 24 covered two common concerns that arise when trying to make new friends: feeling desperate when pursuing friendships and believing you have to hide your loneliness. Here are some other ones. As with any insecurities, being aware of and challenging the counterproductive thoughts beneath them can help, but in the end, it may take several positive firsthand experiences to finally get rid of them.

"I don't feel desperate, but I'm worried about coming across as desperate and putting people off."

Alternative: No one will see you as desperate if you do typical friendly things like starting conversations with people you don't know, trying to chat with acquaintances, inviting someone out, or texting friends to catch up. You have to act blatantly desperate to be seen that way. Desperate acts can include inviting people out after they've already turned you down seven times; texting someone way more frequently than they text you; or telling them how much their friendship means to you after knowing them only a few days.

"It feels weird to ask around to see what people's weekend plans are."

Alternative: Asking around about others' weekend plans is completely normal behavior. If you're already close friends with someone, you have an unspoken okay to ask them what they're up to or try to join a group outing they're planning to attend. It's two equals sharing information and figuring out something to do together. (Once more, it's emotional reasoning to believe that because you *feel* desperate about doing something that it *is* desperate. See Chapter 5 for more details about emotional reasoning.)

"If I ask around to see what people's plans are, I'll reveal I have nothing going on."

Alternative: There's nothing weird or rare about not having plans for later in the week. Being open about not having plans is something people do all the time, and they aren't embarrassed about it. Their thought process is, "Oh, it's Friday, and I didn't think to organize anything yet. I'd better see what my friends are up to."

"Asking around to see what your social circle's plans are is fine if they're your friends. But I want to hang out with some people I don't know that well. It'd be inappropriate to ask them what they're up to."

Alternative: That may seem inappropriate, but you have two perfectly acceptable options: 1) Take a calculated social risk and ask these acquaintances what their plans are, even though it might not work out perfectly. Be sure to ask in a casual, low-pressure way; 2) Play it safe and get to know them a little better first, and then take a stab at making plans.

"Asking someone to hang out makes me feel like I'm 'one down'."

Alternative: If you invite someone out, it doesn't automatically mean you're lower on the social totem pole; it just means you have something fun in mind that you want to do and are trying to round up some people to do it with. More popular people try to organize plans too. They don't sit back and wait for everyone to come to them.

"I'm really not sure if I know the other person well enough to invite them to hang out."

Alternative: Use your judgment. If you think you may not have spoken to someone enough for the invitation to be justified, maybe get to know them a little more first. On the other hand, you can sometimes become friends with people faster than you think you can, and inviting them out can be one way to do that. Also, think about whether you truly don't know them that well. That worry may just be your nervousness talking.

"What if people say no when I invite them out? That means they hate me, right? I don't think I could handle it."

Alternative: If you invite people out, you will get turned down some of the time. If you're arranging a larger activity, it's almost a given that some people won't be able to come. It's often not personal. People may turn down a plan because

- they're not up for the activity you suggested;
- they just don't feel like going out and want to have a quiet night in;
- they've already made plans with other people, but would have been up for it otherwise;
- they have other non-social things they have to do;

- the logistics of the event are inconvenient (for example, they'd have to take the bus for an hour to get there);
- money is tight, and they can't afford to attend;
- they don't know anyone else who's going and aren't in the mood to try to get to know a bunch of new people;
- they like your company, but not in that situation (for example, they like talking to you one-on-one over coffee but not going to bars with you);
- they have their own insecurities (for example, they're older than you and your friends and worry about seeming lame by tagging along with a younger crowd).

Even if they turn you down because they don't think the two of you are compatible, everyone experiences that kind of rejection, and it's something you can learn to manage.

"What if I arrange something and only a few people show up? I'll look bad, and the event will be awkward with so few guests."

Alternative: There's no law that says all of your events have to be big or get a huge turnout. Getting a lot of people to come out is often as much about offering an enticing activity and being lucky enough to have everyone's schedules line up as it is about how popular you are. You'll often have an idea of what the attendance will be ahead of time, so you can always postpone if no one bites when you first suggest the plan. If you don't initially frame the event as big, it doesn't look weird if not many people show up. If the event does end up being smaller, it can still be fun, just in a different way than a giant get-together. You can always improvise too; for example, "This party is pretty quiet. Let's just go out instead."

"What if I arrange something and no one shows up? I definitely couldn't handle that."

Alternative: It's rare to be left waiting for people who will never arrive. More commonly you'll get a bunch of last-minute cancellations. Many people have had the odd plan fizzle out like this. It doesn't mean you're a failure for all time, just that you should try again, and maybe change up your approach by suggesting something that's more convenient or appealing to your invited guests. Most big plans end up with one or two flake-outs, and everyone cancelling at once may just be an unfortunate coincidence. However, if it seems like part of a larger pattern of your friends not respecting your time, you'll need to talk to them.

"What if things are awkward once the event is under way?"

Alternative: Being worried about uncomfortable moments is mostly run-of-the-mill anticipatory anxiety, and everything will likely go fine, especially if you've previously had good interactions with everyone. If things are awkward, it doesn't mean you're forever hopeless; you may not be meant to be friends with those particular people, or you may need some more practice with your conversation skills.

"I feel like I'm always the one arranging things with my friends. They never invite me out. They must not like me."

Alternative: It's hard to read any one person or group's mind, but sometimes friends never show initiative because they're a bit lazy and disorganized about making plans; they're really busy; they would suggest something, but you always ask first; or they've come to expect you to be the organizer.

"I feel discouraged. I tried to get some people to go out to a bar, but hardly anyone came. Then Maria proposed the exact same thing a few weeks later, and twenty people fell all over themselves to be there."

Alternative: Worry about your own social life, and don't tie yourself in knots comparing your plan-making success to other people's. Some people will be more popular than you. It is what it is. What's important is that you have a social circle that makes you happy, even if you have to work at it a little more at the moment. Don't fall into black-and-white thinking where you believe if you're not the absolute best, you must be completely worthless.

"MY LIFE CIRCUMSTANCES ARE INTERFERING WITH MY SOCIAL LIFE"

Many life situations, like living in a dull, isolated village, can get in the way of your making friends. These unhelpful circumstances undeniably make things harder. However, you probably can do at least a little better than you are now, and you shouldn't be too quick to throw in the towel or turn your circumstances into an excuse. Overall, when faced with one of these barriers, you have three long-term choices:

1. You can try to adapt to your situation and get more out of it.
2. You can wait for things to shift in your favor.
3. You can escape entirely.

If you're not an adult yet, your freedom and choices are limited, and you have to bide your time until more options open up to you. Even if you're stuck in a less-than-ideal situation, you can still use your time to lay the groundwork for the future (for example, saving money for a car, or honing your social skills for university while you're stuck at home during high school). Here are some suggestions for particular situations:

Living in a small, boring town

- Make a real effort to find everything going on in your community, as well as getting to know the locals whom you have the most in common with.
- If possible, get a car and see what's available in neighboring towns or cities.
- If you really feel bored and constrained and like there's no one worth knowing where you live, the only real option is to move. That may not be a possibility now, but it could be down the road if you save up enough money to leave or arrange to attend university or take a job in a far-off city.

Living far away from everyone

- If you've decided that your far-flung location is social kryptonite, try having people over. They may not be as reluctant to visit as you think.
- Hang out at the homes of friends who do live nearby. They may understand you live far away and not care that they can't go to your place. Don't feel you must have people over to your home in order to have a life.
- Hang out with people in spots other than someone's house. The older you get, the more possibilities open up to do things outside of going over to a buddy's place after school.
- Be around people in organized settings such as lessons, clubs, or team sports.
- Try making some friends with the people in your area. Your social circle doesn't have to include only people from your school. Check out what's going on in your part of town.
- Once you're of legal drinking age, living far from all the bars and clubs can mess up a night because you may need to cut it short to catch the bus or train home. You can figure out ways around this: Consider arranging to stay at a mate's place, taking a cab home, or trying to get your buddies to come to a more local bar and then crash on your couch.

Living at home

- Unless there's something obvious getting in the way, like your parents have forbidden you from having guests over, there's no reason to assume you can't invite people to your place.
- If hanging out at home isn't an option, spend time with friends in any number of other spots.
- If you're in your mid-twenties or older, don't assume that living at home automatically carries a stigma. Living with your parents is normal in many cultures, and even in ones where grown children are expected to move out, there's an increasing understanding that not everyone can afford to do so right away.

Living in a run-down apartment or neighborhood you're embarrassed about

▨ Again, if doing things at your own place isn't feasible, hang out with people elsewhere.

▨ Don't be too quick to assume this is a mark against you. Most adults understand that not everyone can afford luxury accommodations and may have to live in a cheaper area to save money.

▨ Do whatever is realistically possible to spruce up your home.

Not having a car or not being able to drive in an area where you need a vehicle to get around

▨ Don't feel you must have a car to have friends. If you're an otherwise solid person, no one's going to judge you because you can't pick them up or drive somewhere.

▨ Get rides with other people (be sure to pitch in for gas on longer trips), take public transit when you can, or take cabs. Arrange to meet people at your destination instead of picking them up.

▨ In the long term, prioritize learning to drive and getting your hands on a vehicle.

Not having a lot of money for hanging out with friends

▨ Realize many people, especially when they're young, don't have a ton of spare cash but still manage to have a decent social life.

▨ Hang out at friends' places as much as you can, rather than going out all the time.

▨ Do free activities like going for a hike or attending a street festival.

▨ Do inexpensive activities like seeing a movie, having coffee, or visiting a local attraction on a day of the week when admission is lower.

▨ Eat at cheaper restaurants.

▨ If you're into drinking, drink at home before going out, rather than paying inflated bar prices (of course, don't put your health at risk and drink too much too quickly just to save a few bucks).

- Go to bars with cheap or no cover. Some venues don't charge a cover if you get there early enough. Learn which bars in your city have cheap drink specials on various nights of the week.
- If it's feasible, get a part-time job. You don't even need to work that many hours a week if you're only doing it for a bit of spending money.

Being underage so you can't get into bars, especially when your friends are old enough

- Look for all-ages events and venues.
- Try to go to more house parties with your friends instead of going to bars.
- Just wait to turn the legal age. Everyone is too young at one point.

Being really busy

- Purposely make time for your social life rather than thinking of it as something you may get to if everything else is out of the way.
- Learn to work or study more efficiently so you can free up some time to go out.
- Spend your social time efficiently: See your friends in shorter, higher-quality bursts; catch up with several people at once; or organize get-togethers that fit between things you already had to do.
- If your hectic schedule is leaving you too tired to socialize, recover your energy with well-timed naps or hits of caffeine.

"PEOPLE JUST DON'T SEEM INTERESTED IN BEING FRIENDS WITH ME, AND I'M NOT SURE WHAT I'M DOING WRONG"

Chapter 9 covered the issue of others not reacting well when you try to speak with them. This trouble area is similar, but the impasse comes a bit later. People respond well enough that you can talk to them for a while, maybe even on a regular basis, but they don't seem interested in becoming closer friends. They may not take you up on your invitations, or they may not invite you out themselves. They may chat with you if they run into you somewhere, but the relationship never goes beyond that. Here are some possibilities that may help you suss out where you're going wrong:

Try making friends in a better way

- Talk to people first, instead of expecting them to come to you.
- Go beyond greeting people and exchanging some quick pleasantries; don't expect them to take over from there.
- Have longer conversations with people and invite them out, instead of expecting them to invite you out.
- Don't think you just have to perform certain social "moves," like taking an interest in people, and then everyone will instantly want to be friends with you.
- Accept people's invitations. If people have invited you out a few times, but you never accepted, they've likely given up on you.
- Get better at making plans. Instead of, say, inviting people out at the last second to events that aren't really their style, consider their interests and ask them to do something a few days in advance.
- Keep trying. Don't be too quick to give up after the first setback ("She said she was too busy to get together on Friday. She must hate me. No point in trying again").

The other people aren't interested in being friends with you

Something many lonely people need to do is to take more initiative to actively build a social circle for themselves. That advice only goes so far, though. Just because you put effort into trying to be friends with people doesn't mean it's always going to work out. Here are a few reasons your friendship prospects may not be keen on being buddies:

- You're not the ideal type of friend for the type of people you usually approach. Some people mainly try to befriend stereotypically popular or high-status types, even though they have little in common with them.

- You're making an interaction mistake of some sort that doesn't put people off immediately, but makes them unsure about getting to know you better.
- You don't seem to enjoy the same activities your potential friends enjoy.
- Someone hung out with you a few times, but eventually decided the two of you aren't compatible.
- The people you're pursuing are your coworkers or classmates, and they aren't interested in being friends with anyone they meet at work or school. They just want to put in their time and leave.

Again, the best way to get to the bottom of the issue is to get in-person feedback on how you're coming across.

"I DON'T HAVE TROUBLE MEETING PEOPLE, BUT I DON'T LIKE THEM"

Some lonely people are overly picky. It's fine to screen out jerks or anyone you have nothing in common with. Choosiness is a problem, though, if you're meeting people whom you get along with pretty well, but you're always left with a feeling of, "Meh, I don't know. I think I could do better." Studies have shown that lonely people tend to be more negative about others in general. Although people with this problem may be somewhat choosy to begin with, the trait is mainly a side effect of loneliness. Being lonely in the longer term naturally makes people unhappy, which can sour the way they view their interactions. It also makes them pessimistic and self-protective. They unconsciously think, "This isn't going to work out, so I won't let it get off the ground to begin with." They reject people before they can be rejected.

If you're really lonely, your initial goal should be to get some sort of social life going. As long as your potential friends aren't a total mismatch, consciously try to override your pickiness and hang out with anyone whom you get along with and who seems interested in spending time with you. Become friends with them first, and then decide if you want to continue the relationship. If you're too choosy, you can come up with reasons not to befriend just about anyone ahead of time. But if you push through your pickiness and start hanging out with someone, you'll often find you like their company, even if they didn't seem ideal on paper.

The first people you meet may not be your ideal friends, but the benefits of having a social life outweigh that. At the very least, it's easier to make more friends when you already have a few. You'll feel more confident about your social situation and be able to meet more people through your existing friends. Also, if you're forming your first-ever group of friends, you probably don't completely know what you like or want in that kind of relationship. You have to see firsthand what different types of people are like in a friend capacity. When your social life and friend-making skills are more established, then you can raise your standards.

Be especially cautious about rejecting people you really click with who don't fit the stereotypical image of a popular person. If you're insecure, you may reject them because you're overly concerned with how your friendship comes across to other people. You may also feel put off because you see traits in them, like being shy or having esoteric hobbies, that you're uncomfortable with in yourself. These relationships can teach you that spending time with a person you really get along with is more important and fulfilling than having a social circle that outsiders approve of. If your new friend is comfortable with the acceptable-but-sometimes-misunderstood traits you share, their attitude may rub off on you. If they have some negative facets to their personality, which you also have and feel insecure about, you may become more at peace with these traits when you can see they're just one part of your otherwise solid new friend.

"I FIND IT HARD TO MAKE FRIENDS BECAUSE I DON'T RELATE TO THE MENTALITY AND INTERESTS OF MOST PEOPLE"

Although not every less socially successful person feels alienated because they don't have the same interests as other people, it's not an incredibly rare issue either. In general, they typically feel most people are more shallow and superficial than they are. They have a distaste for seemingly popular interests like sports, celebrity gossip, trashy TV, fashion, drinking, and nightclubs, and see them as a sign of how much distance there is between them and the average vapid person. This sense of disconnect has consequences:

- It is harder to form relationships when you don't relate to the things many people are into. Some interactions won't go well to begin with. A promising conversation may stall when you reply that you don't follow sports. You may be unfairly judged for not drinking. If you meet someone you click with, a wedge may appear when it becomes clear their first-choice activity every weekend is to go clubbing.
- You may become too choosy and write off potential friends because you're quick to judge them as vacuous.
- Your feelings may translate into bitter and misanthropic behavior.
- Your sense of being different from everyone may morph into an arrogant belief that you're on a higher level than all the mindless sheep. Those feelings of false superiority may stay in your head as nothing more than an ego-protecting way to reframe your loneliness. Of course, if they appear as outward arrogance, that will put everyone off.

Here's how you can handle a sense of alienation:

- More than anything else, look for people who do think like you. They are out there. Plenty of people are intellectual or indifferent to sports or not into getting plastered. You can have a satisfying social life and never get drunk or go to a loud, flashy nightclub.
- Be willing to give people more of a chance. Many of them aren't as shallow as they seem if you can look past the surface impression they create.
- Try to soften your aversion to the activities you have a chip on your shoulder about. You don't have to love them, and you definitely don't have to do them, but work not to have such a hostile perception of them. It doesn't do you any favors to carry that kind of resentment around.
- Stick to your values, but be open to the occasional compromise and generally approaching things in a less absolute way. It's fine if you don't like getting wasted or going to deafening, tacky clubs, but it's

less realistic to try to keep alcohol or nightlife venues out of your life entirely. If your friends want to have a beer or two at a low-key pub, that's not so bad, and keeping them company there is better than not going out at all.

- To be frank, if you feel superior to everyone, you need to get over yourself and develop a more humble, balanced self-image. Yes, you may be a bit more intellectual and refined than some of your peers, but it doesn't make you better than anyone. Many of them aren't nearly as dumb as you assume. Whatever your strengths are, you're not that much of a unique snowflake either. Being intelligent or having discerning taste is great, but people with those traits aren't that rare. Getting more social experience will drive all of this home.

Here are a few more thoughts to support some of those suggestions:

Reasons people may seem more shallow than they are

Many people who seem superficial do have deep interests or tendencies. The problem is that their surface features are easy to see, while their more substantial traits are hidden. Here are some things that may make layered, intelligent people come off as shallower at a glance, and cause you to pass on them too quickly:

- They belong to a social group that's stereotypically thought of as dumb and shallow.
- They've fallen into a style of dressing that's associated with shallow people.
- They have an accent or style of speaking that's stereotypically associated with less-cultured types.
- They have a naturally crude, bubbly, or scatterbrained personality.
- They don't use proper spelling and grammar when they text or email because they're more concerned with speed over perfect legibility.
- They tend to act loud and dumb when they're drinking and having a good time.
- They're in a place in their life where they want to do lots of shallow things like partying a lot.
- They're capable of discussing heavy, cerebral topics, but have learned

that those discussions can cause arguments or hurt feelings, so they save them for the appropriate time and place.

- They're intelligent, but not interested in stereotypical intellectual topics like logical fallacies or Game Theory.
- They're content in life, and not in an "ignorance is bliss" way. Some people think someone can only be deep if they're angsty, cynical, and preoccupied with existential questions.
- Their thoughts are concealed. It's easy to think other people are less deep than you because you only see their surface behaviors. You, on the other hand, have access to all of your inner thoughts, many of which are profound and insightful.
- They have good social skills. Some people go so far as to think that anyone who seems comfortable with social interaction, and who is at home in a group, is automatically a brainless follower.

In defense of "shallow" traits and interests

In moderation, shallowness isn't inherently bad. If you're vapid to your core, that's no good, but in reasonable doses, shallow things are fine:

- Shallowness is part of the lighter side of socializing. Sometimes people want to make childish jokes and gossip about celebrities. It isn't better or worse than being reflective and serious, just different.
- Shallow things can be fun. Most people enjoy the odd dumb movie or video game. Nothing wrong with that.
- Shallow things can be a guilty pleasure. Lots of people realize that some of the things they like are fluffy and trashy, but they're enjoyable and harmless, so why not?
- Shallow people can be fun. Even if you may never want to have a long, involved discussion with them, more vapid people can still be entertaining enough to idly chat with or to keep you company when you go out.
- Some shallow things aren't really shallow at all. Sports and video games often get written off, but they're full of nuance and strategy. Real art, skill, and passion go into designing fashionable clothes. Some TV shows or comic books can have deeper plots than many people give them credit for at a glance.

- Some shallow things have positive benefits. For example, a guy who gets into natural bodybuilding so he can take his shirt off at music festivals is improving his health in the process.
- Some shallow things work for other people. Just because it may not appeal to you, it doesn't mean it isn't rewarding to someone else. For example, you may think a 9-to-5 job, a house in the suburbs, and 2.2 kids is soul sucking, but other people may find it fulfilling.

Some thoughts on developing a more balanced view of drinking

To be very clear, nothing in this book is trying to tell you that you need to drink to be socially successful. If you have an overly angry black-and-white view of the activity, it's just trying to get you to see it through softer eyes.

If you're not into alcohol, look for friends who aren't big drinkers either. If you are in a social situation where people are pressuring you to drink, know you're doing nothing wrong and use the assertiveness skills covered in Chapter 23 to stand your ground. Feeling bitter about alcohol is particularly a problem around college age when it seems all everyone cares about is getting hammered. Realize that lots of people besides you aren't keen on drinking. The ones who are into getting wasted make a lot of noise about it and claim a disproportionate amount of attention, but not everyone is like that.

Drinking isn't inherently bad. All kinds of people consume alcohol; many have a glass of wine with dinner. Sometimes you can think of drinking, any kind of drinking, as being more lowbrow or sinister than it is. It's more about how you go about it. There are different levels of alcohol consumption. Someone who has a beer or two while seeing some live music isn't consuming it on the same level as a guy who gets blackout drunk at a party and puts his hand through a window. It's often not drinking itself we feel negative about but the things it can become associated with. When you're young, underage drinking has all this baggage attached to it that it doesn't when you're 45 and sipping a scotch in the evening. You may have come to dislike drinking because it's a favorite activity of a type of person you resent.

It would be foolish to say there's nothing wrong with alcohol. It has a lot of potential downsides, from serious ones like addiction and drunk driving accidents, to more minor annoyances like losing your phone when you're loaded or putting on weight after two semesters of partying. However, most of the time nothing bad happens to people when they drink in moderation. They go out, share a few pitchers, feel the effects, and then head home for the night. Even when they get pretty drunk, most people still behave themselves. They may be louder, sloppier, and goofier than normal, but that's about it on most nights. If you're someplace where a lot of people are drinking, it's easy to spot the handful of people who are acting embarrassing or being self-destructive, but for every one of them, there are fifty who have their act together.

Some thoughts on developing a more balanced view of clubbing

If you can take or leave giant, gaudy nightclubs, you're not alone. They can be loud, crowded, expensive, and full of people who aren't your style. Lots of people don't like them but still manage to have great social lives while setting foot in them as rarely as possible. As with drinking, complaints about clubbing are most commonly heard from people in their late teens and early twenties, when everyone is most enthusiastic about going to them.

Most people who go to clubs are good, regular folk. If you've been dragged to a club, it's easy to think that everyone but you is empty-headed and lives for that kind of scene, but a lot of people are occasional club-goers, who may have been cajoled into going too. The clubbing environment also makes people seem more ditzy than they are. Who doesn't come across as more superficial in a clubbing outfit? Everyone's also there to let loose and have fun, so they're not showing the more refined side of their personality.

Don't be too quick to dismiss specific aspects of clubbing. You may not like dancing to thumping dance music, but that doesn't automatically mean everyone who does is a mouth-breather. Similarly, many people go to clubs for face-value reasons like wanting to see their friends and cut loose after a long week. Not everyone has a less-flattering hidden motivation like wanting to get laid or soak up attention from strangers. Finally, not all clubs are the same. When people first start going out, they often gravitate to the biggest, most stereotypically club-ish clubs and mistakenly think they're all like that. You may not like huge venues that play Top 40 hits, but who's to say you wouldn't appreciate a smaller venue that plays more alternative music and attracts a crowd that's more your style?

31

LOOKING FORWARD
AS YOUR
SOCIAL SKILLS IMPROVE

If you consistently apply this book's ideas over time, your social situation should get to a good place. You'll be reasonably confident and comfortable in your own skin. You won't be completely fearless, but you'll be able to get through most social situations without feeling too shy or nervous. You'll be able carry on most conversations just fine, and you'll know that if one doesn't go well, it's not entirely your fault. You'll have a social life that works for you. What are some things you can expect as your social skills develop in a positive direction?

PITFALLS THAT COME WITH BEING
MORE SOCIALLY SAVVY

As your social skills get better, there aren't any major pitfalls you have to worry about. It's almost all positives. One potential problem is that as you expand into fresh social territory, you may develop some bad habits. For example, if you previously nervously hung back in conversations but now enjoy taking the lead, you may discover you tend to interrupt people or make inappropriate jokes. You can catch and correct those mistakes like you can any others.

MAINTAINING YOUR PROGRESS

After you've improved your conversation and friend-making skills, the gains are here to stay. When you have the knowledge about how to handle a particular situation, you won't forget it. It's not like losing weight where there's always a risk that you'll put the pounds back on if you aren't diligent. If you don't use the skills for a while, they can get rusty, but it won't take long to shake that off. Practically speaking, conversation skills are used so often in day-to-day life that you'll be able to maintain them without trying too hard. Your courage to put yourself in uncomfortable social situations will atrophy more quickly if you don't keep stretching your comfort zone. Though again, it's easier to get that comfort level back than it is to earn it in the first place.

If you've always liked spending time alone, your new-and-improved social life might dry up after a while. This can happen if you become less intrinsically motivated to make new friends because you no longer have anything to prove to yourself. In the past you were pushed by the pain of wanting to get past your loneliness and social skills gaps. Now you may be stuck in a rut; you know you could go make more friends if you really wanted to... but there's no rush. So for now you're going to stay in for another weekend and watch some movies. If you catch yourself in this situation, it will be easier to get out of it a second time, once you re-establish your motivation to meet people.

Your social life may also level out due to a course correction. When you get the hang of socializing, you may go through a phase of going out all the time and making lots of friends. You're having fun using your new abilities, making up for lost time, and proving to yourself you can do this. In time, however, the novelty of having "bloomed" will wear off, and you'll settle back into your true, more low-key social preferences.

COPING WITH CHALLENGING TIMES

Though your more polished social skills won't tend to backslide much, there are a few situations in which socializing may be tougher. The first is if other aspects of your life get particularly stressful or difficult. All of that extra stress and discouragement might temporarily make your shyness and anxiety worse than normal. Second, your life circumstances may change down the road, and you may find yourself in a spot where it's tougher to make friends. You'll know the strategies you need to use, but the deck will still be stacked against you. For example, you may move to a small town after college and find it hard to meet people, as anyone would.

If you hit a stressful patch, give yourself permission to temporarily function at a lower level. It may take time for your life to settle down, and it's not a knock against you if you feel a little more insecure or socially anxious than normal during that time. Think of it as if you injured your ankle and had to ease back on your physical activities for a few weeks—it doesn't mean you're crippled forever. To take the edge off any stress you many feel about socializing, use some additional stress-reducing techniques from Chapter 6. Dust off any anti-anxiety or confidence-boosting principles and techniques you may have applied in the past but haven't had to use as much lately (for example, you may need to go back to consciously questioning your counterproductive thoughts).

When you find yourself in a situation that's more practically challenging than what you're used to, be patient and don't put pressure on yourself to solve it right away. Take the time to try out different ways to adapt your existing skillset. Accept that you may never get the same results as you would under easier circumstances, and don't hold that against yourself (for example, acknowledging there will rarely be an opportunity to meet as many potential friends as easily as you did in college).

WHAT TO WORK ON NEXT

It's not uncommon for socially inexperienced people to think they won't feel happy and "fixed" until they've become incredibly popular and charismatic. However, when they reach a functional, average level of social skills, they often realize that's all they need. If you want to try to take your people skills to a higher level, nothing's stopping you. As the beginning of the book said, being charismatic is more about doing all the basics a bit better than average than employing a set of special high-end techniques. Basic social skills also provide a foundation for more specialized subskills. If you haven't started working on them already, you could begin honing skills like flirting and dating, public speaking, sales, or leadership.

"WHY HASN'T ANYONE NOTICED HOW DIFFERENT I AM NOW?"

When you set out to improve your social skills, you may have wanted the validation of having your family or old high school classmates being amazed at how much you've changed. You have to accept you may never get that recognition. New people will tend to respond to the different you, but people you've known a while will often see you as you've always been. That's partially because if someone has a fixed idea of what you're like, they'll look for instances that confirm their old view of you and ignore whatever doesn't fit. Also, there may be a dynamic around certain people where your changes can't really show. When you're having dinner with your family, they won't see how much more confident you are when meeting strangers at parties.

SELF-IMAGE

Our self-image tends to lag behind our current level of success. Even after you have better social skills, you'll feel like you're still "awkward," a "geek," or whatever label you used for yourself, for a while. You may even feel like an imposter and worry that at any moment everyone will snap to their senses and realize you're really just a dork who's faking it. You may find yourself shoehorning the fact that you used to be shyer into your conversations because you want to pre-emptively explain away any gaffes you may make or because you feel it's such a central part of your identity. These feelings may never fully go away, though they won't outwardly affect you. They may also fade over time, and you'll start to see yourself as a regular person and not define yourself by your old interpersonal problems.

At the moment, your social issues may seem like an overwhelming, all-encompassing storm that's ruining your life. If you work on fixing them, there will come a time where all they'll be is an off-handed, single-sentence summary of something from your past. You'll be talking to someone and mention, "Yeah, I was pretty shy in high school and college... Anyway, as I was saying..."

APPENDIX A:
ASPERGER'S SYNDROME / MILD AUTISM

ASPERGER'S SYNDROME / MILD AUTISM is an inborn difference in brain wiring that, among other things, makes socializing intuitively harder to grasp. It also predisposes people to committing certain types of social mistakes. Although Asperger's syndrome has a big effect on the social abilities of the people who have it, it's a relatively rare condition. Most people who struggle in social situations don't have Asperger's. This chapter briefly describes the symptoms of Asperger's syndrome. It then explains how people with Asperger's can adjust the way they try to acquire better people skills.

CONSIDERING THE DIAGNOSTIC CRITERIA
FOR ASPERGER'S SYNDROME

Below are the official criteria for diagnosing Asperger's syndrome. They're taken from the fourth edition of the *Diagnostic and Statistical Manual of Mental Disorders*. (The DSM-5 came out in mid-2013. It doesn't include Asperger's syndrome, and instead absorbed it and a few other conditions into a more general diagnosis of Autism Spectrum Disorder. However, the decision to take away the standalone status of

Asperger's was somewhat controversial. Members of the public and many professionals still think in terms of Asperger's syndrome, so this book will use it as well.)

Even if you recognize some of your own traits in the criteria below, you should never self-diagnose. Plenty of people have a handful of Asperger-ish traits, but that's often a far cry from having the full condition. If you suspect you're on the autism spectrum, you should see a mental health professional who specializes in the area for a proper evaluation.

Not everyone with Asperger's syndrome is the same. The condition can vary in severity, and each person will exhibit a different mix of symptoms. All the other facets of a person's past and personality and interests will come into play too. An outgoing "Aspie" from a poor, abusive household may come across very differently than one who's more naturally reserved and from a stable upper-middle-class background.

DSM-IV Criteria for Asperger's Syndrome

A. Qualitative impairment in social interaction, as manifested by at least two of the following:
(1) marked impairment in the use of multiple nonverbal behaviors such as eye-to-eye gaze, facial expression, body postures, and gestures to regulate social interaction
(2) failure to develop peer relationships appropriate to developmental level
(3) a lack of spontaneous seeking to share enjoyment, interests, or achievements with other people (for example, by a lack of showing, bringing, or pointing out objects of interest to other people)
(4) lack of social or emotional reciprocity
B. Restricted repetitive and stereotyped patterns of behavior, interests, and activities, as manifested by at least one of the following:
(1) encompassing preoccupation with one or more stereotyped and restricted patterns of interest that is abnormal either in intensity or focus

(2) apparently inflexible adherence to specific, nonfunctional routines or rituals

(3) stereotyped and repetitive motor mannerisms (for example, hand or finger flapping or twisting, or complex whole-body movements)

(4) persistent preoccupation with parts of objects

C. The disturbance causes clinically significant impairment in social, occupational, or other important areas of functioning.

D. There is no clinically significant general delay in language (for example, single words used by age 2 years, communicative phrases used by age 3 years).

E. There is no clinically significant delay in cognitive development or in the development of age-appropriate self-help skills, adaptive behavior (other than in social interaction), and curiosity about the environment in childhood.

F. Criteria are not met for another specific Pervasive Developmental Disorder or Schizophrenia.

SEEING THE SOCIAL DIFFICULTIES ASPERGER'S SYNDROME CAN CAUSE

The official criteria for Asperger's syndrome don't capture the whole picture. People with Asperger's are interested in socializing and connecting with others, but they often have trouble doing so. Until they've had more practice and guidance, they tend to come across as stereotypically socially awkward. Below is a list of common Asperger's syndrome social challenges. Although some of them are objective difficulties, others aren't inherently bad but can cause problems because they go against the grain of what most people expect.

Problems with overall understanding of socializing

People with Asperger's have an intuitive understanding of socializing that's lower than that of neurologically typical people. Most people, even if they're shy or less socially experienced, instinctively grasp many unwritten aspects of the social world. Someone with Asperger's doesn't have this knowledge and can struggle to comprehend or navigate situations most people take for granted. They often compare their condition to being an alien trying to blend in with the culture of a strange planet.

They're also unaware of many social rules. This is a side effect of their lower ability to unconsciously pick up unspoken guidelines through observation and experience. For example, someone with Asperger's may make simple mistakes, like not saying good-bye to a friend after they're done talking to them, because they didn't know it was expected. They can feel uneasy in unfamiliar social situations because they assume there will be hidden rules they're going to inadvertently break.

They have a greater tendency to get drained by socializing because it requires mental resources that most people's brains can process on autopilot.

Empathy

As Chapter 16 explained, empathy is the ability to get in touch with another person's perspective and emotional reactions. People with Asperger's have trouble seeing things from someone else's point of view and adjusting as needed. For example, they may tell someone a story, but not consider how the listener isn't familiar with the background context necessary to understand it.

They also have a harder time recognizing and expressing their own emotions. Asperger's doesn't turn people into emotionless robots, but they may not always be totally plugged into how they're feeling. If they are aware of their feelings, they may struggle to get those emotions across.

Nonverbal communication

Asperger's can cause difficulty reading and understanding other people's nonverbal communication. For example, a person with Asperger's may not pick up on someone's bored facial expression and tone of voice. As a result, they may go on and on about a topic the listener isn't interested in instead of changing the subject.

Their own nonverbal communication comes across as "off" to many people. For example, they may have unusually stiff body language, poor use of eye contact, an inexpressive face, a monotone voice, or a peculiar cadence to their speech.

Thinking style

Individuals with Asperger's tend to have a particular style of thinking, which can extend to and affect many of their daily activities:

- A tendency to be very literal and concrete in their thinking. For example, you ask them if they could pick up some milk at the store. They reply with a yes and go back to what they were doing. In their mind, you asked them a hypothetical question about their ability to get milk, which they answered.
- A desire for structure, routine, and predictability, and trouble deviating from their schedule and going with the flow.
- A reluctance to disobey rules, and a tendency to get agitated and come across as uptight when other people want to skirt them.
- Difficulty compromising. They see many issues as black-and-white and don't want to budge.
- Trouble planning and organizing their time.

Use of language

There are also recurring ways they tend to use and interpret language, which can throw people off, or interfere with their ability to follow and react to conversations:

- A tendency to use language in a nontypical way. Examples include being verbose and using a lot of big words, or speaking in an overly formal and proper manner.
- Trouble grasping humor and idioms. People with Asperger's have senses of humor, but theirs can be on a different wavelength from everyone else's. They may not see what's funny about something their friends are all laughing at. Because they think so literally, figures of speech may not be immediately clear to them.
- Trouble following the flow of conversation from one topic to the

next and seeing the hidden connections between subjects. For example, if someone mentions a sport, and then the other person brings up something a mutual friend did, the person with Asperger's won't necessarily see the unspoken connection that the mutual friend plays the sport.

Interaction style

The following are common features of the social interaction style of individuals with Asperger's syndrome. Their approach can make their conversation partners feel uncomfortable or unsure of how to react.

- A tendency to be very blunt and straightforward in their communication. They'll sometimes say things that other people find inappropriate or hurtful, like casually referencing someone's double chin. If they're bored in a conversation, they may simply walk away.
- A tendency to "talk at" people and deliver monologues about the things that they'd like to speak about, rather than having a conversation with back-and-forth dialogue.
- A tendency to value truth, logic, and accuracy. Aside from contributing to their bluntness, this trait can lead them to feel compelled to correct people on minor facts in conversations. They may have trouble going along with the little white lies and niceties people use to keep relationships on an even keel. Overall they can come across as very detached and analytical, or anal-retentive and tightly wound.
- Trouble stating their thoughts in a concise, coherent way. They may start to explain a point and then ramble or go off on tangents. This is partially because they're thinking out loud about what interests them and are not considering what the other person needs to find the explanation interesting and comprehensible.

Interests

People with Asperger's often have special interests—subjects they're intensely focused on and devote a lot of their time to learning and thinking about. Their interest may be a fairly common one, like video games or wine making, but they can also be quite esoteric, like knowing every-thing about medieval printing presses or collecting memorabilia related to an obscure 1970s country singer. There's nothing objectively wrong with having one interest over another, of course. The issues this trait causes are more indirect, like if people think their choice of hobbies is strange, or they talk about it at length to someone who isn't interested.

Physical

Asperger's leads to physical issues as well. People with it tend to be physically clumsy and uncoordinated. They're often bad at sports (and we all know how rough it is for those kids in gym class). They can also have sensory sensitivities to things like loud noises, particular smells or tastes, or the feeling of certain fabrics on their skin. Places like night-clubs may trigger negative emotions or reactions for them.

Any of the usual possible side effects of having social difficulties

No one—with or without Asperger's—is immune to common difficul-ties that can arise while navigating social situations. Other challenges people with Asperger's may face include
- poor self-esteem
- shyness and social anxiety
- depression
- bitterness at being rejected and misunderstood

IMPROVING YOUR SOCIAL SKILLS
IF YOU HAVE ASPERGER'S

If you have Asperger's syndrome and social difficulties, the best way to improve your people skills is simply to focus on the areas where you're behind. For the most part, that involves standard things like reading up on what to do differently and getting lots of real-world practice. How-ever, you can keep certain things in mind for your unique circumstanc-es. Here are some additional Asperger's-specific considerations:

Don't feel like having Asperger's makes you a hopeless case

People with Asperger's can develop solid social skills if they work at it. There are countless examples of individuals who have done so. However, learning interpersonal skills won't come as naturally to you, so you'll likely have to put in more effort than a typical person. Give your diagnosis the right amount of respect. Don't use it as an excuse or think it dooms you to failure, but don't think you can casually disregard it either.

Make peace with your Asperger-ish traits

Many people with Asperger's struggle with their identity. They might put a lot of work into improving their social skills so they can pass as "normal," and their sense of self-worth may be very tied to how successful they are at doing that. Although it's understandable that someone would want to work on their social problems, their self-esteem may be so wrapped up in getting past their Asperger's that they suppress some of their other traits, which ultimately leaves them feeling unfulfilled. Don't think of Asperger's in either/or terms. Work to move past the parts of it you don't like, but keep the good aspects. Many people with Asperger's say they became a lot happier when they accepted their obscure interests and quirky tendencies.

Work to address your legitimate weak spots and decide how you'll handle subjective social differences

Some of the differences Asperger's causes are real social weaknesses, while others are variations from the norm, but not objectively bad. Many people would agree that not being good at reading nonverbal communication is a handicap. Focus on identifying and correcting clear-cut issues, like having trouble telling one facial expression from the next, making poor eye contact, or tending to monopolize conversations.

For your more subjective differences, you'll need to decide where you want to land on the spectrum between being true to yourself and being pragmatic. Some of these calls are easy to make. There's nothing intrinsically wrong with being into one hobby over another, so don't waver on that—though you probably want to learn not to go on and on about it to people who don't care. Other differences don't have easy answers. What if correcting people is important to you, even though some people find it irritating? Maybe you'll find a middle ground where you'll be your fact-correcting self around friends who have shown they're fine with it, but hold back around anyone you don't know because randomly upsetting strangers is more trouble than it's worth.

Find people you can go to for social explanations and clarifications

The most wide-ranging way Asperger's makes improving your people skills difficult is in how it lowers your initial grasp of the social world. You may feel some social advice, which an inexperienced-but-neurologically-typical (neurotypical) person may have no trouble grasping, is too vague for you. That may include some of the suggestions in this book.

If a piece of advice leaves too much unsaid for you, you may be able to find the detailed breakdown you need in another source. However, it's possible the area you want clarification on is too specific and unique to you to have been covered elsewhere. In those cases, it's most useful to ask someone to give you a personalized, in-depth explanation. That someone could be a friend, family member, counselor, or support group member. If no one like that is available, an acceptable substitute is to ask your questions online on a social skills–related forum. A good "explainer" doesn't need to be incredibly socially savvy themselves, just someone who can break down the reasoning behind everyday social rules and who will be patient and not brush you off with a "That's just the way things are!"

Accept that some social guidelines may never fully make sense to you

People with Asperger's tend to be logical. They're usually fine with following a social rule if they can see the rationale behind it, but they may be resistant to going along with ones that don't make sense to them (for example, why people say niceties like, "We should grab lunch sometime" when they don't mean it). If you really don't like a social rule and are willing to accept the consequences of not following it, that's your choice. For some social rules, you may have to tell yourself, "It doesn't make sense to me, but when this guideline is broken, it causes people's feelings to be upset and I'd rather avoid that."

Learn as many of the broad principles behind socializing as you can

People with Asperger's sometimes try to learn to socialize by attempting to memorize rote responses to use in every situation. For example, they'll come up with a script to use when they run into a coworker in the break room. As Chapter 9 explained, it isn't practical to predict and create a response for every eventuality. Rote replies come across as robotic and are easily thrown off if the circumstances are different from what your template had accounted for (what if the coworker is a new employee or the CEO?). Taken too far, a memorization mentality can lead you to see people as impersonal obstacles to get past through the right sequence of inputs, rather than fellow humans to connect with.

Instead, you should try to identify and understand the underlying principles behind each situation. That will give you more ability to adjust and improvise as needed. For example, if you run into a coworker in the break room, it helps to have an idea of what needs to happen in the interaction (that is, acknowledge them and have a brief, light exchange to show you're friendly; possibly talk about relevant work-related topics). Figuring out the broad goals behind each situation will take some time and memorization, but not to the degree that memorizing word-for-word responses to countless situations would.

Don't rule out canned responses entirely

Rote-memorizing what to say in conversations is clunky and a less-than-optimal option, but some people with Asperger's claim it has its uses. Their reasoning is that because their instinctive understanding of socializing is lower, they can't always grasp the underlying principles they need to use in some situations, at least not right away. Some of those conversations lend themselves to premade responses, so they go with what works. For example, they may use the same three questions whenever they start a conversation at a party. They know they're not being as creative or flexible as they could be, but it helps them get through that situation.

Most people have certain conversations they get into over and over again, like being asked about their job, and have developed a standard set of responses. They'll slightly vary the wording each time they go into longer explanations, but may deliver shorter lines word for word. It isn't inherently a problem to have some preloaded material. You just shouldn't over-rely on it.

Be open to "good enough" alternatives to more confusing social rules

Some social situations have an ideal way to handle them that involves knowing a lot of subtle, unwritten rules, as well as the right times to apply them. If you have Asperger's, you may find it takes too much effort to get your head around it all. Luckily, social situations usually aren't black-and-white in the sense that anything less than the best is a total failure. There may be alternative ways to act that are a bit more crude and simplistic, but get the job done, don't drain your mental resources, and don't cause too many negative outcomes.

For example, it's not the smoothest move to directly ask people you're just getting to know, "Do you want to be friends with me?" That angle will often be viewed as too up-front and clumsy. It can put people on the spot. It's seen as how little kids make friends, not adults. However, under the right circumstances, someone could use this question and have everything go fine. A person with Asperger's may decide, "Trying to make friends gradually and with a light touch is too much for me to think about. I've found that once I seem to be getting along with someone, asking if they want to be friends does the job well enough. Plus, I'm a direct person who's not always socially perfect, so if anyone is put off by my asking, it's a sign they wouldn't be a good fit for me. Maybe I'll lose a good potential friend here and there with this method, but I can handle that. In the future, I may get better at being subtle, but this works for now."

Possibly tell other people about your Asperger's

This one has its pros and cons. Telling people about your diagnosis is getting more feasible by the day, though, as more and more people learn what Asperger's syndrome is and realize it's not a big deal. The pros are that if other people know you have Asperger's, they can be more understanding and adjust their expectations accordingly. They may also be better able to help you with your social skills. Naturally, the negative side is that some people won't understand, think even worse of you, or get the wrong idea about what the condition means. Therefore, you'll need to think about whether you should tell someone like your boss as opposed to a stranger at a party you'll never see again.

FURTHER READING

Hᴇʀᴇ ᴀʀᴇ sᴏᴍᴇ ʙᴏᴏᴋs that go more in-depth about some of the topics this book covers. These aren't the author's one-and-only recommendations, just good examples of books on the subject. Of course, in this day and age, you can also find a lot of solid information on the Internet, though it's sometimes hard to find one comprehensive resource as opposed to a bunch of short, summary-level articles spread across several sites. This list doesn't include any websites because they come and go relatively quickly, but if you do a search on a particular topic, it shouldn't be hard to find some advice on it.

Introversion

Quiet: The Power of Introverts in a World That Can't Stop Talking
by Susan Cain

The Introvert's Way: Living a Quiet Life in a Noisy World
by Sophia Dembling

Asperger's Syndrome

The Complete Guide to Asperger's Syndrome by Tony Atwood

Cognitive Behavioral Therapy for shyness and anxiety

Overcoming Social Anxiety and Shyness: A Self-Help Guide Using Cognitive Behavioral Techniques by Gillian Butler

Shyness and Social Anxiety Workbook: Proven, Step-by-Step Techniques for Overcoming your Fear by Martin Antony, PhD, and Richard Swinson

Mindfulness for shyness and anxiety

The Mindfulness and Acceptance Workbook for Anxiety: A Guide to Breaking Free from Anxiety, Phobias, and Worry Using Acceptance and Commitment Therapy by John P. Forsyth and Georg H. Eifert

Self-Esteem

The Self-Esteem Workbook by Glenn R. Schiradli

The Six Pillars of Self-Esteem by Nathaniel Branden

Assertiveness

The Assertiveness Workbook: How to Express Your Ideas and Stand Up for Yourself at Work and in Relationships by Randy J. Paterson

Listening skills

The Lost Art of Listening, Second Edition: How Learning to Listen Can Improve Relationships by Michael P. Nichols

Body Language

The Definitive Book of Body Language by Barbara Pease and Allan Pease

What Every BODY is Saying: An Ex-FBI Agent's Guide to Speed-Reading People by Joe Navarro and Marvin Karlins

Counterproductive "niceness"

No More Mr. Nice Guy by Robert Glover*
* This book is primarily for men, but it goes over some concepts that are applicable to everyone.

Healing from abuse and trauma

Healing the Scars of Emotional Abuse by Gregory L. Jantz and Ann McMurray

Healing the Shame That Binds You by John Bradshaw

Surviving Childhood Sexual Abuse Workbook: Practical Self-Help for Adults Who Were Sexually Abused As Children by Carolyn Ainscough and Kay Toon

The PTSD Workbook: Simple Effective Techniques for Overcoming Traumatic Stress Symptoms by Mary Beth Williams and Soili Poijula

Toxic Parents: Overcoming Their Hurtful Legacy and Reclaiming Your Life by Susan Forward and Craig Buck

Made in the USA
Lexington, KY
05 June 2017